D1442867

HIGH SCHOOL 1980

HIGH SCHOOL

1980 / *The Shape of the Future in American Secondary Education* / EDITED BY

ALVIN C. EURICH

AND THE STAFF OF *The Academy for Educational Development*

PITMAN PUBLISHING CORPORATION

New York   Toronto   London

ACKNOWLEDGMENTS

The editor gratefully acknowledges the permission to reprint selections from the following sources.

Kenneth Clark, "Alternate School Systems." Copyright © by the Presidents and Fellows of Harvard College. *Harvard Educational Review*, 38, Winter 1968, 110–113, and also in the expanded edition of *Equal Educational Opportunity* published by Harvard University Press, 1969. Reprinted by permission of the *Harvard Educational Review*.

Lawrence Ferlinghetti, *A Coney Island of the Mind.* Copyright © 1958 by Lawrence Ferlinghetti. Reprinted by permission of New Directions Publishing Corporation.

Robert Frost, "What Fifty Said" from *The Poetry of Robert Frost* edited by Edward Connery Lathem. Copyright 1928 by Holt, Rinehart and Winston, Inc. Copyright © 1956 by Robert Frost. Reprinted by permission of Holt, Rinehart and Winston, Inc.

William Butler Yeats, "The Second Coming" from *Complete Poems of William Butler Yeats.* Copyright 1924 by The Macmillan Company. Copyright renewed 1952 by Bertha Georgie Yeats. Reprinted by permission of The Macmillan Company.

Contents

SPECIAL EMERGING PROBLEMS AND OPPORTUNITIES

HIGH SCHOOL 1980

Introduction

The high school is the pivot of our public education system. For some youths it must offer the academic background necessary for college. For others, it must provide the sound vocational training so necessary for success in the job market. For all youth it is the training ground for adulthood, and the high school's success or failure will reflect itself in the fate of society.

Yet, high schools are in trouble. In the cities, many students drop out, many graduate unable to read at grade level, tragically few go on to college. The shocking fact is that 80 percent of the nation's high school students never complete post-secondary education. In both suburbs and cities searching questions are being asked about the curriculum. Is it relevant to today's students? Does it focus on the interests of the students? Does it train them to comprehend and control a rapidly changing and very confusing world? The spread of student unrest to the high schools adds urgency to these questions.

We are entering a new era of school reform. The old issue of upgrading suburban schools to better equip students to enter college and the professions is giving way to concern with ghetto youth and their failure to cope successfully with high school. Concern with the academic quality of the curriculum is giving way to the fear that the curriculum simply is not relevant as it stands. School reorganization is still an issue, but the emphasis has shifted from efficiency to assuring that the schools do not actually thwart learning.

Ole Sand writes that "1980 is already here," and he is right. In John Gardner's words, "the pieces of an educational revolution are lying around unassembled," and it is up to us to put them together. We can project the economic and demographic facts which will both limit and challenge high school 1980, and we have available a range of innovations which, if brought together, will define high school 1980. Now is the time to create that school. If we wait ten years it will be too late.

Several major themes raised by our writers weave in and out of each others' essays, complicating the task of an introduction-writer who would like to tuck these 23 essays into a smaller number of pigeonholes to aid the reader's approach to this volume. Five such themes are education in the cities, the changing student, curriculum, professional staff, and finally, managing educational resources.

EDUCATION IN THE CITIES

One of the people most qualified to discuss education in the cities—Samuel Brownell, former school superintendent in Detroit and now professor of urban educational administration at Yale—writes that city schools must meet a quite specific agenda by 1980 if they are not ". . . to be supplanted by a more effective social institution to aid youth in making a successful beginning in independent urban life." The urban schools' physical plant must be rebuilt not only to provide decent learning facilities for city students, but to stem the flight of white families to the suburbs. The schools must act as focal points for community organization, bringing people together to solve local problems, end racial segregation, and build a climate conducive to change. Pressures for uniformity in large school systems must be regulated so that they do not stifle creativity, inhibit experiment, or obscure the diversity of human needs.

While agreeing with Mr. Brownell that reviving urban education requires massive rebuilding, integration, and a new look at curriculum, former U.S. Commissioner of Education Harold Howe II argues that American education must "completely reexamine and reorient itself to meet challenges quite different from those it has struggled with during the past decade." Principal among these challenges is that of bringing America's poor into the mainstream of our national life by focusing on them a "critical mass" of educational resources; small-scale efforts won't do the job, and if paying more attention to the education of poor youngsters means less attention to suburban youth, then the trade-off, Mr. Howe implies, is a price worth paying.

Picking up Mr. Howe's plea that high schools should revise their programs to serve this majority, Marvin J. Feldman of the Ford Foundation argues for much more varied, thoughtful programs of vocational education. The middle-class youngster's academic success rests largely on his verbal skills and an upbringing that stresses deferred gratification; many inner-city youngsters, however, do not learn easily through the printed or spoken word, and require a stronger motivation for learning than grades provide. Vocational education utilizing graphic, manipulative, or affective teaching techniques to supplement verbal instruction could help them learn better and, by holding out the promise of a job upon graduation, offer such youngsters the motive they need.

Such vocational education need not be separate from "academic," according to Mr. Feldman; a truly comprehensive curriculum that allows for more variation in learning styles could serve the needs of both college-bound and noncollege-bound youth, and could make school more congenial for the latter by removing the "poor learners" stigma from vocational education.

James Conant also argues that the high school must serve a useful social purpose, it must be "an instrument for furthering unity and democracy in an entire community." Reminding us that "The comprehensive high school is an American invention of some 50 years," Mr. Conant, who has long been the leading advocate of the comprehensive high school, asks whether the comprehensive high school will be relevant in 1980. His emphatic answer is yes. By 1980 the comprehensive high school will emerge as the key to solving metropolitan educational problems, "the best way out of the present segregated situation in many areas is to consider as a goal the creation of high schools which shall be widely comprehensive not only in regard to the economic backgrounds and the vocational desires of the students, but in the color of the skins of those attending." To assess the merits of the comprehensive high school for 1980, Mr. Conant carefully examines the obstacles posed by parental opposition to integration, limited resources, and small schools.

Providing equal educational opportunity and achieving integration have proved agonizingly difficult. Kenneth Clark, president of Metropolitan Applied Research Center, addresses himself to these problems and writes about the obstacles to "effective, nonracially constrained" education. He finds the difficulty in the very patterns of public school organization and argues that it may well be necessary to find "realistic, aggressive, and viable competitors" to the present public schools. He examines some alternatives—state and federal regional schools, industrial demonstration schools, labor union supported schools, university supported schools, and army schools—and concludes that "if we succeed in finding and developing these and better alternatives to the present educational inefficiency . . . we will . . . demonstrate the validity of our democratic process. We also will have saved our civilization through saving our cities."

OUR CHANGING STUDENTS

Whether rural, urban, or suburban, today's students are more sophisticated than past generations of high school students—largely because of communications media that have exposed them to social and global concerns at an early age. As Frank Jennings of Teachers College, Columbia University, notes, society is itself a teacher, the "great Sophist" that offers educational possibilities we have not yet learned to take advantage of. High school 1980, he believes, "will not be a place, but rather a growth period and a social condition. The students designated as high school students will have the whole of the city for a classroom."

Echoing Mr. Jennings' theme that the community should be the curriculum, Charles Weingartner, professor of education at Queens College, believes that focusing instruction on community problems rather than on compartmentalized subjects would help meet students' criticisms of education as "irrelevant" to their deepest concerns. High school today, he writes, is "witless work," imposing on students "the same task class after class, year after year, doing the same monotonous job: telling back to the teacher what the teacher told them." In addition to offering students a problem-centered curriculum, the high school of 1980 must give students responsibility and the opportunity to engage in constructive social action outside the classroom.

Perhaps as important as allowing students to act is the necessity for allowing students to *be*, according to Edgar Friedenberg, professor of education at the State University of New York at Buffalo. The schools and adult society, he writes, must offer students respect and power. "What is most repellent about education in America and elsewhere is directly attributable to the fact that the institution so far has been able to count on social pressures and legal coercion to provide it with a captive clientele and a mandate to train that clientele in servility. Servility creates unhappy and resentful students and these attitudes spell the failure of humane education."

Mr. Friedenberg outlines several correctives for this enforced docility, such as allowing students to choose their school, offering them the chance to work outside the classroom and return for periodic tests, and paying students to attend school.

CURRICULUM

As with high school 1970, the heart of high school 1980 will be its course of study. Yet the schools' extension into the community and their use of its resources for instructional purposes imply radical changes in the curriculum—and the rapid growth of knowledge will require still more. The proliferation of academic disciplines will force the high school to reexamine both the kinds of subjects taught and the reasons for teaching them. Traditional subjects may be thrown out and new ones introduced. The instructional emphasis will shift from teaching facts to teaching students to learn on their own.

Ole Sand, director of the National Education Association's Center for the Study of Instruction, offers an overview of the curricular changes in store. No longer will curricular revision simply add more "bits and pieces" in the process of updating specific areas, such as science; educators will shape the curriculum around a theoretical framework that relates isolated items of information to each other and assembles them in a significant context.

Several authors expand on these broad ideas about curriculum by taking a detailed look at individual areas of instruction. One thread will run through the high school 1980 curriculum—an absence of the traditional division-by-subject in favor of interdisciplinary, problem-oriented work. Robert Davis, director of the Madison Project, suggests that we "consider whether the ancient trivium and quadrivium have not shaped our school programs too tightly, and whether the identified disciplines have not become large, inflexible units that impede our efforts at reshaping the over-all student program." High school 1980 will integrate the study of math with other subjects: if a student needs a certain mathematical skill for use in a social sciences project—statistical analysis, say, to help him investigate community attitudes—he will learn that skill in the course of his investigation. Such a combination of learning with immediate applicability, Mr. Davis feels, would give math a new vitality and excitement for students.

Paul Brandwein, of the Center for the Study of Instruction at Harcourt, Brace & World, examines science teaching in today's high schools and reviews seven myths that have impeded instructional improvement. Contending that "By the 1980s, if not sooner, devices for *continuing, sensible,* and *sensitive* review of curriculum and method should be established," Mr. Brandwein foresees widespread acceptance of recent innovations such as learning activity packages, computer-assisted instruction, and learning resource centers. He also recommends a blend of humanistic vision with practical curricular innovations on the ground that "Americans want their children to be compassionate as they are competent."

Neil Postman, professor of English at New York University, takes the extraordinary position of suggesting that his subject be abandoned. Urging that we drop a discipline that is "shallow and precious" as now taught, Postman suggests an alternative: media ecology—a "study of media as environments" that would help the student understand how various media structure what we see, think, and do. Media ecology would be a field of inquiry, not a subject—for the word *subject* implies to Postman a fixed content and methodology.

The content of social studies and foreign language instruction should also be radically revised, in the opinion of our authors. Charles Keller paints a picture of a social studies class that will identify specific issues for study—the cities or protest movement, for example—and will use the community as a classroom. Interdisciplinary humanities courses will be central to social studies curricula, and will help students grapple with the "Who am I?" questions—those most important to every human being.

Similarly, foreign language will begin to disappear as a separate subject and will instead be merged with the rest of the curriculum. Bilingual schools will teach everything from history to chemistry in two languages. A. Bruce Gaarder of the U.S. Office of Education makes this prediction and, though he points out there will still be a need for formal instruction in foreign languages, his speculation holds out an intriguing vision of students learning foreign languages easily and naturally.

PROFESSIONAL STAFF

All these changes in the educational program will, of course, require changes in the training, duties, and outlook of the people who do the educating. Perhaps most important, making high school 1980 a reality will require strong leadership.

The principal is the key figure. He is closest to the school, has an over-all view of its particular strengths and problems, and knows the staff, the community, and students. He is, in short, the man best equipped to provide direction for the effective and humane education prescribed in these pages.

Lloyd Michaels, professor of education at Northwestern University, sees five chief functions for the principal in 1980. He will determine school organization, manage the school, work to improve instruction, work closely with parents and involve them in policy making, and will act as change agent.

Charles Brown of the Ford Foundation reviews the education of educators, starting with the premise expressed by William Arrowsmith in *Campus 1980** that "We lack . . . Socratic teachers, visible embodiments of the realized humanity of our aspirations, intelligence, skill, and scholarship." Mr. Brown examines teacher certification, undergraduate and continuing education of teachers, and institutes for future teachers, and offers specific suggestions for improving professional preparation. Perhaps most stimulating is his suggestion that the development of good teachers should begin early, through elementary school programs that allow students to teach their own classmates and younger students. "It is the teacher's qualities as a person," Mr. Brown argues, "rather than a particular pattern of previous experience that counts."

For all the modern student's sophistication, he will still need help in appraising the remarkable variety of programs and opportunities open to him; hence, according to Douglas D. Dillenbeck, director of guidance services for the College Entrance Examination Board, guidance in 1980 will move "toward a central position in the school's educational program." Guidance counselors will use testing not to rank students, but to help each one discover his strengths and weaknesses; the emphasis of their efforts will shift from remediation to promoting mental and social development.

Technology will play an important role in the student's self-diagnosis; Mr. Dillenbeck treats us to a 1980 scenario of Sam Sophomore in his learning laboratory, using a video machine and recorder to test his ability at math and help him decide whether to pursue the field.

MANAGING EDUCATIONAL RESOURCES

One of the most familiar but nonetheless serious challenges facing high school 1980 will be the continuing challenge of numbers. Sidney Tickton, executive vice-president of the Academy for Educational Development, sees a dramatic increase in high school en-

* *Campus 1980*, edited by Alvin C. Eurich, Delacorte, New York, 1968.

rollments over the next decade. Fortunately, he also sees an increase in the supply of teachers, and thinks there will be "space enough and time enough in many school systems to consolidate the gains of the sixties, to expand educational programs moderately, and move them forward. . . . But this will happen only if the education community and the people of the nation decide to make it happen."

Making "it" happen in the face of increased student enrollments will require educators to devise ways of increasing teacher efficiency in 1980. Instructional technology, writes John Loughary, professor of education at the University of Oregon, may provide the key here. "We are really only in the mechanical phase of the technological revolution in education. Nearly all of the man-made systems now being operated in education are clumsy. They are exciting—but so was the Model T compared with the horse."

In view of greater expenditures for instructional technology, probable increases in professional salaries, and the higher costs that educational improvement always entails, school personnel will also have to sharpen their administrative and managerial expertise. J. Lloyd Trump, associate secretary of the National Association of Secondary School Principals, outlines the new ways in which high school 1980 will allocate its resources of personnel, material, time, space, and money.

It will, for example, increase the number of teachers—but it will also increase the specialization of teachers' functions to capitalize on individual interests and skills. High school 1980 will create new staff positions (such as instructional assistants and general aides) to free the teacher for supervision and planning. Much more efficient use of community resources for instruction will make the schools "docking areas" to which students return after spending large portions of their time in libraries and museums. These and other suggestions in the areas of technology, finance, and administration make Mr. Trump's essay an excellent guide for the practical schoolman of 1980.

A theme running through almost every essay in this book is the value of encouraging diversity in student and school performance, rather than making individuals and institutions toe a predetermined mark drawn by national averages of one kind or another. Refreshing as this new tolerance is, it also creates problems for the evaluation of educational performance. With the repudiation of rigid norms, how can educators judge which schools perform most effectively, or measure student progress?

It is clear that new methods of evaluation will have to be developed to accommodate this new individualism in education. William

Turnbull's article offers some excellent clues to what we can expect in evaluation, 1980. He clarifies the distinction between evaluating school systems and individual students, and offers models and criteria for both.

Whatever forms secondary education takes in 1980, it will have to take place some*where*—and educators as well as the general populace tend to underestimate the importance of appropriate buildings for learning. Unlike so many of our physical plants today, high school 1980 must not suggest that its occupants are "naturally destructive, that the place is designed to protect the taxpayer from the natural ravages of youth. The environment [must say] . . . we trust you." After surveying likely changes in libraries, science laboratories, gymnasiums and cafeterias, Harold Gores, president, Educational Facilities Laboratories, concludes that ten years from now "the best school will be one that not only supports learning, but nourishes the spirit. Unlike the schools of the mid-twentieth century which focused on efficiency and the fast processing of youth, the schools of the 1980s will seek both light and warmth."

THE CHALLENGE

These essays add up to a provocative guess at our educational future, a hopeful outline based partly on a review of our past successes and failures, and partly on a fresh vision of possibilities for which the past offers no guidelines. The question is whether the high school portrayed here will get off the drawing board by 1980, or whether it will remain a blueprint even then.

Perhaps as a needed antidote for the optimism of most of our authors, Anthony Oettinger, author of *Run, Computer, Run*, takes the pessimistic position that American education is unlikely to change substantially in the next decade. "The American school system," he writes, "seems almost ideally designed to resist change . . . ten years or so from now, the schools will be pretty much as they are today."

To support his gloomy forecast, Mr. Oettinger focuses on instructional technology and shows how school economics, national organization, internal school hierarchies, inadequately trained staff, and simple human inertia all militate against substantial change. American schooling, he argues, is organized as if someone determined the most efficient way to facilitate change—and then did just the opposite. "We will simply have to grit our teeth, try as hard as we can to implement change, but muddle through as best we can no matter what happens."

But muddling through as best we can is not likely to be nearly good enough, for our high schools—and the society that supports them—are in serious trouble. The comprehensive education that was designed to support and preserve the American experiment in democracy by giving all its young citizens a reasonable chance to secure the fruits of a classless society for themselves and their progeny now seems threatened anew by old divisions we had hoped to overcome: of race, of social background, of economic station. Viewing the resurgence of these ancient enemies, James Conant pleads for us to develop a sense of urgency in adapting the comprehensive high school to new social conditions because ". . . the entire structure of our nation may be at stake."

The pages which follow do *not* constitute a blueprint for meeting the educational challenge facing high schools. No one of the innovations mentioned nor any present combination of them constitutes *the* answer to the problems of American secondary education. John Gardner put it best:

> I'm convinced that 20 years from now we'll look back at our school system today and ask ourselves how we could have tolerated anything as primitive as education today. I think the pieces of an educational revolution are lying around unassembled, and I think we're going to put them together in the next few years.

I would add to this only one thought: that the missing ingredient, the essential catalyst to assemble this "unassembled revolution," is not any one of the pieces. Rather, it is something which transcends the separate elements, the diverse approaches to reform.

The critical factor is the *idea* of reform itself, the notion—new in education but hardly so in our national experience—that we can do better than we are doing or have ever done, and that we can achieve this through innovation, through exploring *new* ways to achieve our objectives. The innovative spirit is the key to assembling the unassembled revolution.

We cannot wait ten years to begin building high school 1980, we must begin now to invent the future. Every American educator and parent sufficiently concerned about the shape of the future to want to do something about it, must realize that he must begin work today.

THE CONDITIONS
OF CHANGE

Towards a More Human Secondary Education

Edgar Friedenberg

What do schools really do? If you watched them, as a very, very intelligent Uganda native of the eighteenth century might watch a dynamo, would you say that they were in the society for the purpose of doing something you thought was desirable?

In the first place, under what conditions and circumstances do we have schools?

POLICE, GARBAGE-MEN, AND SCHOOL-TEACHERS

Look, for example, at the 1967 New York City teachers' strike. One of the most extraordinary aspects of the strike, it seems to me, is the fact that according to the press reports there was almost universal concensus among the people of New York City that some dreadful emergency had arisen because the schools were closed. Now as the teachers' strike continued, the garbage collectors also went out on strike, and that *is* an emergency: you don't notice the change very rapidly, but ultimately you can't get down the street any more and then you really do have to make other arrangements. The police were also on strike, and that is a situation that has, after all, the qualities of its defect. What people did was lump the strikes together, believing that the police, the garbagemen, and the schoolteachers ran institutions which had not only legitimate, but also indispensable purposes. Thus for all the strikes there was great urgency to settle.

With the school strike, the urgency of settling became as great as it did because nobody thought to ask "Look, what do these schools do anyway besides baby-sit?" And if we can't get along without that for a while (which may be true in a society so organized that both parents have to go out to work to have a decent living) then you ought to look at that situation instead. However, instead of asking this question, the city went ahead and endorsed the teachers' assumption that education is something cumulative, that each day missed in school was a slice off the child's learning life. If you think back to the moments at which you learned relatively important things in your life, you'll find that the things that are, let us say, of grade B importance on the usual scale of 26 you learn in about a second. And the things that are of grade A importance, of course, you don't even know you know; you couldn't even say when you learned them. The notion of the cumulative effects of educational routine, however, is rooted deep: you should never miss a day.

The question immediately arises: why so much concern about the effects of cumulative education if the important things in life are known outside this process. What do the schools really do?

DO YOU HAVE TO BE AN ELEPHANT?

In the first place, let's remind ourselves that the school is a relatively new kind of institution. At least a school which is supposed to include any very large proportion of the population is a relatively new kind of institution; but I don't think I have to modify the first statement that much. In the U.S. in 1870—with the Kalamazoo decision—there wasn't any question of compulsory attendance at high school. The only question was whether you could pay for it out of public funds for the people who had the money and the marks to go. Obviously, there have been other social changes that make the high school a more—here I hardly know what to say—I started to say a more useful institution, but if you're an elephant obviously you need a trunk, but this doesn't mean you have to be an elephant.

Let's say that social evolution has developed in such a way that the society certainly wouldn't work without wide-spread public compulsory education. There is no large industrial society, whether in the free world or in the Eastern world, using the conventional designations for these, that can get along without compulsory school attendance. They all seem to have agreed on a fairly similar number of years' limit on the age range.

The question is then, what do schools do that requires compulsory education? that requires cumulative education? What are their social functions?

The most important social function of the schools, it seems to me, is in defining *youth as a social role*. I would like you to consider what that may really mean. We generally think that youth is a natural category. There aren't any natural categories, however. There really are not *any*. I mean, if you are reasonably comprehensive in your survey of anthropology, you will find that even the living and the dead do not constitute for all societies, all cultures under all circumstances, two distinct categories or groups. In fact, with a different view of the supernatural there may well be little attention paid to the distinction. Obviously, a corpse presents certain practical problems, but they are not insuperable. The transition may be looked on as something having very little significance in the relationship of what we would call the survivors and the persona of what we would call the departed. The difference between men and women seems to be relatively more stable, but by no means always certain. The difference between races, however, is notoriously artificial. There are no Negroes in any part of Africa except Liberia and The Union of South Africa; for the rest of it there are black people who become Negroes if they fly to New York.

Youth is very much the same thing, and one reason that youth is youth is because (as with black people) it is subjected to certain specific, invidious, legally institutionalized distinctions, of which the school is the major source.

For example, since The War Between the States it has not been unlawful simply to be anywhere because you are black. But this is obviously not true of young people. It is an offence to be anywhere but in school during school hours. Since it is an offence, you can be and will be apprehended, and you can be sent away to what we call a juvenile hall or detention home; the names vary. At any rate, there isn't any way you can hang loose. This isn't true of any other element of the population. It has even been elaborated in some jurisdictions in the States in ways that still astonish me. What compulsory school attendance does is to define young people as a subject category, and puts on both their movements and their perceptions certain kinds of restrictions which no one else is subject to at all. It does so, moreover, in a way which is remarkably total since even a veritable Sampson has not the strength to grow out his hair within two hours between 3 and 5 in the afternoon when he may want to pursue some activity among his own peers, for which long hair is a desiderata.

The schools manage by virtue of manipulation of the authority invested in them by the education code. In other words they usurp or intrude upon their students' life space—not just his time in school—and this action they justify. This is often justified as character building, though America is getting a bit more liberal and the explanation of character building doesn't go down so well anymore. It would have 30 or 40 years ago, but there have been a few Court decisions on the question, and American schools are not supposed to go around building your character without your consent. They have to say that long hair is so distracting that it interferes with the educational function of the school. The wife of one of the students who came with me to Buffalo from California, and who is now teaching in the schools of a lower middle class suburb of Buffalo, had the odd experience of having the principal come into her room a few days ago and ask her to search a young girl. The principal said he was being distracted beyond his capacity to perform his duties by the fact that somewhere on her person this girl had a bell. She knew she wasn't supposed to wear a bell at school, so she put it under a sweater or something; but he could still hear it tinkle. It was found and confiscated.

It is reasonably clear that the hegemony of the school situation is really a good deal greyer than it would be if it was only a place to which you go of your own choice because you want to learn something you are curious about or that is useful to you for purposes of your own. Once you put it in the context of your being the client (society supporting you in this definition of your own role) then it seems obvious that education takes on a totally different function than defining a social role for youth.

The second major function of the schools, one which is obviously related to the first, is the legitimization of a form of economic discrimination. The best piece of writing on this subject is by John and Margaret Rowntree in an article called "The Political Economy of American youth." It's in *Our Generation*. (It is published in Montreal under the guidance of an editor with the formidably bilingual name of Demetrios Roussopoulos.) I very strongly recommend this article. It is a cool, clear analysis of the way what the Rowntrees call the "education and military industries" make use of the role definition of people below 25 as young. Their arguments seem to be directed to the workings of capitalist society, although I think they can be equally well applied to the industrial societies of the East.

The main thing the school is supposed to do for children is to guide them in investing in their own future. Once you get people to agree to this then you can avoid the question of having to pay students for what is, after all, a form of involuntary servitude. By assuming that what goes on in school prepares young people to earn more money and have higher social status in the future, you can get out of any implication that they ought to be paid for the

labor of doing it: the school, the argument goes, is already contributing to what the students are laying aside, if you regard their
higher income as a return on capital investment; and what else
could a good North American regard a higher income as? This
makes everything perfectly just and okay.

However, pieces begin falling off the above little model as soon
as you begin turning it around so you can look at it closely.

Now all the books on the subject of income, status, and schooling, even the relatively sophisticated ones, will say that one thing
about schooling is that it does indeed assist you in getting a higher
standard of living; it contributes to social mobility; it is necessary
if you are going to get ahead in the world. The best of the books
may be rather wry about that and say "Isn't it a shame that our
traditional cultural faith in education seems to come to so little in
comparison to the nitty-gritty issues of everyday life, and we wish
people really were interested in ideas, but maybe we can't expect
that. . . ." Yet once you've shown a tight correlation between the
number of years of schooling completed and the average income for
the rest of your life and particularly, of course, for the highest
level of income achieved, what have you really proved?

What you've proved, it seems to me, if you've proved anything,
is the existence of a conspiracy. Because you are faced on the one
hand with a very widespread agreement that you are not going to
hire people who don't have the credentials, and on the other hand,
if you don't hire people who don't have the credentials you'll never
find out if they could have done the job or not, with no alternative
ways of earning the credentials on the job. Increasingly we have no
way outside the school system of legitimizing participation in the
process of growing up, much less getting a license for a trade everyone agrees you need a license for.

What we need to justify educational participation is not the
correlation of higher income to higher levels of schooling, but
rather some direct indication of where or what the skills really are
that enable a person to make it through life, and to what extent
the school does in fact contribute to learning these skills. Further,
if there are such skills, and there is no other place than school to
get them, that still does not really prove that schools are the best
method of passing on these skills. In fact, the argument that schools
are the only channels for opportunity in American culture is a little
bit like the argument that David would have made a suitable and
pious husband to Bathsheba. There is still the question of his com-
plicity in Uriah's fate and whether there would not have been some-

thing even better available except for what he did. In this case it isn't the schools themselves that provide the economic and social rewards, but then, in the biblical story, David isn't the murderer either. He's simply the influential administrative official.

If this were not enough to weaken the argument for schools as places for getting ahead, there is the fact that the statistics are interpreted in a kind of phoney way. In the first place, most of the arguments linking higher incomes and schooling are directed toward high school, concentrating on those who have or have not completed high school. The data for completing high school includes everybody who completed high school, which means people who go on and get university degrees. When you look at those who completed high school and didn't go on to college and those who didn't complete high school the difference in earning potential isn't very great. It averages out to something like an extra $20.00 per month for those who completed high school; not enough probably to make up for the aggravation.

Of course, you can say "Yes, but we think everyone should go to college, and you can't do that unless you go to high school." But then you are faced with a couple of other things that a reasonably bright lawyer would raise in countering such an argument in a court of equity. You see, the financial value of a high school degree was great only at a time when the high school degree was relatively scarce and was a symbol of an elite position. So again we do not know that it was the high school education that caused the higher income. All we can say is that the people in the top 10 percent of the society, with the resources to not earn money and go to school, are likely to earn more money over the long run than those who didn't have the resources and didn't go to school. Further, when education becomes universal, everyone going to college, then it's possible that its fiscal utility will diminish; this seems, in fact, to be what does happen. You can't, I think, use any part of this argument to conclude anything with certainty except that the schools are a sentinel. They provide the check points along which you progress.

From the point of view of the corporations, however, the schools do perform a useful function: they instill or induce you to develop certain characteristics which are marketable, the kind of characteristics that allow you to work comfortably within the corporation. Of course, if you have a mind to, you can then argue that this means that the schools constitute a subsidy for so-called private enterprise provided by the taxpayers' dollars. So maybe students ought to get paid much earlier, and by the people who use them.

I think probably in order to understand the relationship between our corporate society, our schools, and our students in a general way—as to how schools do what they do—there is no better source than the sage of Toronto and two of his most familiar aphorisms.

In the schools, more than in most of the other mass media, it is indeed true that the medium is the message, which is one reason I haven't said a word about curriculum. What is taught isn't as important as learning how you have to act in society, how other people will treat you, how they will respond to you, what the limits of respect that will be accorded to you really are. What the schools teach is the experience of being a school child, and once you get used to that it's unlikely you will run amock among the inhabitants of Yorkville.

The other McLuhan point that seems to me to provide an even deeper source of insight is the observation that we don't know who discovered water, but we're pretty sure it wasn't the fish. What I mean by this is that the schools, by providing a continual social substrate—a kind which is, in effect, a caricature of the society— makes the society seem so natural that you don't notice the awful things that it does. In fact, even your ways of fighting the school are determined by what it teaches you to regard as propriety—or obscenity—whichever you happen to want to employ. In any case, it's essentially true that what the schools do is teach you how "it's spozed to be," particularly in a liberal democracy, where the schools embody the society's central contradictions.

We have a written constitution to which the first ten amendments constitute the Bill of Rights. Most states have laws—laws made before the Supreme Court went over to the 'communists'—that compel you to teach the constitution. However, if you learn the constitution in the American public school system, you certainly are not going to go around thinking that the Bill of Rights applies to you. There has been a little research study, as a matter of fact, on what children really think the pledge of allegiance to the flag means, and there was a very wide divergence of opinion. A masters' degree student, who was more imaginative than most, simply went around and asked children to tell him what the pledge said, to repeat it for him. The nicest result, I think, was "One nation indivincable, with liberty and death for all." We have been trying to fulfill that promise alright, but when it comes to promises, say of freedom of speech in situations in which it creates real social disruptions, we've been less than careful in keeping our word. I don't want to put down the quite remarkable and creditable degree of freedom of speech in the United States in the sense that you are unlikely to be subjected to official sanctions for anything that you say. The point is that the functions of the school are to teach you about the unofficial sanctions, to prepare you for the blacklist, to make sure you understand the implications of being labelled a "trouble-maker," which is the worst thing a school can call you.

The schools perform this kind of function, it seems to me, in a society that is lying about its traditions. A nicer way of putting it is to say the society still honors or likes to draw from components of its tradition that are nobler than it can in fact hope to institutionalize in everyday practice. But it still comes out lying. One of the reasons this has happened is that we have included into the social process, with some degree of influence, people who would in an earlier, more conservative organization of society, have been declassé and nonvoting. Here, I think, we are at the heart of the matter. The schools have succeeded in becoming mass organizations, serving a much larger proportion of the population, and are as bad as they are because of their response to this process. The problem is not that they are serving people now who have less ability than before, but that they are serving people who in earlier days were treated by decision-makers as victims. When a society becomes more democratic and no longer feels comfortable about treating people as victims, yet still retains essentially the same exploitative social arrangements, then it has to create institutions that will induce people to choose to be victims. Choosing out of anxiety or out of a lack of sense of what their own resources might be or out of a realistic sense that they might not be smart enough to be rulers if they don't choose to be victims.

In the most general terms then the schools, like the society, hold in tension the contradictions of the liberal tradition as it grew out of British and later, American society. They emphasize both the individual and the sanctity of getting rich, and so they obscure moral issues and at the same time tend to favor continual enlargement of the in-group.

There is real conflict, it seems to me, between provision through the school of increased economic opportunity and the support of cultural values that might treat all people more generously. The schools have been set up to avoid this conflict, although lately they don't seem to be having so much success. A serious polarization seems to be happening in America, for which I am glad, but then I'm not a liberal. The schools have tried to evade this polarization by defining the difference between the rich and the poor, not in terms of their relationships to the means of production and the consequent real conflicts of interest, but rather in terms of cultural deprivation. They take the sting out of this deprivation by making the authority of the things that really are associated with what is left of high culture so tenuous and so ridiculous that there wasn't much left but the implication that, of course, you must learn this culture just as you have to learn to put on a coat and a tie and comb your hair and have it short, because otherwise you won't get a job. Thus not having this culture doesn't have to mean you're inferior to anyone else. Now, it seems to me that a more valid human message would have been that you have the right to dress in a way you think becomes you, but no matter how you dress, it may indeed be true that you are inferior to other people. And this inferiority may be a consequence of experiences that happened so early and that were so intense that they will never be reversed. No school can be magical. There will be some things that you don't understand, that you will never understand, that certain kinds of schools could help certain other people understand if you would shut up. You have been permanently deprived of something that is of inestimable value.

The possibility of such deprivation we can't face up to. We are very suspicious of the cultivation of the kind of subtlety that builds only on antecedent association, very suspicious of going off with a few people to explore meanings that might be private, letting these people select themselves. You get everyone uptight if you form a self-selected group to talk about issues of importance to you. In American society this is a real violation. The whole thing is set up with the schools as a prime part of it, to keep anyone from fearing that there may indeed be a hidden treasure that they aren't going to find. As a result, it may have been destroyed, at least the one that came down through high culture.

The kids, on the other hand, aren't buying this loss and are re-building other modes of communication. Here we get into the best of folk-rock, the sound of groups that are communicating private experience. They are put down as hippies because the experience has to be private rather than political. Yet it is privacy that is being destroyed, not isolation. What we have increasingly lost is our social right to do our own thing with our own kind of people. Society's institutions are there to stamp it out. The result is that new forms of personal experience have to come in from areas that are not legitimized. If they were legitimate, they would be seized and democratized. It can only be done the other way—by working with materials which were assumed to be of no value until they are finally noticed, and one hopes that it will take years as it did in the case of the Beatles. With them it was finally noticed that there were enough people who shared their illicit longing for subjective communication to make someone rich. At that point the thing falls into the commercial pile and you have the Maharishi appearing, Brian Epstein committing suicide. In this way Western Civilization is carried on.

Nevertheless, there are some suggestions for making high school 1980 more flexible, humane, and *instructive* that are worth considering, and that are in fact under consideration by persons with a professional interest in education at the present time.

First, students by 1980 might be allowed to attend any school they chose, either at state expense or under a fixed state subsidy that they or their parents could augment if necessary. Some proponents of this approach urge the abolition of the public school system as such. But this seems too drastic an action for what it would accomplish; since most public schools would simply have to learn to operate competitively as private schools, in order to fill the demand for places until society began to grasp the idea that young people might be doing something entirely different than going to school—which would take years. A less drastic change might be made by continuing *local* support of the public schools, but assigning the state-aid funds now allotted on the basis of average daily attendance to the school pupils actually chose to attend—including, of course, their public school if they wished to remain there.

One argument advanced against this plan is that white-racist parents would use it to achieve de facto segregation. But I think this is mistaken. What white parents flee to the suburbs to avoid, I am convinced, is *not* Negro children; but the often demoralized and occasionally brutal personnel who have been assigned to, or permitted to accumulate in, such schools, and the atmosphere of hostility and contempt for students that pervades them. Under a system of adequately subsidized free choice the black students, surely, would move, too, unless their school became a decent place. Black people have no preference for bad schools when they are afforded the means to attend better ones—the proportion of the relatively small group of middle-class Negroes who send their children to private schools is far higher than the proportion of middle-class whites who do so. But the loss of the financial support from the state that their withdrawal would occasion is a powerful sanction against schools which mistreat them.

Another device for increasing flexibility of educational opportunity in 1980, which would require less administrative revision but might encounter greater resistance from hostile adults, would be for the school to undertake to *license* off-premise educational projects.

Students might then submit either a proposal for independent study or an application to participate in an ongoing extramural project; if approved, this would free them of attendance requirements for the duration of their project. They might, like grantholders, be required to submit regular progress reports for evaluation; they might also be required to report semi-annually to test centers in order to demonstrate that they were learning the basic curriculum satisfactorily despite their absence from classes. During this period they should also have access to the facilities and staff of the school as, in effect, research consultants. The difficulty with this plan, however, is that one of the major functions of the school is to keep students off the streets and out of the way of adults who really know quite well that submission to school routines, rather than the required course of study, *is* what constitutes the basic curriculum. There is, however, no way around the fact that *any* significant improvement of educational policy must reflect a corresponding improvement in the relative status of youth in society, and will therefore affront those adults whose needs are expressed in present policy.

A much more ambitious proposal now being widely considered is that wholly publicly-supported residential schools be established by 1980, especially for students whose homes provide neither the quiet and privacy nor the basic nutrition and rest needed for study or, what is more important, for health and a decent life. This is a tantalizing question. The drawbacks are serious enough. For one thing, this proposal assumes that our society cannot or will not attack its economic problems radically enough to eliminate the slums and provide decent accommodation for the people trapped there—whether or not they fit a social-worker's conception of a stable family unit. Still, this may be true; and if so, some children might be saved by attending boarding school. They might also be destroyed; the possibilities for making education really totalitarian are horrifying. School personnel, already convinced that they were dealing with the "disadvantaged" or "culturally deprived," might well treat these students the way the teachers and staff of the boarding schools run by the U.S. Bureau of Indian Affairs treat the children of the Oglalla Sioux. These schools, as the anthropologist and sociologist Murray and Rosalie Wax describe them, may be the most oppressive in the world; and the Waxes themselves point out that what makes them so is the prevalence among their staffs of attitudes toward Indians as dirty, shiftless, and uncouth; and an enthusiastic determination to make them clean, responsive, and middle class, which closely resembles the attitudes that prevail among teachers in slum schools.

On the other hand, the very best schools I have observed are boarding schools primarily for high-school students from "disadvantaged" homes; and although—or because—they are highly exceptional, there is a great deal to be learned from them as to what the possibilities are. They are temporary, summer programs, held for about seven weeks on the campuses of colleges and universities, partially or wholly funded by the Office of Economic Opportunity, with some assistance from foundations. They are intended to prepare students for college who almost certainly would not otherwise get there. Those that I know at first hand—the PREP program at Franklin and Marshall College in Lancaster, Pennsylvania, and the Yale Summer High School held on the Divinity School campus in New Haven—have been held for several years consecutively, which makes them real pioneers in the rapidly shifting and sometimes tricky scene of educational service to the culturally deprived.

Among the lessons to be learned from them are:

1. *It is possible to cut through the stultifying mass of value judgments that accumulate in the form of a high-school record and identify creative often disaffected, intelligence underneath.* The intellectual style of these students is more aggressive than that usually found among their peers in high school. It is also more cogent; they stick closer to the heart of the discourse. But they readily learn the conventions of the seminar room, for what these may be worth.

They have bad academic records, both on disciplinary grounds and because their achievement is so spotty. They are likely to have been put down as either an overachiever or an underachiever, depending on whether their regular school was initially impressed by their apparent brashness or their IQ score. To find them, therefore, one must learn to discount the academic record and turn to other sources of appraisal: persons nominated by the student himself as knowing what he is really like; or members of newer bureaucracies, with value-patterns different from those of the school, with which he has had contact—OEO project-directors, for example. When this is done, recruitment is so successful in attracting promising people that one can only regret that the program is directed toward college admission rather than more diverse and original educational purposes.

2. *Bureaucracy is probably as important a source of educational stultification as it is thought to be.* The Yale and PREP programs have been gifted with leadership that both "digs" and respects underclass youth. But there are people in the public schools who do, too—they write very good books about their experiences; thereafter they get fired. What saves the summer programs is the fact that they cannot conceivably provide their staffs with a career-line. Everybody who teaches there has a "real" job somewhere else which pays most of

their living and defines their social identity—and which they probably do worse. In the summer institute, they are much freer to define their educational mission and work directly at it; just as temporary research teams at Arthur D. Little or SRI, unhampered by departmental lines and permanent, built-in status factors, often get more satisfaction and work more efficiently than their academic counterparts.

3. *High school students should be paid.* Students in these summer programs receive stipends of $5 or $10 a week as well as, of course, room and board. It is essential, for reasons that apply to high school students generally. Money is euphoric, psychedelic and, though addictive, the addiction is not regarded as an offense under law. It is the most nearly universally honored claim to at least minimal dignity in our society. It provides genuine independence. At a deeper level, being paid would afford students some protection from the schools' often outrageous moral pretensions. If students were paid to go to school they would be far less implicated in the school's assumption that its demands express moral, as well as social, authority.

4. *Student participation in the governance of the institutions they attend is meaningful and desirable only insofar as it derives from real power.* These summer institute students participate very actively in running their program. But in any real conflict they are still regulated by adults. Some of the students at Yale Summer High School complained seriously against the regulation forbidding boys and girls access to each others' rooms—a policy the director justified simply and honestly as a necessary concession to local custom, rather than on moral grounds. His candor could not, however, prevent his actions from revealing the pretentiousness of student participation in governing the institute, since there was no process by which he could be overruled and the regulation changed, and students who disobeyed were subject to dismissal.

Persons who accept a spurious involvement in the authority that governs them must ultimately face the bitter fact that by doing so they have legitimated that authority and made themselves weaker rather than stronger with respect to it. For this reason, it seems to me especially fortunate that students now think in terms of power rather than authority, and attempt, when they are aggrieved to counter authority with power—real power to affect the operation of the schools to which they have so long been subject. Negotiation, to be sure, is preferable to hostile confrontation; but no real negotiation takes place if either party to it is convinced that his adversary has no power to rebuke his intransigence. The question is not whether students should be permitted a voice in appointments, curriculum design, relations between school and community, and other major issues in the operation of schools and universities, but whether the entire process of education is not becoming more decent and more relevant because it is no longer possible to *deny* them a voice in matters that affect them so profoundly. Whether they should be given it I do not know—for then it might not really be theirs— but I am quite sure that they should take it if they are not, for their own sake and for that of the institution.

That they are doing so is, in my judgment, the most hopeful indication that education may become more decent as the decade passes. I take this position not because I impute to students wisdom superior to that of the faculty or administration or because I believe them to be in general, nobler and less self-seeking—though, at times, both these conclusions do indeed seem justified. But that is not the reason; even if I thought students largely fools and knaves I would still want them to have real power to influence the course of their own lives. What is most repellent about education in America and elsewhere is directly attributable to the fact that the institution has so far been able to count on social pressure and legal coercion to provide it with a captive clientele and a mandate to train that clientele in servility. Nothing so poisons a society as the prevalence within it of a petty and resentful citizenry that has been made to relinquish, through force or guile—and the schools have used both—its sense of moral authority over its own life. Education cannot be improved except in a society that respects the young; and ours respects no social group that is powerless and without resources. Yet, American society has rather consistently worked in such a way as to make it possible—difficult, but possible—for each successive discriminated group to gain enough real power to command respect and some of the elements, at least, of a decent life. With the exception of the Indians, who thought they owned the place, this has been the experience of all—even, at long last, of black people. If—and only if—it is also the experience of youth in America, schools in 1980 will be more decent, less rigid, and less *total* in their segregation from and immunity to the demands of ordinary life. Then, there may come a time when you can't even tell education from living.

Society: The School Without Walls

Frank G. Jennings

One of man's most urgent endeavors is to try to find some clue about what tomorrow will bring. He has used tea leaves, sheep's livers, and systems analysis with indifferent results, but he persists in the quest, driven by a hope that grows out of some modest successes in another line of inquiry. There are, after all, certain regularities in the world about him: the round of the seasons; birth, growth, and death; the agricultural rhythms; and the causal relationships between activities and their consequences. All of this allows man to plan for tomorrow, and in his planning he employs language that reflects his hopes and fears.

Today's systems analyst, racetrack tout, and real estate investor all attempt to understand and, if possible, to control the future. Their impulses are identical with the earlier efforts of Babylonian astrologers and medieval necromancers. Their major difference from these distant ancestors is in the hardware they use. Their major similarity is in their desire somehow to improve the quality of human life.

Ever since education became professional, its practitioners have been "future oriented". Simply by deciding what a child should learn and what kind of an adult it might become inevitably forces the teacher to accept the heady notion that he can affect eternity. This leads him to assume or to accept the awesome responsibility of changing the shape of things. He attempts to do this by occasionally assessing his role as teacher and by seeking ever more sophisticated means for improving the quality of his performance. He is, however, constantly disabused by the measurable results of his endeavors, and thus seeks to find someone or some agency with which to share the blame.

During the high noon of the Greek miracle Socrates asserted that society was "the greatest of all Sophists." Depending upon how the word "Sophist" is defined, he could have meant either the "twister of men's minds" or the "enlarger of man's vision." However, it is certain that he viewed society as the most potent educative force in men's lives. For the Greeks during their greatest period did not distinguish sharply between formal and informal education, and so the school undertook merely one portion of the child's and the citizen's education. It is this view, in fact, that has persisted with more or less force to the present day. Certainly Thomas Jefferson expressed the belief, shared with the founding fathers, that the whole of the community educates and that the teacher instructs only in certain specific skills and understandings. Thus, formal schooling, whatever the promise or protestation of its practitioners, is concerned with the education of only some part of the minds of some of the citizens. This is true today despite the contemporary world's insistence on such noble aims as "the education of all the people." The very partisans of this view confess in their behavior that no formal system of education can affect the totality of any individual or can even shape his public personality.

From the turn of the century when public education became increasingly a field for professionals, and since public schools have become compulsory and pervasive, many tasks that the school undertook were taken away from other institutions, including the family and the church. The services that schools sought to provide went far beyond the confines of the classroom. Thus, schools today, whether in the United States, in the Soviet Union, or in Communist China, attempt to provide not only instruction but the meeting of social, psychological, and even physical needs of the students. In every instance, however, regardless of the structure of the educational or political system, educators everywhere are plagued by ancient doubts and dissatisfactions. They are unable to provide "the right education for every child." They are unable to offer "education for all American youth." They are inadequate in attempting to guarantee that every student would leave every school with "certain marketable skills." Most serious of all is their recognized failure to mitigate the corrosive consequences of life in a mass society. For, in spite of vastly increased efforts and quantum leaps in the expenditure of government monies, the plight of the least fortunate in every society does not appear to be responsive to the exclusive ministrations of formal education.

Some social critics (and this is in every country) insist that the present state of education is a direct result of the social acquisitiveness of its professionals, who have presumed too much and in so doing have either alienated or bypassed some of the most potent sources of instruction that exist in every society.

Examples are numerous, but one need only advert to Socrates' observation to realize the nature of the problem. The most human part of human nature is that, except for its basic genetic endowment, everything that makes man human is learned, is taught, is caught from experience, whether that experience be planned or "accidental." We know so much in detail about the human animal. There are so many things that we can do to it and for it that will improve its ability to survive and to increase the quality of the life it can live, and yet there are so many variables that enter into the "making of the modern mind" over which only minimum controls are possible, that one is driven to the naïve position of many contemporary artists who see wanton chance as the undisputed ruler of the universe.

What haunts the social and the behavioral scientist and what plagues the professional educator (who sees himself as carrying on the engineering functions of these "disciplines") is that the physical scientist appears to them to have accommodated himself to the chance nature of reality and with powerful statistical tools appears even to have domesticated it. Neither the educator nor any scientist concerned with human behavior can approximate this success, and yet each suspects that this failure (if it is indeed a failure) must be the result of asking inappropriate questions. Further, it is just possible that educators, especially, have become trapped in their methodology and victimized by the very technology they have enlisted in their undertaking. They appear to be hag-ridden by the old alchemists' dream of controlling the future. They seem to be driven by the race track tout's compulsion to believe that every new hunch is a key to limitless riches.

Robert Maynard Hutchins, that life-long critic of the "professional educator," in his most recent book, *The Learning Society*, points out that ". . . since the real test [of schooling] is what the students are in later life, an educational system can claim to have succeeded in its own terms only after a quarter of a century." Hutchins writes that even such a claim would probably be false, since the behavior of any individual throughout adult life can only in a rather small measure be attributed to the experiences undergone during years of schooling. He appears to agree with Benjamin S. Bloom (*Stability and Change in Human Characteristics*) as well as with the almost universal folk wisdom of the race in believing that what happens to the child in its first five years of life literally determines what it

can become as a man or woman, and that the deprivations it under-
goes or the supports it enjoys do more to shape both its personality
and its intelligence than all of the organized efforts of all of the
teachers in all of the schools the individual ever attends.

Yet, there persists among those who, in Aristotle's phrase, "have
thought long upon the fate of empires," the conviction that we
have resources now at our disposal to effect for the good of man-
kind some vast and positive changes in the way we consider education as a function of the total society, and as an experience that
continues throughout life. What is required, they believe, is an
inventory of these resources and some dependable assessments of
their differential worth, and the collective wisdom to select appropriately from among these resources to be employed for sound
social and humane purposes.

II

Any discussion of the organization and function of the high school
in 1980 must be limited by the recognition that *we are not dealing
with prophecy,* but merely with rather short-term projections. Most
public school systems already have on their "future books" more
or less detailed plans for most aspects of the educational undertaking
as they will be elaborated over the next decade. With the exception
of occasional flights of controlled fancy on matters of architecture
and technology, these projects have a sober actuarial cast.

For example, every large city is possessed of fairly dependable
demographic data which indicate quite clearly what the population
makeup of the different sections of the city will be like five, ten,
and fifteen years hence. Every major city is today confronting the
no longer avoidable necessity of reorganizing its educational administration and of redeploying its educational resources to meet the
anticipated shifts in citizen needs. Every major city, whether or not
it employs a master plan, is possessed of fairly accurate information
about anticipated shifts and growth in business and manufacturing
areas, in transportation systems, the size of the tax base, and the
measurable needs for increased social and welfare services. Every
major city has warrant to anticipate an increase in state and federal
tax support to meet the rising costs of social and welfare services,
among which education will continue to loom the largest.

Therefore, the arguments for decentralization which are today so heavily freighted with real and putative racial issues have an intractable economic base which must be contended with. Put very simply, the cost to the city and to the financial community of real estate that is withdrawn from tax production will have to be reduced. In many of the larger central cities it is today not unusual to find more than 50 percent of the real estate being employed on a tax exempt basis. In some instances, such as downtown Milwaukee and Manhattan island, the figure either approaches or exceeds 75 percent.

The State of New York is tentatively experimenting with legislation permitting public schools to be housed within buildings that also provide rental space for either business or residence. Whether or not this will provide a viable alternative to present arrangements remains to be seen.

In the slums of most of the great cities one finds an increasing number of "street academies." Most of these grew out of earlier tutorial programs and Headstart projects, some from beginnings in storefront churches. All of these undertakings are in direct reaction to the communities' judgments that the public school has failed. It is almost incidental that these "academies" are beginning to appear as a possible alternative to the leviathan public school bureaucracy that seems to be incapable of disassembling and recreating itself.

At the other end of the economic spectrum, the past decade has seen a sharp increase in the number of private schools, whether church supported or independent. While many of these schools have been created with a poorly hidden purpose of avoiding the "terrors" of integration, an increasing number are being established for the opposite purpose, by people both black and white who are persuaded that the public schools in large cities are victims of demography and can never be responsive to the leveling and egalitarian urgings of educational idealists.

Thus, both the street academies and the new private schools represent the emergence of educational systems competitive with the public system, and, as indicated above, must inevitably present an additional threat to the ever-shrinking real estate tax base. They may, however, also offer some salutary challenges to the hitherto seemingly monolithic boards of education.

Another source of challenge in this regard is beginning to appear in industry. Starting with interesting experiments in cooperative education, which are designed to compensate for the dismal failure of vocational education, these programs (in some instances harking back to earlier apprenticeship and guild systems) provide part-time on-the-job training, balanced with a modified and compressed secondary academic program. It is conceivable that this as yet very modest movement may become associated with the growing number of community and junior colleges, many of which have vocational emphases.

There are other pressures that will reshape the schools which will come from society's efforts to meet other civic needs. Public and private housing must be vastly expanded in the coming decade. The federal government has moved on this through the new departments of transportation and of housing and urban development.

In the *New York Post* of September 3, 1968, Sylvia Porter wrote of "the most far-reaching, gigantic, potentially revolutionary housing law in the entire history of the United States . . . ." It is a grab-bag law with something for everybody and every section. It is in part probably unworkable, but the major features will produce profound and positive changes in the economics of the building industry, change the shape, size, and complexion of the suburbs, re-create the centers of our cities, give aid and comfort to the comfortable middle class, extend the range of job opportunities downward to the ranks of the unskilled—but most important, it assures the almost continuous creation of new towns in this country throughout the remainder of this century.

The Housing and Urban Development Act of 1968 will be the most dramatic instance of society functioning as the school-without-walls we have ever seen. This is not prophecy. This is simple social budgeting. The early changes in the American housing picture will be both modest and bungling, but they will increase algebraically. Whether an informed intelligence guides them or not, they will come. Whether or not there is a central planning agency to guide them, they will develop. The social, political and economic consequences will be cumulatively vast, but they will consist in the early years of polyp-like accretions. Very few of the public school systems now operative in the country will not have their geography altered; very few of them will have their population mixtures remain stabile; very few of them will be able to resist for more than four or five years new community pressures to alter their structure, change their administration, re-create their curricula, and modify their educational goals, nor will many of them be able to remain uninvolved in the larger affairs of their host communities.

Perhaps this is expecting too much from a single act of Congress, but the point is made here to underscore the vulnerability of the schools to pressures for change. After all, the history of secondary education in the United States is one of challenge and response (even more so than is that of higher education).

Although the American commitment to the public high school was established by the Massachusetts Law of 1827, it was not until 1864 that New York required the maintenance of high schools, and by 1890 there were only 2526 high schools in the nation, which had a population of 63 million. That information appears in *The High School in a New Era,* edited by Francis S. Chase and Harold A. Anderson (University of Chicago Press, 1958). One of the authors, Henry Steele Commager, writing only a decade ago, is more congratulatory than our present temper would allow:

> Looking back on the American experience in the perspective of a century or so (about the time we have been at the job of comprehensive education), we cannot, I think, but be dazzled that we have managed so well in so short a time. If we look only to the educational achievement, we see that we have provided more education to a larger portion of society than did any other country in history; we have built a magnificent physical plant and equipped it with educational apparatus, for example, gymnasiums and school libraries; we have supplied more than one million teachers (and who will deny that they are better prepared for their jobs than were the teachers of half a century ago?). If emphasis seems to be laid too heavily on quantity, may we not add that, qualitatively, the products of the American school system compared favorably with the products of German and French school systems both in competence and in judgment in the great crisis of World War II and its aftermath? (Pp. 5-6.)

It is patently unfair to expose such a citation removed from its textbook context, except for the possible therapeutic value. This is the way we have addressed prospective teachers. The real world is more disorderly than it is represented to be in such shining paragraphs. The educational problems are more fraught with difficulty than it would appear in texts which assert that progress is always linear and always assured.

In spite of all that we have learned during the past half century about the nature of adolescence and about the complex and interrelated issues of attitude formation, motivation, habit formation, and learning, our strategies for teaching tend in practice to be regressive. Whatever the classroom teacher's own education suggests, however sophisticated the new curricular designs may be, the ancient rule still has very few exceptions. The teacher stands before his class and talks and talks and talks.

But there is a new education that has become far more widespread and far more effective than most educators care to admit. It is informal. It is affective. And it is pervasive. And it comes from the "great Sophist." Every contemporary high technology is now teaching and has been teaching with increasing effectiveness all of its citizens for the past half century. This is not merely an historical phenomenon. It is the consequence of a radical change in the quality of life and in the increasing richness of options available to all citizens. It is most crudely described by Marshall McLuhan. It has been narrowly conceived by those general semanticists who view all aberrant behavior as functions of language misunderstanding and language disorders. It is often described in metaphysical metaphors by activist social scientists as a "creatively destructive impulse attending the birth of the new world." The public language of even high school youth appears to offer testimony in support of this "new reality." They are "antiestablishment"; they are against the "power structure"; they see all great societies as part of a new imperium. They see class distinctions of the most egregious sort, and they see the dominant majority as essentially racist in all of its actions. They are persuaded that the middle-class values are valueless. In short, contemporary youth appears to be behaving like primordial Christians who view the world's end as necessary and near.

Such a mosaic description as the foregoing is born of a near hysteria. Our contemporary social realities are not quite that disorderly.

Item: For the first time in the history of the United States we have a sizable and potentially long-lived youth movement. The high school in 1980 will have to function with respect to such a youth movement which by then will have accumulated a tradition of five school generations.

Item: As indicated earlier, our youth today are taking our "democratic house platitudes" seriously. They see them as programs for action with a vividness comparable only to the vision of our founding fathers and of the democrats of Periclean Athens.

Item: Contemporary students in high school as well as in college increasingly want a piece of the social action. They see themselves as capable of accepting and undertaking socially responsible work, and they resent the deferral of adult roles into early middle life, as is presently so common in our society.

Item: Contemporary youth, despite its needs for permanence and stability, are quite at home in the presence of change and tend to look upon conflict even as Alfred North Whitehead did, not as a portent of disaster but as an opportunity for creative growth.

Now consider the contemporary high school curriculum that is only marginally responsive to the needs of youth. Bear in mind their reaction against attenuated adolescence. Consider the prevalence of the Pill, of military service at the end of high school, of the inevitable lowering of the voting age to 18, of the present and increasing preference for youthfulness throughout the whole of society. And add to all of the foregoing the inevitable increase of socially useful undertakings even among children. Then one is bound to realize that the institution we now denominate as "high school" will even in so short a space as the 12 years ahead of us undergo such profound changes that its basic functions will have to be altered beyond our present powers of recognition.

Although the foregoing comments might be criticized as overly dramatic, and the implied forecasts unwarranted in the face of the hard data of the social and behavioral sciences, it should be clear that children and youth today are already in possession of far more useful knowledge and understood experience than our existing educational institutions can help them learn to manage.

The young men and women now being recruited into the teaching professions and into the behavioral and social sciences, and those who are attracted to and committed to careers of political action, not only are dissatisfied with the present use of our social tools and techniques, but are already undertaking the redesign of the institutions within which they have chosen to function. We are thus in the midst of profound social change which is under way in a world society which is essentially so large and so stable that its technological and cultural foundations will withstand the shocks and be able to support whatever new social edifices are built upon them.

One can specify some of these social changes exclusively in terms of our present understanding of the function of the high school as it now operates within our great cities.

Although poor people are in a distinct and shrinking minority in the country at large, they are a growing and increasingly costly minority in our great cities. While the causes of poverty are many and complex, the elimination of poverty seems to be possible through a combination of effective education and the orderly application of welfare services which our society is now able to offer and which in themselves are essentially educational in nature.

Early childhood education is rapidly being extended into infancy, and techniques and insights that have been available for more than half a century are now being employed in designing what might be called emotional life-supporting systems. These systems can assure that no child, whatever his conditions of birth, need be limited by those conditions, or debarred by them from a socially satisfying and personally productive life.

Secondary education on the whole has not yet been appropriately redesigned or effectively coupled to the programs of childhood education. But that redesign and coupling is imminent. It will come

about as it is already beginning to develop, as we reorganize, redefine, and redeploy our public school resources in the great cities.
Such activity goes far beyond mere "decentralization" or the increased involvement of community groups in the affairs of schools.
It implies in fact the creation of *community* within the city, and this
creation is itself the acceptance of the city as the great Sophist.
All of our social resources, our hospitals and welfare agencies, our
cultural centers, our political organizations and governmental bureaus,
are moving towards increased effectiveness in meeting private needs
and satisfying public requirements of the citizens to the degree that
they accept citizen participation in their direction.

It is quite probable that the high school in 1980 will not be a
place, but rather it will be a growth period and a social condition.
The students designated as high school students will have the whole
of the city for a classroom, and their instruction will be provided
by things and events that are under the orderly control of teachers
who are themselves secure in their understanding of their own professional capacities, and in the recognition they receive from the
larger community as effective practitioners. Under their guidance
student learning may under appropriate conditions be "decoupled"
from practice; that is, there will be continual concern on the part
of teachers to provide islands of privacy for the growing adolescent
and periods of quiet in which the learning adolescent will have time
to "make sense" out of the occasional disorder that attends the
acquisition of rich experience. But perhaps most important of all,
teachers and students, never in isolation from their community, will
engage in adventures with ideas and in explorations of those constantly receding horizons which are the best indicators of approaching maturity.

The Urban Challenge and the High School

Samuel M. Brownell

Twelve years ago I started a ten-year term as superintendent of the fourth largest school system in the nation. Twelve years ago some of the current challenges to urban schools were clearly visible. Others were only slightly visible if at all, and I am sure entirely invisible to many. A review of some of the current concerns about urban schools and the weight given them in 1956 may make us wonder how clearly we foresee today the nature and concerns of High School 1980.

ON THE ONE HAND

It was clear in 1956 that urban schools would enroll an increasing proportion of the youth of a growing nation. We may expect this to continue through 1980.

We knew twelve years ago that youth emerging from high schools would need to have more and better schooling than ever before to make good lives for themselves, economically and otherwise, and to fulfill the national manpower needs. This requirement will be even greater in 1980.

We could discern, without much documentation, the great disparity among urban schools in resources, in facilities, in programs and output. The disparity is now well documented, and eliminating the educational deficiencies concentrated in poor urban areas is now a major effort. The nature of the variations may well be quite different in 1980 from the present.

BUT ON THE OTHER HAND

There was little recognition in 1956 outside the cities that available financial resources were inadequate to provide essential school services to urban schools, let alone to those who dropped out of school. Even in the cities, only a few educators fully grasped the problem. Current recognition at the federal, state, and local levels may lead to some action of significance by 1980.

In 1956 few cities recognized the need for decentralization of some aspects of large city school systems and for more participation by citizens. The need has reached the action point in many cities by now. What and how extensively to centralize will probably still be an issue in 1980.

No one foresaw in 1956 that there would be the coming impact of civil rights and racial integration on urban schools generally. To assume that by 1980 these problems will be wholly resolved or unchanged in their manifestations would seem unrealistic.

No one predicted in 1956 today's extensive militancy of teacher organizations, of high school pupils, and of parent organizations in most urban school systems. Let us hope the urban schools of 1980 will have evolved better ways to recognize and resolve dissent and frustration.

There seemed little possibility in 1956 that slum conditions, which had been exposed by crusading writers for generations, would become a major national concern. By 1980, we may hope, slums will be much reduced and the slum high school of 1956 will no longer exist.

In 1956 only a handful of reformers dreamt that city school systems could become leaders in educational research, experimentation, innovation, and improvement of teaching. The dream is still far from realization, but perhaps it may be realized by 1980.

All of these developments made themselves felt throughout the school system. What was done to modify one part of school operations inevitably influenced what was or could be done in another part. Change in the elementary school curriculum influenced the high school curriculum. Change of class size influenced the number of classrooms needed. Change in the rate of dropouts at once influenced school practices and was influenced by them.

But one fairly constant component was the children themselves. They came to school in greater numbers, but with the same basic abilities as did their parents. Their physiological growth rate and structure for learning differed little or not at all from their ancestors. It was home, community, and school conditions and expectations which changed, or did not change enough to suit many persons, not the learning capacity of youth as active, growing adolescents.

High school students of the 1980s, even more than the present crop, will have grown up in an urban environment. They will not be adjusting from rural and small town living. They will accept as routine and substandard what this generation considers as change and improvement. They will be impatient to bring about the changes which appear most important to them.

We can anticipate a number of changes in the students' lives that may well place greater responsibilities upon the urban high school:

—Many may become voting citizens at the age 18.
—Families and friends may be less and less helpful in finding job opportunities.
—Moving about the community almost on an anonymous basis will make for early independence.
—Opportunities for direct action in civic and social causes will grow.

The latin grammar school was supplanted by the academies, largely because it only provided for youth who would either complete their job preparation in college or would continue with some other type of preparation for adult responsibilities. Because the academies in their turn came to be chiefly college-preparatory institutions, the high school emerged as the social agency designed to offer youth the chance to add to his capabilities enough to enable him to take the next step—be it further schooling or transition directly into a job.

Unemployment of urban youth cannot be tolerated, for their sake and for the sake of the cities. Transition into full citizenship, into jobs, into union membership, into active participation for social betterment, recognition as a person with identity and responsibility; these are challenges to the urban high school of 1980. If the high school does not meet these challenges, it may be supplanted by some other kind of institution better equiped to prepare young people for successful and useful lives.

In trying to look ahead over the next 12 years, therefore, it seems advisable to examine some of the urban conditions which influence and will influence the probable characteristics of the urban high school in 1980.

CHALLENGES OF URBAN LIVING

Urban areas and cities are not synonymous. Neither are cities homogeneous. Not all parts of cities are slums. Not all suburbs are homes of the wealthy. There are suburbs predominately composed of low-income, poorly educated families. There are areas in the cities where the wealthy, the well-educated, and the culturally motivated predominate. The urban area contains the complete range in population from the affluent to the poor, of all races, occupations, and beliefs. Urban problems depend largely on how these differences are distributed in the area, how decisions affecting people are controlled to bring about economic and social benefits, how people in one section of an urban area are and feel related to the interests and concerns of people in other sections.

Urban problems involve much more than making provisions for adequate food, housing, transportation, public utilities, and parking. Also needed are established institutions which bring residents together around common human interests. These provide anchors for stability, and ways for the development of common concerns which make the difference between family isolation in a sea of impersonal humanity and family participation in a friendly community, between a place to live and a place to exist. It may well be that this community function will assume great importance in the urban high school of 1980.

Making school conditions adequate in all parts of an urban community presents special problems because of the way in which urban areas develop. As urban population has grown, it has been easier and more economical to build at the periphery, rather than rebuild in the established city. It has been easier to develop a separate town government for the new area than to change the city boundaries with the complexities of making adjustments in tax rates, bonding for capital improvements, relationships to "city hall," etc. Local controls and access to decision-making power has appealed to suburban citizens. Thus, while the proportions of low and high income families in the total urban area may not change greatly with population growth, larger and larger proportions of the lower income, the unemployed, the elderly, and the in-migrants tend to concentrate within the city limits. Public service expenses—for health, safety, recreations, welfare, special education—become proportionally larger in the inner city than in the outer urban and suburban areas.

The disparity between different sections of the city has grown gradually, and not by design. The limited public funds available have gone to provide streets, sewers, street lighting, schools, parks for the outlying growth areas that lacked these facilities. As a result, there has not been enough money to bring up to contemporary standards the street lighting, the recreation areas, the schools, etc., in the older areas. As the metropolitan area spread, the disparity between the old areas and the new was not just due to wear and tear and neglected maintenance. The new areas were better adapted to contemporary needs, and the contrast between the old and the new increased apace.

OLD SCHOOLS AND EDUCATIONAL NEGLECT

The central high school built for a congested population was modern for the time in which it was built. It was designed for the assigning and oral reading of textbooks to well-motivated youth who were expected to meet examination requirements and presumably enter college or find a job on their own or with their families' help. A meagerly equipped science laboratory and limited library were about the only additions to the standard class or recitation room. There might be an auditorium, too, perhaps on the second or third floor. There was little or no lawn or athletic field space adjacent to the school. Such buildings have continued in use in the older sections of cities.

But newer urban sections have constructed new schools on sites large enough to have athletic fields and parking areas and well-landscaped lawns. The newer buildings contained modern science laboratories, well-stocked and well-lighted libraries, cafeterias, attractive classrooms with ceilings treated to reduce the noise level, with built-in audiovisual aids, language laboratories, music and art rooms especially designed for these subjects, gymnasiums, swimming pools, locker and shower facilities. Indoor and outdoor lighting, toilets, and ventilation controls conform to contemporary standards, far exceeding levels provided in the old buildings. Shops for industrial arts and special rooms for home economics, business education, electronics and service trades training, offices for counselors and teachers, make possible instruction that goes beyond the old conventional lecture, textbook recitation, and checking of homework assignments. Urban extension has tended to leave the old schools less and less adaptable to new conditions.

It is only within the past decade, as the contrast of old and new in central city housing and business building has come into focus, that the contrast between inner-city school and outer-city or suburban school has begun to receive attention. Whether the urban area has one large city school system, or is a constellation of a core city surrounded by suburbs, the growth pattern has been essentially similar. High schools built years ago to house the educational program of their day cannot match, in new or remodelled facilities, the school plants provided in newer urban areas, nor are they apt to attract staff eager to try out new ideas. Traditional programs and procedures have tended to continue in the older schools along with the outmoded plant. The contrast among inner city, outer city, and suburban secondary schools was dramatized by Conant's *Slums and Suburbs* and reiterated by other more recent reports. While some large cities have begun to replace the older, inner-city schools with new school plants designed to serve contemporary school needs, only a small start has been made on closing a dramatic gap.

If, by 1980, urban high school students are to have educational opportunities adequate to their needs, massive school building and rebuilding programs need to be undertaken without delay.

The planning of these school buildings must be closely related to urban planning for housing and transportation of increased population so that new schools are ready for those who occupy new housing. But even greater efforts are needed to replace or update existing obsolete, inadequate buildings, often overcrowded, which cripple teaching and learning. To their communities these buildings symbolize outmoded education. The solution in some urban situations may well be the complexes called educational parks. In others, modern high schools serving essentially the same city areas may be what the community decides is best suited to meet its needs.

In areas of old homes, many persons left behind consider that their lot is always to have the old house with used furniture, hand-me-down clothing, a decrepit church building, an old school, a leftover teacher—everything that has been discarded by those with enough money to move out. It is pretty hard to convince them that their children have an equal chance to make the most of themselves through taking advantage of the available educational opportunities when all of the tangible aspects of the school are inferior to that which is supplied to pupils who come from new homes, who wear new clothes, drive new cars, and who have school facilities more extensive, more modern, and more attractive.

If urban areas are to avoid successive concentric deterioration, with consequent spreading of slums, there is need not only to replace on adequate and attractive sites the obsolete, incomplete, and unattractive secondary-school buildings of the central city. Schools in middle-aged areas of the city must also be provided with physical and instructional resources equal to or better than those in newer parts of the urban area. To do otherwise is to persuade parents to move outward if they want to provide the best education for their children. In so doing they hasten the outward march of the slums.

These parents must have convincing evidence that their children will receive as good or better schooling by staying where they are.

Any one who has worked with parents in all parts of a city school system is well aware of one universal drive on their part. It may be expressed in different languages, the form may vary from conference to petition, to demand, to boycott, or to rugged demonstration. It is that their children—*now*—receive the best possible education. They associate old and crowded buildings with poor education, and evidence shows that very often they are right. A parent who shouts four-letter words at a school official may, if the official will listen, calm down and listen. He may eventually understand that it takes time to convince enough citizens of the need for increased taxes to pay for the new buildings and new teachers, time to acquire the land, plan and erect the new building. But he sees his daughter and his son who need good education today perhaps losing interest in schooling, in the crowded outmoded building in which he can take no pride. The parent may understand that the school authorities cannot perform miracles. But he also knows that a new building, a new school program by 1980 is too late for his child and reacts: "Damn it! My child needs the education now. He can't wait." And he is right.

The foregoing has stressed the urgent need in all parts of an urban area for an up-to-date, quality educational program, in an adequate, efficient, and attractive building. I have emphasized school plant to many people because buildings are the visible evidence that an attempt is being made to keep the school program modern. And they are right: it is necessary to make the physical plant and equipment up-to-date in order to take advantage of modern technological advance. For citizens of the slums, the significance of a new school building or a new addition is far greater than to those who live in areas where new homes, stores, and churches are a part of their normal living. The achievement of the urban high school in 1980 depends much more than we might like on the efforts made from now on to overcome the physical obsolescence of inner-city school buildings.

ISOLATION VERSUS COMMUNITY

Bigness in population and area affects what schools can do and how efficiently they can operate. Urban high schools are inevitably big.

Large school districts and large enrollment increase the resources and options available for education. The idea is appealing that within the large urban area with its multitude of persons and agencies it will be possible to develop these resources in a mosaic use pattern in which each discrete part maintains its identity in relation to others and provides configurations more beautiful and interesting than where resources are fewer. But this has characterized only a small number of urban high schools to date.

As the high school of the growing urban areas attempts to find ways to utilize these resources and realize these possibilities, it has to deal with several hazards generated by bigness. One is fractionalization of interests, which tend to be focused on a small part of the area. One section is as unaware of others as if they were cities far removed. People react to what happens to come to their attention, on the basis of their limited experience or what is provided through news media.

As communities become urban, the common school no longer brings together the children of the butcher, the baker, the banker, the lawyer, and the candlestick maker. Population and area growth encourage the division of the city into separate sections that are economically and socially homogenous. There are separate high-rent, medium-rent, and low-rent districts. This is segregation by economic level—and inevitably by racial group as well. Churches, shopping centers, schools, and movie theaters serve each section, further restricting community-wide contacts. There are enough butchers and bakers and bankers and mechanics and candlestick makers in the urban area so that the bankers' families tend to live in one section, attend the same church, have their own social clubs, and go to the same school. The mechanics and the candlestick makers do likewise. The pieces for the mosaic are present but the white pieces are largely separated from the black and the yellow and the brown. The large pieces are mostly apart from the little ones, the clean ones from the unwashed. Even the chance meeting on the street car and the bus and on the street which formerly served to bring together common elements and some cross socialization is eliminated by the universality of the private car. Bigness of the urban area thus fosters economic segregation in addition to racial segregation. The extent to which this segregation now exists and how it continues needs to be reckoned with by the high school of 1980. The urban challenge is to have all parts of the urban area contribute to the other parts, to have unity of concern because there is mutuality of understanding between those who live in the different parts.

Some look upon the news media as a means of providing common experiences for all, and thus serving as a unifying influence in the urban community. To a degree this idea may be true, but in some ways the bigness of an urban area reduces the unifying impact of news media and even creates new problems of communication and mutual understanding that concerns the schools. Expectation that the news media will enable people in an urban area to understand each other and develop common interests and attitudes does not appear realistic. Urban understanding, as well as world understanding, presents a challenge to the schools.

There is not the universality of coverage by news media in an urban area that at one time I thought existed. This is generally true of the press and the radio, and to a lesser degree of TV. Some portions of the city read a foreign-language paper and listen to foreign-language radio broadcasts. The union paper and the union radio, or the press and the radio operated by and for the black population, are the exclusive purveyors of news to some sections; they are not seen or listened to at all in other sections. Some people depend upon what are considered the metropolitan news and radio stations. One who compares presentations of the same events by these different media sources is bound to be impressed by the variation in emphasis and interpretation. Size of the urban area makes it economically possible for these varied news media to exist and for special constituencies to have their differences thus extended and exploited.

There are other aspects of news media coverage, too, that are related to urban bigness. First, the news media give highest priority to that which is dramatic, controversial, unusual, and a possible occurrence. Those who seek to know about other parts of the urban area through news media are largely limited to the unusual, the different, and the controversial aspects of life.

Second, in covering news of the urban area, media are limited in the space and time they can devote to providing background and follow-up to situations which may be of great import to citizens in one school area, but seem remote and of minor importance to persons in other sections. One high school among 20 to 50 others cannot count on the news media to reach its particular constituency with news of school accomplishments, school needs, or the background information on school incidents. By 1980 such a school will have to provide other means to inform its patrons of its accomplishments, activities, operations, and needs.

Third, because news media in urban areas are big, they are organized to provide "instant news." This practice creates problems for urban school systems in several ways as they try to develop and maintain an understanding relationship with parents, staff, and citizens generally. Instant news usually means capsule news with little explanation: an unusual incident in one school is thus broadcast to the constituents of all schools. It can and often does reach the public before responsible authorities are able to gather the background facts and present them to the school staff, the student body, or parents of an affected school. Fear, indignation, resentment, or confusion may be engendered throughout the urban area which could have been avoided if the pressure for instant news had been balanced against the significance of complete news.

The urban school system cannot expect the news media to provide the full information needed by parents, school staff, and citizens generally if they are to understand what is going on. The urban school system needs to have procedures which will respond to instant news situations in ways to make them as accurate and as complete as is possible.

THE CHALLENGE OF CENTRALIZATION, STANDARDIZATION, AND BUREAUCRACY

The urban high school is part of a large educational enterprise whether it is located in the central city or in the suburbs. Pressures of one sort or another work for conformity in many aspects of schooling. Curriculum similarity, identical textbooks and school calendars, uniform graduation requirements are urged as ways of easing transfers as families move from one part of the area to another. Social mores of pupils in one school have a way of influencing neighboring schools in a hurry. Pressures bear on administrators and the school board to provide for all schools any advantage introduced in one, to deal with problems of student behavior through a common code of conduct, and even to adopt standards of dress that apply to all schools. The individual teacher and administrator or their organizations frequently appeal to the central administrative staff or the school board for the adoption of rules and regulations which would provide uniformity of decisions on matters that include salary rates, assignment of responsibilities, methods of handling grievances, numbers of subjects in which a pupil may enroll, length of class periods, and the procedures and rights of teachers in dealing with unruly pupils in the classroom.

In the name of efficiency, consistency, and equal treatment, the school in the urban area finds itself as a part of a bureaucracy in fact or by association. The larger it becomes as a school, the greater are the pressures within the school itself to become bureaucratic, so that organizational processes determine decisions and relationships rather than judicious consideration of what may be most desirable to the individuals involved. Decisions by rules made by groups or persons apart from the facts of the immediate situation thus tend to frustrate individuals who seek to provide and to maintain in school operations the conditions of teaching and learning which respect and encourage each person to develop his uniqueness. This remote control applies especially to frequently recurring situations. Unity in effort and response does not necessarily require uniformity in action. Use of common policies as guides does not mean that there should be the abrogation of decision-making based upon assessment of facts in the case, or exercise of judgment in fairness to the individual.

One approach to protect urban schools against over-centralization and over-standardization is to decentralize operations and controls in schools. Presumably current steps in this direction in several of the large cities will have progressed or been suppressed by 1980, but the forces favoring centralization and standardization will continue.

As more and more individuals and groups want to participate in educational decisions, it will be important to recognize the limitations of centralization and standardization in urban schools. Many persons must share responsibilities as bosses of some portion of the school enterprise. Conflicts in authority and responsibility can be avoided and resolved, to a considerable degree, if there is careful analysis of the types of decisions involved in the school enterprise and agreement on who is in the best position to make each type of decision.

One of the major obstacles tending to prevent the acceptance of some decentralization is the handling of dissent from decisions. In centralized, large operations the right of appeal through channels may lead to appeal from a teacher decision to the principal, then to a regional executive, to a central administrator and finally to the board of education. Piling up of appeals at the several levels leads to delay. Often those who appeal feel that each authority feels heavily inclined to support those who made the original decision. They are also often concerned that pressing an appeal will work against their interests in the future or against the interests of their children. Along with the allocation of decision-making responsibility, then, is the need for an appeals authority which can hear and consider appeals promptly and which has the authority to make final decisions or recommendations. Such an appeals authority would appropriately include parents, teachers, and student representatives. Decentralization, with decision-making authority allocated and appeals opportunity of this type provided, could do much to enable the urban high school of 1980 to overcome handicaps of centralization and standardization.

THE STRUGGLE FOR RACIAL INTEGRATION

It would be overly optimistic to believe that 1980 will witness full achievement of racial integration in this nation. But one cannot review 1956 through 1968 without hope that there will be major progress toward racial integration which is much more than merely having black and white pupils in the same school. The objective of racial integration is to have all persons possess the knowledge, understanding, and spirit which enables them as a matter of course to associate in life activities with those who differ in race so as to respect and to consider them for what they are and do so without regard to race.

For high schools in 1980 it seems fair to assume that administrative vigilance will be necessary at all times to see that every aspect of the school contributes positively to the spirit and practice of respect and understanding among the different races, nationalities, and religions. Included are recruitment, assignment, and transfers of staff, especially in areas where residents are predominantly of one race, and where school contacts may be the most intimate and continuous opportunities students have for association with members of the other race on the basis of free and equal contributors to common enterprises.

In curriculum and instruction, schools will still need to be on the alert to provide authentic information which recognizes the contribution of all races, and materials which portray racially integrated activities of children and adults as a normal way of life. High schools enrolling students who are all or nearly all of one race will have the special problem of providing good interracial experiences in both the regular and in the extracurricular program.

Presumably by 1980 we will know more about the kinds of racially integrated experiences for high school students that are most effective in fostering attitudes of mutual respect for others. We do know that if a pupil grows up in a home and neighborhood where respect for people of all races prevails, the task of the school is relatively light. But elimination of racism, conscious or un-conscious, will still be an important objective of the high school in 1980.

To those who predict that the direction of American society is toward separatism of the races and that by 1980 integration will no longer be acceptable to blacks or whites, I would call attention to the study made by the Center for Urban Education of "Com-munity Attitudes in Bedford-Stuyvesant," Brooklyn's Harlem, and to the editorial comment on this study in *Crisis* (The N.A.A.C.P. official organ) of June–July 1968.

The survey's interviews were conducted by a corps of 80 residents of the predominantly Negro community. Their findings reaffirm the continuing commitment of Negro Americans to integration as a goal.

This observation is another indication of the extent to which the strident voices of the minority black separatists have misrepresented the aspirations of the black community and have succeeded in misleading the easily deceived news media. Four-fifths of the Negro residents interviewed ex-pressed a preference to live in a block with people of every race rather than in an all-Negro block. The stated preference of this 80 percent belies the contention of those angry black spokesmen who discount as meaningless the housing provision of the Civil Rights Act of 1968 and the United States Supreme Court ruling of June 17 validating the right of Negroes to acquire property on the same terms as white citizens.

The Center for Urban Education's survey is only the most recent of a series of independent studies of Negro attitudes. In one way or another these polls have uniformly endorsed integration as a major goal of the nation's black population. Included in these surveys are two national polls by Louis Harris, one in 1964 and the other a year later; a 1964 *New York Times* poll of attitudes of New York Negroes; "Protest and Prejudice," a survey of four cities by Gary T. Marx, published in 1967; and the *Fortune* magazine national poll, January 1968.

THE HIGH SCHOOL OF 1980 WILL STILL BE IN THE MIDDLE

What the high school does and can do is only in part within its power to control. It will and must continue to receive and accept from the elementary and junior high schools children who have had 13 to 15 years in and out of school, to develop and establish attitudes toward school and learning, and toward their own potential and their relationships to others. They have also acquired, in varying degrees, knowledge and skills basic to further learning. High schools traditionally have not been satisfied with the competence and the attitudes of many entering students. As more and more of the students in central city high schools have come from disadvantaged homes, and from schools which all too frequently have been inadequate, the high school has been confronted with new tasks and new demands on its resources.

Teaching basic skills of reading, arithmetic, spelling, and language at elementary levels, but to youth mature in experience, is a need resisted by many high schools as an elementary or junior high school responsibility. Others have tackled the job with vigor, imagination, and resourcefulness.

At the same time, urban high schools have received many pupils who have been given unprecedented opportunities to develop special skills and interests. New curriculums, new methods of instruction, and opportunities for individualized learning have widened the span of competence of beginning high school pupils. Foreign language for many in the elementary grades, special science curricula taught by specialists, the new math, team teaching, special ability and interest groups meeting out of school hours or during the regular day—these are some of the innovations introduced by elementary schools to enable those with ability and high purpose to progress at full speed or to gain broader experiences.

The high school of 1980 will probably be enrolling students even more diverse in knowledge and skills than those entering high school today.

The record of the urban high school shows that it is graduating more pupils better prepared and more competent than at any time in history. It is retaining a higher percent of high school youth than ever before. It is also graduating more pupils less competent in skills basic to learning than ever before.

As a result of the improved preparation of those in the upper ranks of high school graduates, colleges generally have raised their requirements for entering the freshmen year and have admitted many high school graduates to advanced standing classes. Because of the graduation from high school of more students with less academic competence than when unskilled jobs were more available for dropouts there is great criticism of urban high school lack of quality production.

To the extent that the high school assumes the responsibility to accept all adolescents and provide them with the best opportunity to develop knowledge, skills, and attitudes needed to make the most of their lives, high schools of 1980 will range more widely in the performance levels of those they accept and in those they send forth.

By 1980 high schools will have had an opportunity to develop, extend, and perfect many of the structural, curricular, and operational changes instituted during the past few years as innovations. The new math will no longer be new. Language laboratories should be technically more efficient and teachers have been trained to utilize them far more effectively. Learning-resource centers, electronically aided so that pupils can retrieve easily and quickly audio and visual materials of many varieties, should be commonplace. There will, no doubt, be even more dramatic developments spurred by computers and other devices to augment the learning resources of teacher and pupil.

The high school of 1980 can be this nation's chief institution devoted to giving every youth the best possible chance to make the transition from dependent childhood to that of an independent adult. Obviously it cannot and should not assume all of the responsibilities in serving this all-important objective. Rather it can supplement and complement what others do, or open avenues to further and augment what the high school is able to do. This role will require that each urban high school constantly study urban conditions and urban changes. The high school must be willing to make changes in its emphases, in its programs, and in its operations. It will need more than ever to measure success far more broadly than by achievement test scores. If it lives up to these goals, the urban high school will indeed have met the urban challenge. If it does not, the urban high school may well be supplanted by a more effective social institution to aid youth in making a successful beginning in independent urban life.

Relevance and Spirit: The Student's Viewpoint

Charles Weingartner

High school students are stuck essentially with the same task class after class, year after year, doing the same meaningless, monotonous job: telling back to the teacher what the teacher told to them.

And what students *do* is critical because, whether we like it or not, it is true that we learn only what we do.

It makes little sense to talk about "curriculum" as if it does not actually consist of what teachers do and what—as a consequence—students do.

The response of students to this witless work is amply cataloged. Look at any dictionary of quotations in the sections on "school" or "teachers" or, even, "educational". The dreariness of these observations is ominous. Schooling, in our culture, is a mean and demeaning process—for everyone involved. And not all of the students who complain, or who refuse to conform to the role of a ventriloquist's dummy, can be dismissed as dullards "not interested in or capable of learning." It may even be that the dullest are the ones who are best rewarded in the school game.

H. L. Mencken, a source of pungent comments on various foibles, made several observations about schools, teachers, and students, including: "It is one of the tragedies of youth, and youth is a time of real tragedy, that so much of it must be spent in school in the presence of adults whom the youth do not quite respect."

And composer Richard Rogers, commenting on his high school experience said: " . . . it was a terrible and depressing place. I hated it. If I learned anything during the time I attended high school, I learned it outside."

Holden Caulfield, the "catcher" in what is still one of the most widely read books by adolescents, *The Catcher in the Rye,* said: "Even the couple of *nice* teachers on the faculty, they were phonies, too."

And in their recent *Authorized Biography* the Beatles (except for Ringo who "has few memories of . . . school aside from playing truant. . . .") are quoted as follows on the subject of school and teachers.

"Never once did anyone make it clear what I was being educated for."—Paul McCartney.

"All teachers . . . are ignorant. Yet because they were old and withered you were supposed to believe they weren't ignorant."—George Harrison.

"They were all stupid teachers, except one or two."—John Lennon.

Whatever else the Beatles might be called, they cannot be called dumb. They were all driven out of school by what they perceived to be its massively dull irrelevance.

And on this point, in America we have some ominous statistics of our own. New York City might be cited as an illustration of the kind of problem that seems to be increasing in American cities, the problem of the increasing gap between black adolescents and the process that comprises the city high school. In New York City about half of the entering high school population is black. Less than 25 percent of this population ever completes high school. Less than 1 percent of the student population of the City University of New York is black. One of the few members of this black population to record his thoughts on the subject of school is Claude Brown, author of *Manchild in the Promised Land.* "School," he says, "what a joke that was! With those terrified slinky people who hated you. They knew as much about human beings and education as I know about growing flowers. They just became teachers because it was an easy dodge! Man, were they miserable! They were real psychological defectives, and of all the places they should wind up, in a school with kids needing help. Oh, Lord!"

It is also interesting to note that most of the seminal and creative thinkers of the nineteenth and twentieth centuries (so far) were considered to be "poor students" by their teachers. Most probably because they would not hold still while intellectual genocide was perpetrated on them.

But, it is commonly said, they constituted a small minority of the student body, just as the total student body today are only a small percentage of dissenters and rebels. True, but without romanticizing about the needs of adolescence it is not too much to say that while the record of the human group so far makes few points clear, there is one that is made sharply clear, if only by its repetition, and it is that all of our intellectual and social milestones are the result of the efforts of a "minority" and frequently a minority of one, though this is less and less common as our environment increases in complexity.

The majority of any group at any time, including our present group of high school students, not only has no conscious perspective on how things are, much less how they ought to be, but will resist, usually by merely doing nothing, any attempt to change even those routines they find uncomfortable or meaningless. The "majority" is "average." And average high school students have no conscious point of view about high school or much of anything else. They are simply—and at their average worst—merely reflections of the operational values of the society in which they are denied a chance to play an active, responsible, productive role. Like most of us who have been taught American values via television, film, radio, magazines, and even schools, high school students are interested in acquiring with as little effort as possible as much stuff as possible for the purpose of enhancing their personal comfort and amusement. Period.

In the cosmic account book that nature keeps, this kind of value system produces certain inexorable debts that may be difficult to pay off. We are already in default on several payments, but so far show little sign of having the inclination to pay, irrespective of our ability to do so. But the bell is tolling.

Most high school students, of course, would resent and resist any attempts at substantive change in their schooling, especially if it required them to think about how they think and of the results of this process.

There are two student minorities in high school, however, who are seriously concerned about the way things are, and who are interested in effecting serious and dramatic changes in their schooling. They seem, so far, to be a fallout from the more visible and audible efforts of college students concerned about doing the same thing; but while they are a minority, they are increasing in numbers and visibility. Our response to them, as to other minorities seeking planned change to permit responsible participation in the great society in the global village, had better be less stereotypic and autocratic than indications up to this point suggest, or we may find ourselves using the line that the marine major used in describing what happened to one of the oldest cities in Vietnam in the process of defending it: "We had to destroy it in order to save it." Orwellian rhetoric such as this characterizes most of our problem-solving efforts on all levels—domestic, international, economic, social, political, and, most of all, military. Our rhetoric about our youth has the flavor of our military rhetoric about "the enemy." Ominous? It gets ominouser and ominouser.

These two aforementioned high school student minorities are two in a socioeconomic sense, but in an operational intellectual-emotional sense they are one. In any case, these are the students who do have a conscious view of high school—similar to those quoted earlier—and it is unequivocally critical.

These students think and say and write that the high school is a malignant and meretricious place, maintained by and for bureaucratic functionaries who are obsessed with the idea that everybody needs to be kept quietly in line, and anonymously alike in appearance, attitude, and behavior, and all for the curious purpose of temporarily memorizing and simultaneously regurgitating passing portions of the trivia that they have been told. Much of this trivia, it should be noted, is not trivial in its effects since it is not uncommonly inaccurate, misleading, and flatly untrue, in order to avoid offending the biases and prejudices of those who purchase textbooks and run schools.

These students who are not sleepwalking in lockstep include many who are "lower class" and "disadvantaged," as well as many who are upper-middle class and advantaged. The former usually drop out of school—at the rate of about one million a year. The latter usually just tune out. But this may be changing, too. There have been recent indications of substantive student dissent in high school, with the leaders coming from this latter group. While dissenting college students do not usually include among their numbers many who are majoring in technical subjects or engineering, dissenting high school students include exceptionally high achievers, even in technical subjects.

The largest single distinction between the two groups of activists is the socioeconomic one. The most radical students come from the upper layers of this kind of stratification. Students—including blacks —in the lower socioeconomic layers are much more conservative. Indeed, for whites, a virtual formula could be devised to show the inverse relationship between high radical attitudes and actions and low socioeconomic status. The situation is different for blacks.

A curious anomaly exists between black and white radicals, and it is leading to serious difficulties in the attempts by the whites to work with blacks.

The white radical student is motivated by humanistic concerns of a much more abstract nature than are the blacks. The white radicals find an articulation of a philosophical rationale for their radicalism in men such as Marcuse, Camus, Beckett, Genet, and Thoreau, as well as in popular translations of similar views by Bob Dylan, the Beatles, Tom Paxton, Phil Ochs, Buffy St. Marie, Joan Baez, and Janis Ian. These young, singing philosophers play a crucial role in the emergence of the white radical student, especially of the girls. None of these spokesmen for the white radicals hold any interest for the blacks. The black radical is motivated by a much less abstract, much more personal philosophy. It is simply to break Charlie's monopoly on the economic game. This is their essential motive, and it is articulated by Rap Brown, Stokely Carmichael, Le Roi Jones, James Foreman, Malcolm X, and even Jim Brown (through such media as the Black Economic Union).

So, these are two quite different forms of radicalism. The black radical fight is to get into the system. The white radical fight is to change the system. The conservative establishment resistance to both is what forces them to take radical steps. The establishment, predictably, doesn't want to respond to the demands of either group.

The radicals, either black or white, are a minority, but a growing minority, of the students. This point is frequently cited by the conservative establishment spokesmen calling for "law and order." It is worth noting, however, that "only" 2 percent of the population was involved in the French Revolution.

Possibly 1 percent of college students are active radicals, but according to figures cited by *Fortune* magazine at least 25 percent of the student population favors their radical activity. The probability is that this latter percentage will increase, for diverse and even irrational reasons.

Through late 1968 and 1969, the similarities between college and high school student radical action increased markedly. The reasons for this may be too obvious to seem acceptable. Most members of the establishment *need* to think, Manichaean-like, of a conscious conspiracy, mostly of a communist origin. Most of us over 30 have been trained for at least 20 years to view any event that is not complimentary to the conservative establishment view of the good, the true, and the beautiful as a "communist plot." This psychopathic oversimplification is now virtually the only basis we have for explaining anything we don't like, from bad weather through Supreme Court decisions to flower children. The paranoia resulting from this kind of tunnel vision has led us to police the whole world, and it may yet turn us into a police state in order to "protect our freedom."

Pogo once noted that "We has met the enemy, and he is us." The politicized high school student feels the same way. It is interesting, isn't it, that the behavior we value so highly when engaged in by students in Czechoslovakia or Hungary we find reprehensible in our own. What we call resistance to totalitarian tactics abroad we call anarchy at home.

Since high school students are legally confined to playing pseudo-politics (although there are some signs that laws enabling 18-year-olds to vote may be in the offing) most of their real political activities seem radical to many. The tactics they use are the only ones they have access to. The politics of the activist students are not party politics; they are the real politics of confrontation and power. A humanistic-political children's crusade has begun, and efforts to repress it will probably intensify it even while making it less visible.

In a literal sense, the campus is a battleground for the generation war and the school is caught between the warring factions. Changes demanded by students are regarded as radical by the establishment, including those members of it who provide the financial support that permits the school to exist. At the same time (and for the same reasons) the questioning activist students regard the school as ultraconservative and repressive and their own demands as just and reasonable. Similarly, what the establishment regards as appropriate the activist students regard as irrelevant. While it may not seem to help much to say so, they are both "right," given their respective value systems and the assumptions and perceptions that result from them. There lies the problem: the lack of agreement as to what is good. The establishment view of the good life is regarded as a Faustian bargain at best and a fraud at worst by the activist students. It may be that what the students have yet to learn is that (especially in a technological culture) the human condition consists of nothing but Faustian bargains. The students, however, may intuitively be striving for a diminution of the price being paid in human terms in these bargains by attacking the—to date—mindless assumptions of what is "good" being made by the establishment.

If we can somehow avoid reacting stereotypically, we might perceive recent modes of student dissent as suggestions as to how the role of the high school student in 1980 should be different from that of today. For better or worse, college students are now gaining a more active role in school politics. They are beginning to share responsibility for developing and implementing policies affecting everything from the curriculum to the selection and retention of faculty. It is most probable that the high schools will follow this pattern.

By 1980, if not sooner, the high school had better plan to make provisions for responsible participation by activist students in its real politics. That is, in making decisions about what the high schools should be doing, how it should be doing it, and who should be doing it.

The activist students are now too sophisticated to be co-opted into settling for a mere expansion of the mickey mouse domain of student government. They have learned—via media outside of school control—to need to participate in real politics responsive to real human problems rather than passively accepting institutional rituals determined solely by convention or tradition. Chicago, 1968, was one manifestation of this need. That this need was repressed may obscure two facts: (1) that a substantive *change has occurred* in national politics because of this need, and (2) that the price paid to effect this repression may be higher than *anyone* wants to pay.

The energy and resources that would be required to continue to repress this need, if that is the decision that is made, would be wasteful not only because it would produce, ultimately, results quite the opposite of those it is intended to produce, but also, and perhaps mostly, because such energy and resources could fulfill a much more reality oriented educational function if used to develop ways in which students could participate responsibly in school politics.

Edmund Burke's statement that "Any condition instituted by force can be maintained only by force" is still true.

The question facing the high school in 1980 is whether it is to be a place of forced detention, isolating the student from responsible participation in real politics and insulating the student (ineffectively) from reality, or educating the student for the role he will ultimately have to fulfill in a democracy by using reality as a focus for student attention and action.

It is not impossible that the activist students may be right in their claims that the high school as it is now is irrelevant and unresponsive to the realities of a rapidly changing environment.

It may even be that their claims do not go far enough.

Can we as a society afford, using *any* criteria as a basis for judgment, to subsidize the high school as an institution that serves primarily to delay the chance for our own young adults to learn how to cope with the way it is? Think of it. The present role of students insulates them from reality and responsible participation in society. They are kept out of all important decision-making processes and are expected to obey older authorities without question and to play nice and be innocent and consume prodigiously. Most of them are happy to escape from freedom—and the responsibilities it imposes—and to let the elders absorb the shock and do the work while they play—not always nicely, since they tend to notice the size of the gap between what the elders moralistically say and what they actually do, and not always innocently—and while they consume.

If you look at this process as an anthropologist would, you might notice that it is devastatingly poor preparation for responsible participation in a complex society, especially one that is supposed to be basically a democratic republic.

For about the first third of their lives, an increasing number of our students are assiduously kept from doing (learning) any of the things they most need to know in order to function in a rapidly changing technological culture.

What the high school of 1980, then, most needs to do is to provide an opportunity for students to do (learn) those things that will equip them to function responsibly and productively in a rapidly changing technological culture.

The high school of 1980 should be more of a process than a place. Its curriculum should be the community and the real problems facing it. The student in 1980 should be an active agent in the process of inquiring into real problems, their causes, their symptoms, and their dynamics, for the purpose of formulating possible solutions and for carrying them out. The student in 1980 should not be a passive ventriloquizer of dead and abstract ideas, but rather an active formulator and user of ideas relevant to the real problems of the community—up to and including the global village.

It seems incredible that the actual energy and potential imagination of millions of our adolescents should be confined to playing meaningless games and engaging in destructive mischief. Why shouldn't the high school of 1980 be primarily a process intended to channel this energy and potential into an active, relevant instrument of constructive social action?

This shift in the role of the student would respond not only to demands of student dissenters for responsible participation in activities relevant to real and immediate social issues and problems, but would also respond to the demands—largely misunderstood and unarticulated—of a rapidly changing culture.

Norbert Wiener noted in *The Human Use of Human Beings* that:

The pace at which changes . . . have taken place is unexampled in earlier history, as is the very nature of these changes. . . . We have modified our environment so radically that we must now modify ourselves in order to exist in this new environment. We can no longer live in the old one.

This suggested shift in the role of the student would be responsive to this change since it would be a step in the direction of modifying ourselves. It would capitalize on the fact that students have the unique advantage of not having as much newly irrelevant stuff to unlearn as their elders. This is unique and an unprecedented advantage when a revolution in thinking is needed as a primary step in the process of modifying ourselves in order that we might survive our unprecedented environment.

Almost all of the ideas and metaphors that have accumulated in Western culture for 5000 years must now be unlearned if we are to survive in our new environment. The modes of thinking explicitly and implicitly taught in school today *make necessary* Pogo's observation that "We have met the enemy and they is us." Students now learn in school that every problem has two sides, and that they are always in opposition. And that every question has one right answer. And that reason and logic and their corollaries objectivity and will power are the ultimate human triumphs. And that the universe conforms to a vertical hierarchy. And that, for example, at the top of this hierarchy is white, Judaeo-Christian culture. And that good and evil are opposites. And that everything and everybody is to be judged immediately by these criteria. And that we are good, and that "we" means white, Judaeo-Christian. And that anyone who is not we is bad, or at least inferior, and in any case a potential enemy. And that we are God's chosen ones. And that nothing is too good for us. And that everything that God put on earth He put there for our taking. And that more is better.

The high school in 1980 must at least provide an opportunity for all students to discover that the kind of thinking cited above can be fatal in the new environment, because almost all of the problems in the new environment were caused by thinking like that. It must help them to become ecologists rather than taxonomists.

And the role of the high school student in 1980 must include an opportunity to use and become sophisticated in using all media of communication, primarily on the producing ends rather than on the consuming ends. The best way to discover what a medium means—or can mean—is to use it as an instrument for producing social action that will enhance rather than jeopardize the survival prospects of the group.

Why shouldn't students use all media as instruments for dealing with the real problems of the community that will comprise the curriculum for the high school in 1980?

Change is the central fact of the world we live in, and it is literally impossible to overstate the significance of this fact.

The Cassandra-like prognoses that characteristically follow most diagnoses of our present plights resulting from change stem almost entirely from the fact that our basic responses to change are not essentially different from those of cave men or medieval peasants.

When *change* becomes the central fact of the world in which we live—as it now has—there can be no task more important for our schools to undertake than to equip students to deal fruitfully with it. This requires thinking of reality as processes rather than as fixed states.

The student in high school in 1980 had better learn disciplines—subjects—as ways of knowing, rather than as catalogs of facts that once got to be known. The high school student in 1980 should be actively inquiring into the present and future rather than passively staring into the past.

The role of the student in 1980 must be modified into that of an active, responsible discoverer, capable of dealing fruitfully with rapid and continuing change; of thinking in nonpolarized ways; of suspending judgment; of dealing with probability rather than certainty; of perceiving multiple causality; of simultaneously entertaining a variety of answers to a single question; of understanding—and accepting—nonrational patterns as valid.

This seems like a tall order, and it is. But the new environment requires nothing less, as Wiener said, than that we modify ourselves. If the student is not helped to achieve this modification then the question might be asked, "Why have a high school in 1980 at all?"

THE CHALLENGE
OF CHANGE

The Comprehensive High School

James B. Conant

The comprehensive high school is an American invention of some 50 years ago. The basic idea was simple. All the youth of a community were to be equally well served by a public secondary school. To that end, the high school would provide a wide variety of elective courses; the boy or girl who wished to take a job on graduation was to be as well taken care of as those who were college bound. Such, at least, was and is the ideal. The arguments in favor of a comprehensive school are two-fold: educational and social. The educational may be summed up by the word "flexibility." Each year, a student may reassess his program of studies. In contrast to a strictly academic or vocational school, the possibility exists that a young person may drastically change the orientation of his education without transferring to another school. For example, a tenth-grade boy who has been planning to be a skilled mechanic may in the eleventh grade change his mind and elect courses required for admission to an engineering school; a girl whose ambition on entering high school had been to complete an academic course, may decide she wishes to seek employment as a secretary and, therefore, makes a new choice of her courses.

The social arguments in favor of a comprehensive school are, today, at least as important as the educational. They merit careful examination since their acceptance or rejection will determine the direction of our planning of tax-supported secondary education. Four premises are usually involved. It is assumed first that in a heterogeneous group, a democratic cooperative spirit can only exist if there is a sympathetic understanding among the members with widely different backgrounds; second, that the healthy growth of American democracy requires the widespread existence of such a spirit; third, that the attitude of an adult is determined to a considerable degree by his or her experiences when young; fourth, that those who attend a widely comprehensive high school do in fact come to know and understand youths from families very different from their own. From these premises flows the conclusion that under favorable circumstances a widely comprehensive school can be an effective instrument for furthering unity and democracy in an entire community. Along some such lines, the proponents of a comprehensive or composite high school have argued ever since the educational reformers first formulated their ideas at the time of World War I.

Ten years and more ago when the American high school was little known in Great Britain or on the European continent, I used to hear from my foreign friends questions which indicated their incredulity when I spoke of the three functions of a widely comprehensive high school. Was it possible, they asked, for one and the same school to provide: (1) a good education for the academically talented, (2) a satisfactory offering of vocational courses, (3) the basis for an understanding among students of highly different backgrounds and vocational interests? I had to admit that I could not name any one school which I would consider excellent in all three respects. But I knew of many that were excellent according to one of the criteria at least, and nearly adequate as regards the others. I always hastened to add that all these schools would become excellent in all three respects with the expenditure of a little more money.

The comprehensive high school may well be regarded as an ideal, the complete realization of which is difficult to achieve in practice. In this case, the question of the relevance of the ideal for 1980 at once arises. In planning for the future, should or should not the effort be made to increase the number of comprehensive schools and to broaden still further the comprehensiveness of those which now exist? The answer to this question turns on the acceptance or rejection of the social arguments I have already listed in favor of the comprehensive principle. If one rejects the arguments, then one can forget about our high schools functioning as instruments of democracy; attention can be directed solely to the task of finding the most effective and least expensive way of imparting knowledge and developing skills; whether the social composition of a student body is heterogeneous or not is a matter of indifference; vocational schools, selective academic schools and general high schools may be welcomed as the component parts of the pattern of public secondary education in the 1980s. The idea of comprehensiveness can be pushed aside. On the other hand, if one accepts the arguments in question, one is committed to a point of view which must be considered every time a decision is made which affects the education of our youth. If the commitment is deeply sincere, the proponent of the widely comprehensive high school will not be satisfied with merely encouraging the improvement of those institutions which now exist; he will wish to examine some tough questions. He will want to explore how schools in the suburbs which are essentially academic schools can be made widely comprehensive; he will ponder what steps could be taken to make a school comprehensive as regards racial origins of the students. In short, he will wish to examine all possible implications of the doctrine he has espoused.

Let me postpone a discussion of the implications of the word "comprehensive" for high school students in a community with a considerable portion of Negro or Puerto Rican or Spanish-speaking families. Let me concentrate first on the difficulties of creating a widely comprehensive high school in a school district which is essentially all white. Until recently, this was the only problem that was considered proper for educators to discuss. All youth were future American citizens and were to be treated as such, it was declared; the fact that some were white and some black was not to be mentioned by educators. Indeed, prior to World War II, any consideration of the socioeconomic status of the families in even an all white community was frowned upon by most writers on education. It was assumed that the student body in a high school would be heterogeneous as regards the educational plans of the graduates, but it was further assumed that the degree of heterogeneity was about the same in all the high schools of the nation. The existence of tax-supported college preparatory schools like the Boston Latin School or the Bronx High School of Science in New York City was ignored. So, too, were the completely segregated schools in the South.

To be sure, the Educational Policies Commission (appointed by the National Education Association and the American Association of School Administrators) writing in the 1940s, recognized a difference between a city and a farming community. In the large volume, "Education for *All* American Youth," two somewhat different organizations of secondary education through grades 13 and 14 were recommended. There is no reference in the book, however, to what we now call the education of members of minority groups; neither segregation nor desegregation are mentioned; racial prejudice is completely ignored, which fact vitiates much of what is written about vocational education. I make these comments not to criticize the book (which I am not in a position to do, as I was one of the authors), but in order to underline the significance of a factor which was largely ignored in the writings of those who sponsored the creation of secondary schools for all American youth. The factor might be called the degree of heterogeneity of the community which the high school serves.

When I started my inquiry into the state of American public secondary education in 1957, I was well aware of the fact that shifts in population in the 1930s and 1940s had created communities which differed one from another in ways significant for those responsible for the schools. I knew from what I had heard that these differences were reflected in the interests and desires of the students. One could no longer ignore the socioeconomic status of the families in a school district or assume that all public high schools were alike as regards the vocational desires of the students. There were schools from which almost all the seniors intended to pursue their formal studies after graduation; there were others in which less than half had the same ambition. I decided to concentrate my attention primarily on high schools with a high degree of comprehensiveness. In these schools, at least half of the students terminated their full-time education at graduation; a variety of vocational programs were available as well as courses for those who were academically talented. Later, I introduced the term "widely comprehensive high school" and included in the classification all the schools in which the precentage of college-bound students was between 25 and 75 percent. Such schools, it seemed to me, were comparable in heterogeneity to those of 50 years ago that the reformers had in mind when they first pointed out the advantages of a comprehensive school. Life in such a school, I was convinced, could be under favorable conditions "a natural and valuable preparation for life in a democracy," to use the reformers' words. In terms of the variable which most affects the instruction provided, namely the post-high school plans of the twelfth graders, the student body could be said to be *widely* heterogeneous.

I have characterized the comprehensive high school as an ideal that is difficult to achieve in practice, yet I do not want to leave the impression that one would have difficulty in finding such schools in the United States. Quite the contrary is true, as shown by the findings of a committee of the National Association of Secondary School Principals. We compiled by means of a questionnaire an inventory of the educational offerings of some 2000 schools of medium size (total enrollment 750 to 2000). Since we were in search of the facts about comprehensive schools, we included only schools from which between 25 percent and 75 percent of the seniors went on for further full-time education after graduation. Practically all the schools provided courses in business and home economics. A little more than a half offered instruction in auto mechanics or building trades. If we had been in a position to make a more detailed examination of the possible vocational instruction, I do not doubt we would have found a still greater number of schools in which a boy could have satisfied his desire for practical instruction. We identified as a minimum, a thousand schools which could without question be designated as widely comprehensive. If anyone had doubts as to whether this type of school still exists, the results of our study were conclusive. Our other findings largely concerned the adequacy of the programs for the academically talented and the instruction in English. They have been published in "The Comprehensive High School: A Second Report to Interested Citizens." (McGraw-Hill, New York, 1967.)

There are at least a thousand widely comprehensive high schools today but anyone who is aware of the present situation knows that unless radical measures are taken, many high schools in the nation which are now widely comprehensive will soon become essentially college preparatory institutions. As a community becomes more affluent, the number of families desiring a college education increases; the fraction of the youth who wish to find employment on graduation decreases. As long as the nature of the student body reflects the housing pattern of the community, the trend in many parts of the country will be towards making the high schools less and less comprehensive. Ten years ago, many welcomed the changes which were going on. These people were convinced that the comprehensive high schools could not provide an intellectual diet suitable for academically talented youth. Even today in spite of the well-known improvements in high school education, some educators and influential citizens in certain localities seem to have grave doubts about the basic principle of the widely comprehensive high school; otherwise, they would not have favored the creation of new vocational schools. Needless to say, I am not among their number. I believe we should start our thinking about the future by assuming that it would be desirable to increase, not decrease, the fraction of the youth who are educated in schools with a high degree of comprehensiveness.

To be quite frank, the case for the comprehensive principle must be far more powerfully presented than it has been in recent years. The truth is that professional educators and laymen concerned with public schools have become so engrossed with one set of extremely difficult problems that all other questions have been largely pushed aside. I refer, of course, to the education of members of minority groups in the metropolitan areas. The issues here are so explosive

and the factors involved change so rapidly that it is hard for anyone to propose a program which is likely to be acceptable for any
length of time. Nevertheless, I am going to assert my belief that
the ideal of the comprehensive high school, if properly extended
should be the model for the future; that the best way out of the
present segregated situation in many areas is to consider as a goal
the creation of high schools which shall be widely comprehensive
not only as regards the economic backgrounds and the vocational
desires of the students, but in terms of the color of the skins of
those who are attending. If this is done, then the social arguments
for the comprehensive high school gain new force. Until it is done,
it is easy for those primarily interested in integration to scoff at
the use of the words "widely comprehensive" to describe any school
which is 100 percent all white. Yet if the ideal secondary school is
defined as one in which the student body is widely heterogeneous
as regards color, then in some sections of the country, the ideal
school is impossible to achieve. It is for this reason that I would
favor continuing to talk about schools which are widely comprehensive only as regards the post-high school plans of the graduates.
One may substitute the adjective "fully" to designate a widely comprehensive school which is, in fact, attended by a considerable
proportion of both black and white students.

Theoretically, schools which are fully comprehensive can be established in all school districts in which the percentage of minority
group students is high. As a matter of fact, the distribution of the
population is often such as to create high school attendance areas,
none of which reflect the social composition of the entire large district. The way the cities have developed since World War II has
created homogeneous areas of disadvantaged Negro and homogeneous
areas of advantaged white families. This fact seems to make the
goal of a widely and fully comprehensive high school impossible to
reach. And so it may be unless one is ready to transfer many youth
by bus. If bussing is accepted, then attendance areas for each high
school in the city can be created which in socioeconomic terms
corresponds to a cross section of the entire district. In some cities,
a number of such areas would have a checkerboard pattern; several
sections would not be contiguous; the different attendance areas
would be outlined and combined with the one clear-cut objective
in mind, namely, that of approaching the ideal of a widely and fully
comprehensive student body in each high school. The same objective
could govern the joint planning of a group of high schools surround-
ing a large city. One could imagine the drawing of school district
lines so that many if not all suburban high schools would serve

both white and black families. The fact that our public schools are supported to a considerable degree by local property taxes is a complication to the realization of the dream. In theory, this obstacle could be circumvented by abolishing local taxes for schools and placing the whole financial burden on the state. Indeed, such a possibility is beginning to be discussed, but it would be inappropriate for me to pursue the matter further in this chapter. Probably the sentiment of the suburban dwellers is today a more formidable block to making all suburban high schools widely and fully comprehensive than the existence of almost unmovable school district lines.

It may well be asked whether the families concerned would cooperate in the scheme proposed. Those in the affluent white areas might rebel and either leave the city or force the school board to give up the idea of making the schools widely and fully comprehensive; those in the black areas might also reject the idea of integration and demand a locally controlled school staff entirely with black teachers. If one assumes that a majority of the schools in all the large cities of the nation must be made widely and fully comprehensive within five or even ten years, I would agree the idea was impossible of fulfillment. I am writing about 1980 and beyond, however, not 1970 or even 1974. It seems to me that it is quite conceivable that in the course of a decade, the electorate in a few places, at least, might be ready to endorse the principle of comprehensiveness and make it the key to the planning for the education of the youth. If a majority of the people in a city and its suburbs become convinced of the importance of widely and fully comprehensive high schools, then providing the necessary funds and revising administrative measures would be relatively easy. I do not minimize, however, the difficulties involved in obtaining a wide acceptance of the principle which is at stake. I suggest, however, that until these difficulties are frankly faced and forcefully debated, the direction of progress for American secondary education will remain uncertain because it is undefined. Is the tradition of the comprehensive high school to be accepted as an ideal or is it to be rejected? It would be well if an answer to this question could be arrived at state by state over the course of the next 10 or 15 years.

I am an advocate of the comprehensive school, yet I must admit that the future of this type of institution is far from certain in the United States. It is strange that the enthusiasm for an American invention is so limited in this country just at the time when other nations are beginning to explore application of the basic idea. In

Great Britain, a citizens' group is actively promoting the establishment of comprehensive schools which, to be sure, are by no means
identical with American schools bearing the same name, but are
organized on similar principles. The Swedes have recently reformed
their educational system; the typically European, highly selective
academic school has disappeared. No longer in Sweden are those
who are headed for the university separated from the others by
examination at age 10 or 11. Instead, all the children and youth
from ages 7 to 16 attend a 9-year comprehensive school. After
graduation at age 16 or 17, the youth may enroll in one of the
three types of schools or cease his formal educational endeavors.
One of the three types is a rigorous academic school whose graduates enter a university with a level of scholastic accomplishment
equivalent to the junior year of a highly selective American college.
At present, 20 percent of the relevant age group are thus preparing
to enter a university; 30 years ago, the corresponding figure was
9 or 10 percent; by 1970, the figure is expected to rise to 25 or
30 percent. The dramatic increase is a consequence, the Swedish
educators believe, of the abolition of selection for a preuniversity
school at age 10 and the introduction of 9 years of schooling in an
institution in which several curricula are connected by a flexible
arrangement. The essence of the change is that a decision to prepare for a university is postponed from age 10 or 11 to age 16. In
those days when the decision was made at the early age, parental
influence hostile to advanced education was often the controlling
factor. After 9 years in a comprehensive school with a wide choice
of curricula, a youth begins to make up his own mind whether or
not he wants to prepare for a university.

Professor Torsten Husén of the University of Stockholm, who
has done much to bring about the changes I have outlined, believes
that in many European countries, between 40 and 70 percent of
the potential academic talent is left undeveloped because selection
for a preuniversity school is made so early. He writes as follows:
"The selective school, i.e., the school which seeks to separate the
book learners from the rest as soon as possible, inflicts a fearful
wastage of talent; in my opinion, the wastage is much greater than
would result from allowing pupils of different gifts to stay together
in the same classes as long as possible." Professor Husén concludes
that a modern industrialized society, if it is to be competitive with
other nations, requires an "*elective* school, not a selective school."
By elective school, Professor Husén means a school in which the
pupils are permitted a choice of electives; they can gradually focus
their studies "in a direction to which they are drawn by their abili-

ties and interests." His words are remarkably similar to those used in 1918 by the authors of "Cardinal Principles of Secondary Education" (A Report of the Commission on the Reorganization of Secondary Education Appointed by the National Education Association). A section on vocational education opens as follows: "When effectively organized and administered, the comprehensive high school can make differentiated education of greater value to the individual and to society, for such value depends largely upon the extent to which the individual pursues the curriculum best suited to his needs. This factor is of prime importance, although frequently ignored in discussions regarding the effectiveness of vocational and other types of differentiated education."

Let me make it plain that I am not claiming that Sweden has copied the United States. Nor do I suggest that in England the experiments with the introduction of the elective principle into secondary education represent a blind imitation of the American comprehensive high school. What I am pointing out is that arguments first heard in the United States are now being repeated in other lands. In these days when the papers are full of the problems of the high schools and highly vocal critics are to be heard on every hand, it is worthwhile to remind ourselves that in the field of public secondary education, the United States has been an innovator. Whatever the future has in store, are we not justified in saluting with pride those educational statesmen who so long ago gave form to the concept of education for all the youth of a community in a single comprehensive school?

It was not only the flexibility of the programs in a comprehensive school which recommended this type of school to the writers of "Cardinal Principles of Secondary Education." They were aware of the significance of what I have called the social arguments as the following quotation makes evident:

In America, racial stocks are widely diversified, various forms of racial heredity come into conflict, differing religious beliefs do not always make for unification, and the members of different vocations often fail to recognize the interests that they have in common with others. The school is the one agency that may be controlled definitely and consciously by our democracy for the purpose of unifying its people. . . . When administered by a principal who himself recognizes the social value of all types of secondary education and inspires a broad spirit of democracy among teachers and pupils, the comprehensive high school is a better instrument for unification. Through friendships formed with pupils pursuing other curriculums and having vocational and educational goals widely different from their own, the pupils realize that the interests which they hold in common with others are, after all, far more important than the differences that would tend to make them antagonistic to others. . . . In short, the comprehensive school is the prototype of a democracy in which various groups must have a degree of self-consciousness as groups and yet be federated into a larger whole through the recognition of common interests and ideals. Life in such a school is a natural and valuable preparation for life in a democracy." (Department of the Interior Bureau of Education Bulletin 1918 No. 35, pp. 22–26.)

Over the years, those who have favored the comprehensive school as a prototype of American democracy have had to struggle with many difficulties, almost all of which were a consequence of the high cost of providing a range of elective courses—a range wide enough to satisfy the ambitions of a widely heterogeneous student body. An example of the consequence of financial limitations is afforded by the plight of modern foreign language instruction in many otherwise satisfactory schools. If only a small number of students wish to elect a certain course, the budget-maker will think twice before authorizing such an expensive arrangement. A few years ago, one often found that the second, third, and fourth year courses in a modern foreign language were combined in a single class because only five or six students in each grade desired the instruction. Adequate instruction by conventional methods is impossible under such conditions.

Providing for satisfactory vocational courses is particularly expensive. To equip a shop means the investment of a considerable sum. If only a few boys wish to enroll, the overhead per student is extremely high. Although the federal government for years has provided a major share of the funds for vocational courses even at the high school level, the state and local administrators are quite properly concerned with the effective expenditure of money. If the cost per student is used as a measure of the efficiency of the school, a strong case can be made for the vocational high school. For a given annual expenditure, more shops can be maintained in a vocational school than in a comprehensive school. The reason, of course, is that in many a comprehensive high school there are often an insufficient number who wish to enroll in any one of the vocational courses; therefore, the classes are small, the costs are high.

Unless one wishes to decry all vocational courses at the high school level, which I certainly do not, one must be prepared to face the fact that a high school must be at least of medium size if it is to be a widely comprehensive school. Some years ago I suggested that a high school should graduate each year at least a hundred if it is to provide adequate instruction at reasonable expense. I am now strongly inclined to double this figure. I can explain my reasons by giving a hypothetical example. Suppose there are three shops (say, one for auto mechanics, one for modern printing and photography, and one for electronics) and that as a minimum there should be 15 students in each shop, a total of 45; suppose further that half the boys in the senior class are interested in these programs, then clearly the male enrollment in the senior class should be 90; the total size of the senior class should be 180. A little arithmetic of this sort makes clear one of the blocks to the development of a satisfactory comprehensive school; a community is often loath to support a high school with a graduating class of more than 50.

There are many limitations on what can be accomplished in a small high school quite apart from the difficulties of offering adequate vocational instruction. Decades ago, leading educators concluded that small high schools should be consolidated and the students from a distance brought to the school by bus at public expense. There are many examples of such consolidation, yet the small high school persists, as it has many friends. Throughout the country, one finds high schools which are much too small to function as widely comprehensive schools, yet each is cherished by the community because it is felt to be a local institution. Pride in the accomplishment of the football or basketball team is often the chief component of the emotional attachment of the local inhabitants to the school. According to the returns of a questionnaire sent by the committee of the National Association of Secondary School Principals to which I have already referred, there were in 1965 over 6000 public high schools, each with an enrollment of less than 500. In some states, over 75 percent of the schools fell in this category; for the entire nation, the figure was 45 percent.

The figures I have just quoted are disappointing to the proponents of the widely comprehensive school. Efforts to reduce the number of small schools will continue, but it is unlikely that the situation will change drastically in the next decade. By no stretch of the imagination can one foresee the time in this century when a majority of those high schools whose total enrollment is now one or two hundred will be replaced by consolidated comprehensive schools of a thousand or more pupils. There are two developments, however, which will help the spread of the comprehensive ideal if the citizens of an area really desire to have their high schools provide adequately for both the college bound and the others. In the first place new developments in vocational education promise new kinds of instruction which will be more popular because they are clearly related to the changing technology. It may well be that these new offerings may require equipment which is far less expensive to maintain and operate than the old stand-bys of auto mechanics, printing, and building trades. In a word, the field of vocational instruction is in a state of flux; there may emerge types of courses which will be better suited to the needs of a heterogeneous student body than what has been available in the past. In the second place, a cooperative effort among several school districts may to some extent lower the cost of providing a variety of shop courses. The scheme could be adopted in the sections of the country with a relatively high density of population. The shop facilities would be so distributed that while no single comprehensive school could offer more than a single shop course, taken together the offerings of the group may number three or four. If a student wished instruction in a field not available in his own school, he would be bussed to one of the cooperating schools which offered the desired course. The schedule would permit the youth in question to spend the necessary hours in a shop, yet allow him to remain a student in the academic elective courses as well as in the required English course in the school from which he would graduate eventually.

As we have seen, the widely comprehensive high school must aim at providing satisfactory education for all the members of a highly heterogeneous student body, yet budgetary considerations place a limit on the planning of the curricula. The problem is well illustrated by the situation in modern foreign language instruction which I have already cited. Small classes are too expensive to be scheduled by any but the richest school districts. The limitation affects adversely not only the ambitious bright boy or girl but also those who are at the other end of the spectrum of scholastic talent. For example, the slow reader should meet with a teacher either on an individual basis or be a member of a group of two or three. There may be many such students in a fully comprehensive school. Indeed, I think it fair to say that the wider the spread of scholastic ability in a student body, the more unsatisfactory is the usual procedure of requiring every teacher to face a class of approximately the same size. Yet no school system could afford to hire the number of teachers required if really small classes were the general rule. It is all very well to talk about individualizing the instruction of the less able youth, but quite another to translate such fine talk into financial terms. As one reduces the size of the average class, the expense per student skyrockets. Before one reaches in imagination a situation which is significantly different from the present, the budgetary figures are of a different order of magnitude from those even in the wealthiest school districts.

In the analysis I have just presented, I have assumed that what will go on in the classroom in the future will be little different from what has gone on in the past. In other words, I have completely neglected the impact of the new technology. If the educators who have been experimenting with the use of computers and similar devices are right in their forecasts, I have overlooked the very development which holds promise of making individualized instruction a possibility at costs that a well-supported school district could afford. It is beyond the scope of my assignment and my competence to amplify this statement. I gather from what I read that though the technology is developing fast, it will be some time before the capital costs of the equipment will be low enough to permit the widespread use of new systems in tax-supported schools. In looking into the future, it is important to note the distinction between new devices which are on the road to individualized instruction and those which serve a class of usual size. The use of a television screen provides a good illustration. Excellent programs, particularly in science and foreign languages, are now available which can be seen to good advantage by a class or by several classes at the same time. They may be broadcast within a school or an open circuit and have been effectively used in this way for a number of years. A new device recently announced by CBS promises to provide the means by which such programs can be the basis for individualized instruction. The usual television receiver is attached to a piece of equipment called a player into which a circular cartridge may be inserted carrying a film on which a program has been recorded. Because the cartridges can be made in quantity, they are relatively inexpensive. Eventually a school would have a library of such cartridges. When a teacher wanted to show a program to an individual or group, the appropriate cartridge would be taken from the library and inserted in a player. What is seen on the television screen could be repeated at any time for any sized group; the presentation could be interrupted for discussion at any point. On a completely individualized basis, a student might select a cartridge and play it without reference to a teacher.

I can imagine that a time may come when a large portion of what is now handled in a class of 25 or 30 would be on an individualized basis. The new educational technology will have made such a revolutionary change possible. Many of those difficulties of a widely comprehensive high school which I have been discussing will have disappeared. Neither individual instruction nor small classes will be excessively expensive. Classroom instruction as we now know it may survive only for one purpose, namely to evoke discussion in a class whose composition reflects that of the entire student body.

Yet this purpose is of cardinal importance in any high school which aims to be widely and fully comprehensive. Indeed, as the systems based on the new technology take over a large share of the present teachers' work, it will be necessary to focus attention on those procedures which do not develop skills or impart information but are directed towards developing mutual understanding among students. As an illustration of the kind of class instruction I have in mind, I might call attention to an arrangement I have found in certain comprehensive schools. The classes in a twelfth grade course in the problems of American democracy are so arranged that each class of 25 or 30 is as heterogeneous as possible. I have heard discussions in such a class under the leadership of a skillful teacher which proved that in that particular school one of the aims of a widely comprehensive school was in process of being realized. An understanding among youth with different prejudices and personal ambitions was being effectively promoted.

As I attempt to look into the future, I seem to see two types of teachers emerging. One would be concerned with the individualized instruction made possible by the new computer-based systems; the other would be interested in working with groups of students (probably organized as classes) to insure that all the students in a grade were exposed to the same intellectual experiences and were stimulated to interchange their views. Admittedly, what I envision assumes a widely and fully comprehensive high school. If that ideal is rejected, the need for courses in which students learn from one another largely disappears. Therefore, if I am right, the future organization of secondary public education including the role of the new technology, turns on the answer to the question I have kept repeating in this chapter. Are the high schools of the United States to be so designed as to be effective means of forwarding the idea of a unity based on diversity in a democratic community, or is the comprehensive concept to be given at best only lip service? Far more than the nature of our schools is involved in the answer to this question. The entire structure of our nation may be at stake—possibly even its survival as an open society of free men.

The Future Scope and Shape of American Secondary Education

Sidney G. Tickton

Today the broad outlines of American secondary education in 1980 have already been shaped. The children who will be enrolled in secondary schools have already been born; the teachers who will instruct them are already preparing to teach; the classrooms in which they will learn are, for the most part, already built; the textbooks they will study are in some cases already written. Barring war or some other calamity, it is clear that the basic factors likely to affect secondary education a decade hence have already been set. Three significant factors remain unresolved. They are:

What will teachers teach?
How well will they teach it?
Who will pay the bill?

Obviously, the answers to these questions depend upon so many variables and unknowns that they are virtually impossible to predict. Some clues to the trends that are to be expected may be found in other chapters of this book. The purpose of this chapter is to document the basic demographic and financial factors we see for the decade ahead. The figures have been assembled and analyzed against the background of a single set of broad assumptions about society and education as set forth in Table 1.

Using these assumptions, an analysis of the wide range of materials on population, economic outlook and the educational perspectives that are available in the files and reports of government agencies and private research organizations lead to the conclusions and projections outlined in the tables in this chapter.

The first of these, Table 2, shows the school-age population in 1965 and estimated for 1980 as well as the change expected to occur during the 15 year period.

As shown in the third line of Table 2, the high school age population, which is already born, is expected to grow by 13.5 percent

TABLE 1

Secondary Education: Assumptions for Projections to 1980

ITEM	ASSUMPTION
1. World situation	Will remain about the same as it was in 1965–1969; no additional wars, widespread epidemic or similar catastrophe will occur.
2. Economic activity	Will continue at a high level. Neither a severe depression nor a major boom will occur during the period.
3. Price levels	Will follow the pattern of the decade 1957–1967, which means moderate increases.
4. National attitude toward education	Will follow the pattern of the decade 1957–1967 including an increasing emphasis on the completion of high school.
5. Birth rate	Will be substantially below the post-World War II level or the level of the fifties. The effects of the birth control pill and the trend toward smaller families will balance off against the increasing number of women of childbearing age.
6. Total population	Will increase at a moderate rate to a total of 235,000,000 persons by 1980.
7. Population by states	Will increase significantly greater than the national average in California and Florida. Will increase significantly less than the national average in the plains states, the South, Appalachia, and most of the Midwest.
8. Population in the cities	Will increase moderately. The proportion of blacks in cities as a whole, and in the inner city especially, will continue to grow.
9. Population in suburban areas	Will continue to increase more than proportionally to 1980. This population will then as now be overwhelmingly white.
10. Enrollment in private and parochial schools	Will decrease in relation to the total enrollment and to the total school age population.
11. Educational attainment	Will continue to increase, particularly in the inner cities and the South with a greater proportion of the population completing high school. By 1980, graduation of 85.2 percent of those who enrolled in the ninth grade in public school is expected.

TABLE 1 (*Continued*)

ITEM	ASSUMPTION
12. Teachers' salaries	Will increase faster than the rate during the decade 1957–1967 because of the organized efforts of teachers' organizations.
13. Student-teacher ratio	Will decrease slightly. By 1980 the ratio in public secondary schools is expected to be 20.3 to 1 compared with 20.8 to 1 in 1965. The ratio in nonpublic schools will drop to 15.4 to 1 compared with 16.7 to 1 some 15 years earlier.
14. Classroom construction	Will follow the trend of construction during the period 1957–1967.
15. The use of technological media for instruction	Will increase substantially but is not likely to provide a major portion of the instructional program by 1980.
16. Federal support for education	Will increase substantially with most of the increase funneled through state and local governmental agencies. Limitations on the use of funds will be less stringent in 1980 than in the late 1960s. Because of the concentration of blacks in the cities, a proportionally greater amount of federal financial support will be directed into those areas.

TABLE 2
Estimated School Age Population 1965 and 1980*

AGE GROUP	1965 JULY 1	1980[a] JULY 1	15-YEAR INCREASE	PERCENTAGE CHANGE
18 years old [b]	3,743,000	4,260,000	517,000	+ 13.8%
14–17 years old	14,113,000	16,005,000	1,892,000	+ 13.4%
Subtotal, high school-age	17,856,000	20,265,000	2,409,000	+ 13.5%
5–13 years old	35,890,000	36,680,000	790,000	+ 2.2%
Total, 5–18 years old	53,746,000	56,945,000	3,199,000	+ 6.0%

[a] The 1980 projections are based on the Census Bureau's "Series C" estimates which assume a gradual movement of the fertility rate toward the 1966 level.

[b] Some young people in this age bracket are in high school and some are in college. The figures are included in this table for a clearer indication of the totals that are relevant for projections and comparisons.

in 15 years. This compares with an increase of only 2.2 percent during the 15 year period for elementary school-age children, as shown in the fourth line of Table 2.*

These contrasting trends on a national basis—a continued growth in total number of high school-age children at a time when the increase in the total number of elementary school-age children is expected to slacken or even decline—are going to be a new development of mid-century education. It will provide most educators with experiences dramatically different from those of their predecessors in the decade after the war.**

This outlook could be of tremendous importance to the long-range planning decisions of the nation's schools. Yet to date its prospect has had little effect.

The figures in Table 3 show that the enrollment totals are expected to increase from 13,010,000 to 15,800,000 in the period from 1965 to 1980, a rise of 21.4 percent. A greater proportion of high school-age children is expected to attend classes in 1980 than in 1965. The ratio of enrollment to population in the high school age bracket is expected to rise from the 72.9 percent level of 1965 to 78.0 percent 15 years later.† There has been a national trend toward staying in school longer and the prospect is that trend can be expected to continue until 1980. In some states, Wisconsin, for example, the minimum age for leaving school has been raised recently from 16 years to 18 years. Similar steps can be expected to be taken in other states.

In view of the nation's increasing demand for the high school diploma as a passport for job entry, there seems little doubt that the trend toward a higher level of educational attainment, including high school graduation for more students, will continue. As shown in Table 3, about 76.5 percent of those who started with the high school class of 1965 were actually graduated, but in 1980 about 85.2 percent of the students who will enroll in high school are expected to receive diplomas. The number of graduates from public and nonpublic high schools will increase from the 2,665,000 estimated for 1965 to a projected 3,706,000 in 1980, a 39.1 percent rise.

* For the 12 year period 1969–1980, a *net decline* in elementary school-age children can be expected.

** As educators consider the enrollment figures in this chapter they should note that the peak in high school enrollment during the decade, 1970–1980, is expected to be in the year 1976. This means that more teachers and classrooms must be available *before* 1980 than in 1980 itself.

† The remainder consists of dropouts, persons who graduate before age 18, the ill and disabled, dependents living overseas of persons traveling in or temporarily stationed in foreign countries, inmates of correctional institutions, etc.

TABLE 3
*Estimated High School-Age Population,
Enrollment and Graduations: 1965 and 1980*

CATEGORY	1965	1980	15-YEAR INCREASE	PERCENTAGE CHANGE
14–18 year olds				
Number	17,856,000	20,265,000	2,409,000	+ 13.5%
Percent of total				
population	9.2%	8.6%		
High school enrollment				
Number	13,010,000	15,800,000	2,790,000	+ 21.4%
Percent of 14–18				
year olds	72.9%	78.0%		
Graduates				
Number	2,665,000	3,706,000	1,041,000	+ 39.1%
Percent of enroll-				
ment as 9th				
graders (public				
schools only)	76.5%	85.2%		
Distribution of high				
school students by sex				
Boys	6,530,000	8,067,000	1,537,000	+ 23.5%
Girls	6,480,000	7,733,000	1,253,000	+ 19.3%
Total	13,010,000	15,800,000	2,790,000	+ 21.4%
Distribution of high				
school graduates by sex				
Boys	1,332,000	1,871,000	539,000	+ 40.5%
Girls	1,333,000	1,835,000	502,000	+ 37.7%
Total	2,665,000	3,706,000	1,041,000	+ 39.1%
Distribution of high				
school-age group by				
color				
White	15,548,000	17,047,000	1,499,000	+ 9.6%
Nonwhite	2,308,000	3,218,000	910,000	+ 39.4%
Total	17,856,000	20,265,000	2,409,000	+ 13.5%

NOTE: Minor adjustments were made by the Academy for Educational Development to the distributions by sex and color of high school-age students and graduates in order to make the totals consistent with other population figures. These adjustments had no significant effect on the percentages of change.

Table 3 also shows that the composition of high school-age graduates is expected to change. For instance, more girls than boys were graduated from high schools in 1965. In 1980, however, the number of boys will be greater. The shift is expected to be caused

TABLE 4

Estimated Number of Secondary School Teachers and High School Students;
Secondary School Pupil/Teacher Ratios and
Secondary School Teachers' Average Salaries: 1965 and 1980

ITEM	1965	1980	15-YEAR CHANGE	PERCENTAGE CHANGE
Number of secondary school teachers	828,000	1,084,000	256,000	+30.9%
Number of high school students	13,010,000	15,800,000	2,790,000	+21.4%
Secondary school pupil/teacher ratio				
Public schools	20.8	20.3		
Private and parochial schools	16.7	15.4		
Secondary school teachers salaries, public schools				
only (average)	$6,761	$10,192 [a]		+42.5% [b]

NOTES: Where possible, figures are for high school grades 9 through 12. However, many sources list only secondary school data. While secondary schools may include as few as three or as many as seven grades, these differences are not considered important for the purposes of this chapter.

[a] Figure shown at the 1967 price level.

[b] Percentage of change calculated using figures at the 1965 price level and therefore show real change, excluding inflation.

by a lower dropout rate for boys as a result of the trend toward higher educational attainment.

Table 3 also provides data on the makeup of the high school-age population by color. On a percentage basis, the increase in non-white children is expected to be greater than the increase in white children.

Table 4 compares the number of high school pupils and the number of secondary school teachers. The number of secondary school teachers, which totaled 828,000 for both public and non-public schools in 1965, will increase to no fewer than 1,084,000 by 1980, a rise of 30.9 percent. In view of the expected large growth in the number of college and university graduates during the next few years,* particularly in teacher education programs, the supply of secondary school teachers should be adequate by 1980. The

* See *Campus 1980*, Alvin C. Eurich, ed., Delacorte Press, New York 1968, p. 18.

pupil-teacher ratio can be expected to drop moderately during the 15 year period—say from about 20.8 to 1 in 1965 to about 20.3 to 1 in 1980. The pupil-teacher ratio in private and parochial schools will drop correspondingly during the same 15 year period: from about 16.7 to about 15.4 to 1.

The increased number of secondary school teachers is expected to be accompanied by higher salaries—expected to rise from an average of $6,761 in 1965 to an average of $10,192 by 1980—as shown in Table 4. Due to the increasingly stronger bargaining power of teachers generally, the increase per year is expected to be greater on the average than the increase reported during the decade from 1957 to 1967.

Table 5 shows that the growth in the level of the nation's economic activity is expected to be accompanied by an increase in educational spending. The gross national product in 1980 is ex-

TABLE 5

Estimated Gross National Product, Total Education Expenditures, Total Secondary School Expenditures, Secondary School Teachers' Salaries and Cost Per High School Student: 1965 and 1980

ITEM	1965	1980 [a]	PERCENT OF CHANGE [b]
Gross National Product	$684.9 billion	$1,407.00 billion	+94.2%
Total education expenditure [c]	46.2 billion	86.4 billion	+76.6%
Total secondary school expenditure [d]	10.0 billion	18.6 billion	+76.0%
Cost per high school student [e]	$827.00	$1,266.00	+44.6%
Total secondary school expenditure as percentage of Gross National Product	1.4%	1.3%	

NOTES: Since nonpublic secondary school teachers make up only 8% of all secondary school teachers in 1980, salary differences between public and nonpublic teachers are not considered in this table.
    Costs have been calculated using secondary school teachers' average salaries since comparable data are unavailable.

[a] 1980 figures are shown at the 1967 price levels.
[b] Percentages of change were calculated using figures at the 1965 price level and therefore show real changes excluding inflation.
[c] Includes public and nonpublic, elementary, secondary, and higher education.
[d] Includes operating, capital, and interest expenditures for public and nonpublic schools.
[e] Costs per public and nonpublic elementary student are estimated at $636 for 1965 and $1,103 for 1980, the latter figure at the 1967 price level. All cost per pupil figures are based on average daily attendance.

pected to be nearly double the 1965 level with inflation excluded —$1,407,000,000,000* compared to $684,900,000,000. Secondary education's percentage of the GNP in 1980 will be about the same then as it was 15 years earlier. The percentage comparisons are shown in the last line of Table 5. These calculations are based on the estimate that expenditures per pupil in secondary schools will rise on the average from $874 per pupil in 1965 to $1421 per pupil in 1980.

In the aggregate, the projections provide an impression of solidity and continued growth in secondary education to 1980. There is likely to be space enough and time enough in many school systems to consolidate the gains of the sixties, to expand educational programs moderately and move them forward, and to provide a more adequate springboard than now exists from which to prepare for the needs of students in the next century. But this will only happen if the education community and the people of the nation decide to make it happen.

---

* 1980 GNP adjusted to a 1967 price level.

Alternative Schools

Kenneth B. Clark

It is now clear that American public education is organized and functions along social and economic class lines. A biracial public school system wherein approximately 90 percent of American children are required to attend segregated schools is one of the clearest manifestations of this basic fact. The difficulties encountered in attempting to desegregate public schools in the South as well as in the North point to the tenacity of the forces seeking to prevent any basic change in the system.

The class and social organization of American public schools is consistently associated with a lower level of educational efficiency in the less privileged schools. This lower efficiency is expressed in terms of the fact that the schools attended by Negro and poor children have less adequate educational facilities than those attended by more privileged children. Teachers tend to resist assignments in Negro and other underprivileged schools and generally function less adequately in these schools. Their morale is generally lower; they are not adequately supervised; they tend to see their students as less capable of learning. The parents of the children in these schools are usually unable to bring about any positive changes in the conditions of these schools.

The pervasive and persistent educational inefficiency which characterizes these schools results in: (1) marked and cumulative academic retardation in a disproportionately high percentage of these children, beginning in the third or fourth grade and increasing through the eighth grade; (2) a high percentage of dropouts in the junior and senior high schools of students unequipped academically and occupationally for a constructive role in society; (3) a pattern of rejection and despair and hopelessness resulting in massive human wastage.

Given these conditions, American public schools have become significant instruments in the blocking of economic mobility and in the intensification of class distinctions rather than fulfilling their historic function of facilitating such mobility. In effect, the public schools have become captives of a middle class who have failed to use them to aid others to move into the middle class. It might even be possible to interpret the role of the controlling middle class as that of using the public schools to block further mobility.

What are the implications of this existing educational inefficiency? In the national interest, it is a serious question whether the United States government can afford the continuation of the wastage of human resources at this period of world history. Although we cannot conclusively demonstrate a relation between educational inefficiency and other symptoms of personal and social pathology such as crime, delinquency, and pervasive urban decay, there is strong evidence that these are correlates.

Increasing industrialization and automation of our economy will demand larger numbers of skilled and educated and fewer uneducated workers. The manpower needs of contemporary America require business and industry to pay for the added burden of reeducating the miseducated. This is a double taxation. The burdens of the present inefficient public education include this double taxation in addition to the high cost of crime and family stability and the artificial constriction of the labor and consumer market.

Beyond these material disadvantages are the human costs inherent in the failure to achieve equality of educational opportunity. This dehumanization contributes significantly to the cycle of pathology—poor education, menial jobs or unemployment, family instability, group and personal powerlessness. This passive pathology weakens the fabric of the entire society.

OBSTACLES TO THE ATTAINMENT
OF EFFICIENT EDUCATION

The obstacles which interfere with the attainment of efficient public education fall into many categories. Among them are those obstacles which reflect historical premises and dogmas about education, administrative realities, and psychological assumptions and prejudices.

The historical premises and dogmas include such fetishes as the inviolability of the "neighborhood school" concept which might include the belief that schools should be economically and racially homogeneous. The administrative barriers involve such problems as those incurred in the transportation of children from residential neighborhoods to other areas of the city. Here again the issue is one of relative advantages of the status quo versus the imperatives for change.

The residual psychological prejudices take many forms and probably underlie the apparent inability of society to resolve the historical and administrative problems. Initially the academic retardation of Negro children was explained in terms of their inherent racial inferiority. The existence of segregated schools was supported either by law or explained in terms of the existence of segregated neighborhoods. More recently the racial inferiority or legal and custom interpretations have given way to more subtle explanations and support for continued inefficient education. Examples are theories of "cultural deprivation" and related beliefs that the culturally determined educational inferiority of Negro children will impair the ability of white children to learn if they are taught in the same classes. It is assumed that because of their background, Negro children and their parents are poorly motivated for academic achievement and will not only be unable to compete with white children but will also retard the white children. The implicit and at times explicit assumption of these cultural deprivation theories is that the environmental deficits which Negro children bring with them to school make it difficult, if not impossible, for them to be educated either in racially homogeneous or heterogeneous schools. This point of view, intentionally or not, tends to support the pervasive rejection of Negro children and obscures and intensifies the basic problem.

There are more flagrant sources of opposition to any effective desegregation of American public schools. White Citizens' Councils in the South, parents' and taxpayers' groups in the North, and the control of boards of education by whites who identify either overtly or covertly with the more vehement opposition to change are examples of effective resistance. School officials and professional educators have defaulted in their responsibility for providing educational leadership. They have tended, for the most part, to go along with the level of community readiness and the "political realities." They have been accessories to the development and use of various subterfuges and devices for giving the appearance of change without its substance and, in doing so, have failed to present the problem of the necessary school reorganization in educational terms. This seems equally true of teachers and teachers' organizations. In some cases, teachers, textbooks, and other teaching materials have either contributed to or failed to counteract racism.

Within the past two years another formidable and insidious barrier in the way of the movement towards effective, desegregated public schools has emerged in the form of the black power movement and its demands for racial separatism. Some of the more

vocal of the black power advocates who have addressed themselves
to the problems of education have explicitly and implicitly argued
for Negroes' control of "Negro Schools." Some have asserted that
there should be separate school districts organized to control the
schools in all-Negro residential areas; that there should be Negro
boards of education, Negro superintendents of schools, Negro
faculty, and Negro curricula and materials. These demands are
clearly a rejection of the goals of integrated education and a return
to the pursuit of the myth of an efficient "separate but equal"—
or the pathetic wish for a separate and superior—racially-organized
system of education. One may view this current trend whereby
some Negroes themselves seem to be asking for a racially segregated
system of education as a reflection of the frustration resulting from
white resistance to genuine desegregation of the public schools since
the *Brown* decision and as a reaction to the reality that the quality
of education in the de facto segregated Negro schools in the North
and the Negro schools in the South has steadily deteriorated under
the present system of white control.

In spite of these explanations, the demands for segregated schools
can be no more acceptable coming from Negroes than they are
coming from white segregationists. There is no reason to believe
and certainly there is no evidence to support the contention that
all-Negro schools, controlled by Negroes, will be any more efficient
in preparing American children to contribute constructively to the
realities of the present and future world. The damage inherent in
racially isolated schools was persuasively documented by the comprehensive study conducted by the United States Commission on
Civil Rights.*

Furthermore, the more subtle and insidious educational deprivation
for white children who are required to attend all white schools is
furthered by both the black and the white advocates of racially
homogeneous schools.

ATTEMPTS AT REMEDIES

In spite of these obstacles in the path of genuine desegregation of
American public schools and the attainment of effective, nonracially

* U.S. Commission on Civil Rights, *Racial Isolation in the Public Schools,* Washington:
U.S. Government Printing Office, 1967.

constrained education for all American children, there have been persistent attempts to compensate for the deficits of racial isolation in the American public schools. A tremendous amount of energy and money has been expended in the attempt to develop special programs designed to improve the academic achievement of Negro children, who are the most obvious victims of inferior, racially segregated public schools.

The United States Commission on Civil Rights report *Racial Isolation in the Public Schools* has presented facts which raise questions concerning the long-range effectiveness of these programs. There is some evidence that these special programs do some good and help some children; but they clearly underline the inadequacy of the regular education these children receive. In addition to the fact that they obscure the overriding reality that underprivileged children are being systematically short-changed in their regular segregated and inferior schools, these programs may also be seen as a type of commitment to the continuation of segregated education.

If one accepts the premise which seems supported by all available evidence, and above all by the reasoning of the *Brown* decision, that racially segregated schools are inherently inferior, it would seem to follow that all attempts to improve the quality of education in all Negro and all white schools would have necessarily limited positive effects. All programs designed to raise the quality of education in racially homogeneous schools would therefore have to be seen as essentially evasive programs or as the first stage in an inferior approach to a serious plan for effective desegregation of public schools. Given the resistance to an immediate reorganization of the present system of racially organized schools so as to create a more effective system of racially heterogeneous schools, however, one may be required to attempt to increase the efficiency of education in all Negro schools as a necessary battle in the larger struggle for racially desegregated schools.

The problem of the extent to which it is possible to provide excellent education in a predominantly Negro school should be reexamined thoroughly in spite of the basic premise of the *Brown* decision that racially segregated schools are inherently inferior. Some questions which we must now dare to ask and seek to answer as the basis for a new strategy in the assault against the inhumanity of the American system of racial segregation are: (1) Is the present pattern of massive educational inferiority and inefficiency which is found in predominantly Negro schools inherent and inevitable in racially segregated schools? (2) Is there anything which can be done within the Negro schools to raise them to a tolerable level of educational efficiency—or to raise them to a level of educational excellence? If the answer to the first question is *yes* and to the second question is *no*, then the strategy of continued and intensified assault on the system of segregated schools is justified and should continue unabated since there is no hope of raising the quality of education for Negro children as long as they are condemned to segregated schools—there is no hope of salvaging them. If, on the other hand, the answers to the above questions are reversed, it would suggest that a shift in strategy and tactics, without giving up the ultimate goals of eliminating the dehumanizing force of racial segregation from American life, would be indicated. This shift would suggest that given the present strong and persistent resistance to any serious and effective desegregation of our public schools, that the bulk of the available organizational, human, and financial resources and specialized skills be mobilized and directed toward obtaining the highest quality of education for Negro students without regard to the racial composition of the schools which they attend. This attempt would demand a massive, system-wide educational enrichment program designed to obtain educational excellence in the schools attended by Negro children.

Recent experiences in New York City, Boston, Chicago, Philadelphia, and other northern cities reveal that this temporary shift in the battleground will not in itself lead to any easier victory. School boards and public school officials seem as resistant to developing or implementing programs designed to improve the quality and efficiency of education provided for Negro children in segregated schools as they are deaf to all requests for effective desegregation plans and programs. The interests and desires of white middle-class parents, and the interests of the increasingly powerful teachers' federations and professional supervisory associations are invariably given priority over the desire of Negro parents for nonsegregated quality education for their children. The interests of the white parents, teachers, and supervisors are often perceived by them as inimical to the desires of the Negro parents. Furthermore, the capture and control of the public schools by the white middle-class parents and teachers provided the climate within which the system of racially segregated and inferior schools could be developed, expanded, and reinforced and within which the public schools became instruments for blocking rather than facilitating the upward mobility of Negroes and other lower-status groups. One, therefore, could not expect these individuals and groups to be sympathetic and responsive to the pleas of Negro parents for higher quality education for their children. Negro parents and organizations must accept and plan their strategy in terms of the fact that adversaries in the battle for higher quality education for Negro children will be as numerous and as formidable as the adversaries in the battle for nonsegregated schools. Indeed they will be the same individuals, officials, and groups in different disguises and with different excuses for inaction but with the same powerful weapons of evasion, equivocation, inaction, or tokenism.

An effective strategy for the present and the future requires rigorous and honest appraisal of all of the realities, a tough-minded diagnosis of the strengths and weaknesses of the Negro and his allies. We cannot now permit ourselves to be deluded by wishful thinking, sentimental optimism, or rigid and oversimplified ideological postures. We must be tough-mindedly pragmatic and flexible as we seek to free our children from the cruel and de-humanizing, inferior and segregated education inflicted upon them by the insensitive, indifferent, affable, and at times callously rigid custodians of American public education.

In developing an appropriate strategy and the related flexible tactics, it must be clearly understood that the objective of improving the quality of education provided for Negro children is not a sub-stitute for or a retreat from the fundamental goal of removing the anachronism of racially segregated schools from American life. The objective of excellent education for Negro and other lower-status children is inextricably linked with the continuing struggle to desegregate public education. All of the public school, college, and professional school civil-rights litigation instituted by the legal staff of the NAACP arose from recognition of the obvious fact that the segregated schools which Negroes were forced by law to attend were inferior and therefore damaging and violative of the equal protection clause in the Fourteenth Amendment of the United States Constitution.

The suggested shift in emphasis from desegregation to quality of education is not a retreat into the blind alley of accepting racial separation as advocated by the Negro nationalist groups, nor is it the acceptance of defeat in the battle for desegregation. It is rather a regrouping of forces, a shift in battle plans and an attempt to determine the most vulnerable flanks of the opposition as the basis for major attack. The resisting educational bureaucracies, their pro-fessional staffs, and the segment of the white public which has not yet been infected fatally by the American racist disease are most vulnerable to attack on the issue of the inferior quality of edu-cation found in Negro schools and the need to institute a plan immediately to raise the educational level of these schools. The

economic, political, military, social-stability, international democratic, humane, and self-interest arguments in favor of an immediate massive program for educational excellence in predominantly
Negro schools are so persuasive as to be irrefutable. The expected
resistance should be overcome with intelligently planned and sustained efforts.

The first phase of an all-out attack on the inferior education now
found in racially segregated schools should be coordinated with a
strategy and program for massive and realistic desegregation of
entire school systems. This more complicated phase of the over-all
struggle will continue to meet the resistances of the past with increased intensity. It will be necessary, therefore, to break this task
down into its significant components and determine the timing and
phasing of the attack on each or combinations of the components.
For example:

The evidence and arguments demonstrating the detrimental effects of
segregated schools on the personality and effectiveness of white children
should be gathered, evaluated, and widely disseminated in ways understandable to the masses of whites.

The need to reorganize large public school systems away from the
presently inefficient and uneconomic neighborhood schools to more modern
and viable systems of organization such as educational parks, campuses,
or clusters must be sold to the general public in terms of hard dollars
and cents and educational efficiency benefiting all children rather than in
terms of public school desegregation.

The need to consolidate small, uneconomic, and relatively ineffective
school districts into larger educational and fiscal systems in order to
obtain more efficient education for suburban and exurban children must
also be sold in direct practical terms rather than in terms of desegregation
of schools.

The need to involve large metropolitan regional planning in the
mobilization, utilization, and distribution of limited educational resources
on a more efficient level must also be explored and discussed publicly.

The movement toward decentralization of large urban school systems
must be carefully monitored in order to see that decentralization does not
reinforce or concretize urban public school segregation—and to assure that
decentralization is consistent with the more economically determined trend
toward consolidation and regional planning allocation of resources and
cooperation.

A final indication that phase one, the struggle for excellent
education for Negro children in ghetto schools, is not inconsistent
with phase two, the struggle for nonsegregated education for all
children, is to be seen in the fact that if it were possible to raise
the quality of education provided for Negro children who attend

the urban schools to a level of unquestioned excellence, the flight of middle class whites to the suburbs might be stemmed and some who have left might be attracted back to the city. Hence, phase one activity would increase the chances of obtaining nonsegregated education in our cities. Similarly, some of the program suggestions of phase two such as educational parks and campuses and the possibilities of regional planning and educational cooperation across present municipal boundaries could lead to substantial improvements in the quality of education offered to inner-city children.

The goal of high quality education for Negro and lower-status children and the goal of public school desegregation are inextricable; the attainment of the one will lead to the attainment of the other. It is not likely that there could be effective desegregation of the schools without a marked increase in the academic achievement and personal and social effectiveness of Negro and white children. Neither is it possible to have a marked increase in the educational efficiency of Negro schools and the resulting dramatic increase in the academic performance of Negro children without directly and indirectly facilitating the process of public school desegregation.

PROBLEMS OF EDUCATIONAL MONOPOLY

It is possible that all attempts to improve the quality of education in our present racially segregated public schools and all attempts to desegregate these schools will have minimal positive results. The rigidity of present patterns of public school organization and the concomitant stagnation in quality of education and academic performance of children may not be amenable to any attempts at change working through and within the present system.

Until the influx of Negro and Puerto Rican youngsters into urban public schools, the American public school system was justifiably credited with being the chief instrument for making the American dream of upward social, economic, and political mobility a reality. The depressed immigrants from southern and eastern Europe could use American public schools as the ladder toward the goals of assimilation and success. The past successes of American public education seem undebatable. The fact that American public schools were effective mobility vehicles for white American immigrants makes even more stark and intolerable their present ineffectiveness for Negro and Puerto Rican children. Now it appears that the present system of organization and functioning of urban public schools is a chief blockage in the mobility of the masses of Negro and other lower-status minority group children. The inefficiency of their schools and the persistence and acceptance of the explanations for this generalized inefficiency are clear threats to the viability of our cities and national stability. The relationship between long-standing urban problems of poverty, crime and delinquency, broken homes—the total cycle of pathology, powerlessness, and personal and social destructiveness which haunts our urban ghettos —and the breakdown in the efficiency of our public schools is now unavoidably clear. It is not enough that those responsible for our public schools should assert passively that the schools merely reflect the pathologies and injustices of our society. Public schools and their administrators must assert boldly that education must dare to challenge and change society toward social justice as the basis for democratic stability.

There remains the disturbing question—a most relevant question probably too painful for educators themselves to ask—whether the selection process involved in training and promoting educators and administrators for our public schools emphasizes qualities of passivity, conformity, caution, smoothness, and superficial affability rather than boldness, creativity, substance, and the ability to demand and obtain those things which are essential for solid and effective public education for all children. If the former is true and if we are dependent upon the present educational establishment, than all hopes for the imperative reforms which must be made so that city public schools can return to a level of innovation and excellence are reduced to a minimum, if not totally eliminated.

The racial components of the present crisis in urban public education clearly make the possibilities of solution more difficult and may contribute to the passivity and pervading sense of hopelessness of school administrators. Aside from any latent or subtle racism which might infect school personnel themselves, they are hampered by the gnawing awareness that with the continuing flight of middle-class whites from urban public schools and with the increasing competition which education must engage in for a fair share of the tax dollar, it is quite possible that Americans will decide deliberately or by default to sacrifice urban public schools on the altars of its historic and contemporary forms of racism. If this can be done without any real threat to the important segments of economic and political power in the society and with only Negro children as the victims, then there is no realistic basis for hope that our urban public schools will be saved.

The hope for a realistic approach to saving public education in American cities seems to this observer to be found in a formula whereby it can be demonstrated to the public at large that the present level of public school inefficiency has reached an intolerable stage of public calamity. It must be demonstrated that minority group children are not the only victims of the monopolistic inefficiency of the present pattern of organization and functioning of our public schools.

It must be demonstrated that white children—privileged white children whose parents understandably seek to protect them by moving to suburbs or by sending them to private and parochial schools—also suffer both potentially and immediately.

It must be demonstrated that business and industry suffer intolerable financial burdens of double and triple taxation in seeking to maintain a stable economy in the face of the public school inefficiency which produces human casualties rather than constructive human beings.

It must be demonstrated that the cost in correctional, welfare, and health services are intolerably high in seeking to cope with consequences of educational inefficiency—that it would be more economical, even for an affluent society, to pay the price and meet the demands of efficient public education.

It must be demonstrated that a nation which presents itself to the world as the guardian of democracy and the protector of human values throughout the world cannot itself make a mockery of these significant ethical principles by dooming one-tenth of its own population to a lifetime of inhumane futility because of remediable educational deficiencies in its public schools.

These must be understood and there must be the commitment to make the average American understand them if our public schools and our cities are to be effective. But it does not seem likely that the changes necessary for increased efficiency of our urban public schools will come about because they should. Our urban public school systems seem muscle-bound with tradition. They seem to represent the most rigid forms of bureaucracies which, paradoxically, are most resilient in their ability and use of devices to resist rational or irrational demands for change. What is most important in understanding the ability of the educational establishment to resist change is the fact that public school systems are protected public monopolies with only minimal competition from private and parochial schools. Few critics of the American urban public schools—even severe ones such as myself—dare to question the givens of the present organization of public education in terms of local control of public schools, in terms of existing municipal or political boundaries, or in terms of the rights and prerogatives of boards of education to establish policy and select professional staff—at least nominally or titularly if not actually. Nor dare the critics question the relevance of the criteria and standards for selecting superintendents, principals, and teachers, or the relevance of all of these to the objectives of public education—producing a literate and informed public to carry on the business of democracy —and to the goal of producing human beings with social sensitivity and dignity and creativity and a respect for the humanity of others.

A monopoly need not genuinely concern itself with these matters. As long as local school systems can be assured of state aid and increasing federal aid without the accountability which inevitably comes with aggressive competition, it would be sentimental, wishful thinking to expect any significant increase in the efficiency of our public schools. If there are no alternatives to the present system— short of present private and parochial schools which are approaching their limit of expansion—then the possibilities of improvement in public education are limited.

ALTERNATIVE FORMS OF PUBLIC EDUCATION

Alternatives—realistic, aggressive, and viable competitors—to the present public school systems must be found. The development of such competitive public school systems will be attacked by the defenders of the present system as attempts to weaken the present system and thereby weaken, if not destroy, public education. This type of expected self-serving argument can be briefly and accurately disposed of by asserting and demonstrating that truly effective competition strengthens rather than weakens that which deserves to survive. I would argue further that public education need not be identified with the present system of organization of public schools. Public education can be more broadly and pragmatically defined in terms of that form of organization and functioning of an educational system which is in the public interest. Given this definition, it becomes clear that an inefficient system of public systems is not in the public interest:

—a system of public schools which destroys rather than develops positive human potentialities is not in the public interest;

—a system which consumes funds without demonstrating effective returns is not in the public interest;

—a system which insists that its standards of performance should not or cannot be judged by those who must pay the cost is not in the public interest;

—a system which says that the public has no competence to assert that a patently defective product is a sign of the system's inefficiency and demands radical reforms is not in the public interest;

—a system which blames its human resources and its society while it quietly acquiesces in, and inadvertently perpetuates, the very injustices which it claims limit its efficiency is not in the public interest.

Given these assumptions, therefore, it follows that alternative forms of public education must be developed if the children of our cities are to be educated and made constructive members of our society. In the development of alternatives, all attempts must at the same time be made to strengthen our present urban public schools. Such attempts would involve reexamination, revision, and strengthening of curricula, methods, personnel selection, and evaluation; the development of more rigorous procedures of superivsion, reward of superior performance, and the institution of a realistic and tough system of accountability, and the provision of meaningful ways of involving the parents and the community in the activities of the school.

The above measures, however, will not suffice. The following are suggested as possible, realistic, and practical competitors to the present form of urban public school systems:

Regional State Schools. These schools would be financed by the states and would cut across present urban-suburban boundaries.

Federal Regional Schools. These schools would be financed by the Federal Government out of present state aid funds or with additional federal funds. These schools would be able to cut through state boundaries and could make provisions for residential students.

College- and University-Related Open Schools. These schools would be financed by colleges and universities as part of their laboratories in education. They would be open to the public and not restricted to children of faculty and students. Obviously, students would be selected in terms of constitutional criteria and their percentage determined by realistic considerations.

Industrial Demonstration Schools. These schools would be financed by industrial, business, and commercial firms for their employees and selected members of the public. These would not be vocational schools—but elementary and comprehensive high schools of quality. They would be sponsored by combinations of business and industrial firms in much the same way as churches and denominations sponsor and support parochial or sectarian schools.

Labor Union Sponsored Schools. These schools would be financed and sponsored by labor unions largely, but not exclusively, for the children of their members.

Army Schools. The Defense Department has been quietly effective in educating some of the casualties of our present public schools. It is hereby suggested that they now go into the business of repairing hundreds of thousands of these human casualties with affirmation rather than apology. Schools for adolescent dropouts or educational rejects could be set up by the Defense Department adjacent to camps—but not necessarily as an integral part of the military. If this is necessary, it should not block the attainment of the goal of rescuing as many of these young people as possible. They are not expendable on the altar of antimilitarism rhetoric.

With strong, efficient, and demonstrably excellent parallel systems of public schools, organized and operated on a quasi-private level, and with quality control and professional accountability maintained and determined by federal and state educational standards and supervision, it would be possible to bring back into public education a vitality and dynamism which are now clearly missing. Even the public discussion of these possibilities might clear away some of the dank stagnation which seems to be suffocating urban education today. American industrial and material wealth was made possible through industrial competition. American educational health may be made possible through educational competition.

If we succeed, we will have returned to the dynamic, affirmative goal of education; namely, to free man of irrational fears, superstitions, and hatreds. Specifically, in America the goal of democratic education must be to free Americans of the blinding and atrophying shackles of racism. A fearful, passive, apologetic, and inefficient educational system cannot help in the attainment of these goals.

If we succeed in finding and developing these and better alternatives to the present educational inefficiency, we will not only save countless Negro children from lives of despair and hopelessness; and thousands and thousands of white children from cynicism, moral emptiness, and social ineptness—but we will also demonstrate the validity of our democratic promises. We also will have saved our civilization through saving our cities.

Agenda for the Future

Harold Howe, II

Between now and 1980, American secondary education must completely reexamine and reorient itself to meet challenges quite different from those it has struggled with during the past decade. If it fails at this task, our high schools will have failed to play a potentially critical role in helping to solve the nation's greatest social crisis—the role of bringing the children of America's 25 million poor people into the mainstream of the nation's economic and political life. If secondary education succeeds—and reviewing the achievements of the past 15 years, I believe it can—our high schools will provide the seedbed for a more decent and more productive American in 1980.

Looking back over the secondary education scene of the past decade and a half, we can find much to be proud of. For example, the major subjects—mathematics, the sciences, the foreign languages, and to a lesser degree, English and the social studies—have been reexamined by independent groups of scholars and educators. The results are hardly final and hardly available on a widespread basis. But they have taken us the first significant steps toward making academic instruction more up-to-date, potent, relevant, and stimulating.

Another example appears in the *organization* of teaching and learning in our schools. Experiments in team teaching and flexible scheduling have cracked the high school's rigid structure. We are deploying students and teachers more flexibly, using diverse patterns, and a wider range of teaching aids—both human and technological—that can contribute much in the classroom. We are no longer trapped (in our thinking, at least) by the classroom's four walls and the six, set periods per day.

Such innovations of curriculum and organization are not pervasive in our nation's high schools, but they are increasingly characteristic of the better schools. And the innovative thrust of recent federal support—earmarking large sums specifically to produce change—also has helped.

THE NEGLECTED MAJORITY

Why, with these good signs cropping up, shouldn't we feel largely satisfied? The answer is very simple. The advances I have mentioned and the myriad others that may occur to anyone familiar with American secondary education, *have not affected most secondary-school youngsters.*

These changes in our high schools since the mid-1950s have helped mainly the students bound for a college degree. They are the ones most affected by the strengthened academic curricula, the more stimulating teaching methods, and the added flexibility of schools. What I call "the neglected majority"—the 80 percent of our secondary-school students who will never receive a B.A.—have gained much less from the changes. The one million a year who drop out of school have gained nothing at all.

What have we done in the last decade for the millions of students —the majority of the student body—who are average or poor academically, or financially, and will not complete college or perhaps even high school for either or both reasons? What have we done for the potential dropout who looks on school as a reformatory where he serves time simply because he is young? What realistic guidance and counseling, or practical technical and vocational training, have we given these youngsters to help them compete for jobs in a highly demanding economy? Most important, what have we done to help them compete with themselves, to awaken the pride and sense of personal worth that is a minimum precondition for effective learning and living? In candor, I think we must say: Not enough. While maintaining our interest in the college-bound student, we also must remember that in our secondary schools we are committed to serve *all* students of all abilities and interests—a point that we are most adept at talking about but not very good at doing something about.

Why have we neglected this majority? One basic reason is that we tend to think of secondary school as a sorting-out operation. We see our job as primarily identifying the probably successful students—and not nearly enough as helping the probable failures. Is it any wonder that, faced with such an institution, students who know or have been convinced that they are slated for failure, rebel? From the minute they enter the high school they feel diminished; they feel confined by an institution that is not a friend. I believe we have paid mainly lip service to the idea of enabling each student to become all he is capable of being. To make this idea a reality we will have to think of the high school much less as a sorting out operation and much more as an institution to serve all kinds and conditions of young people—a place with as many special programs for the potential dropout as for the potential advanced placement student. Let us focus on including rather than selecting, on assuring success rather than punishing failure. The Federal Government had to start the Job Corps to give a second chance to young people who had been failed by our schools. Our schools confront the challenge of making the "first chance" work.

CRITICAL MASS

Whatever the reasons for the neglect of these youngsters, the past 15 years hold the clue to remedying this basic flaw in our efforts at secondary-school reform. Experience under the National Defense Education Act showed that when the nation wants to change a major element of education, it can marshal the forces to start and sustain change. However, such change does require a national commitment of money, public support, and the dedication of educators.

This is the principle of "critical mass." Borrowed from physics and translated into the educational context, this concept calls for a focus of all human and material resources needed to produce major improvement—to make a difference. The concept suggests that any output of resources short of the critical mass will fail to produce a measurable change. Perhaps more important, it implies that human and financial resources must zero in on *a particular problem;* they must not be dispersed generally through every school in the half-hearted hope of over-all improvement.

In effect, the critical-mass concept says to educators: "Select the priority problems you must solve first. Concentrate your resources on them and let other matters go if necessary."

If we put together these two ideas—our neglect of students who are not headed for a B.A. and the critical-mass approach—we can see what we must do. (The U.S. Congress grasped this same need when it passed the Elementary and Secondary Education Act of 1965 and other laws.) In the next 10 years, we must, on the one hand, better prepare this majority both to enter the world of work and to accept the responsibilities of citizenship. On the other, we must prepare many more than now to enter college or some form of post-high school education.

How can our high schools point themselves in this new direction? Again, the past 15 years' experience helps us see the changes we must have. Clearly, to meet this priority purpose, we must make our schools even more flexible and adaptable to the students' real needs. We will have to change the way the schools relate students and teachers to each other; the way they use time and resources; their role in teacher training and retraining; their administrative structure; the chances they provide for successful learning.

TRAIN FOR THE INDUSTRY, NOT FOR ONE JOB

First, let's look at the curriculum. Here, the question is: How do we equip students to live and work in a technological society without a college education? In the case of many, without a high school diploma?

Like the British, we have reached the point where our educational system must assume some responsibility for matching technically demanding jobs with technically competent people. For students who will not get beyond—or even to—the twelfth grade, this training must be gotten in high school. I do not urge training so specialized that the student has one limited skill which may become obsolete with economic and scientific change. I advocate courses that cover principles—in electronics, for instance—that prepare the student for an entry job in that industry, as well as teach him how to prepare for jobs that he may aspire to later on and perhaps for jobs that do not even exist today.

Taking the broader view, I would like to see our secondary schools use the newer federal programs to do for students who do not go to college what they have done under the National Defense Education Act for students who do.

For a start, I would like to see the same upheaval in the vocational and technical curriculum that NDEA has generated in the academic curriculum. I don't see any reason why automotive mechanics, for instance, can't reflect the same critical reexamination, the same innovative responses, the same high standards for students and criteria for teachers that educators used in NDEA-supported academic offerings. We cannot just repaint the Model A—which I think is all too characteristic of some vocational curricula.

Many large school districts have vocational high schools, and many of them are good. Some smaller districts have shown real ingenuity in combining their resources to offer job training each alone could not afford.

This is encouraging, but it is not enough. Secondary education must bring vocational training into the comprehensive high school; it must involve business and industry in curriculum development; it must make all or part of this curriculum available to every student. Time is running out for the development of a comprehensive curriculum, one that gives vocational offerings equal time—and I might add, equal status—with academic programs.

Equal time, equal status, equal quality of instruction for vocational education. These goals require educators to review and revise our own attitudes. To many of us, vocational training has always been an awkward appendage of the academic curriculum. It never quite fitted and it was never really wanted. We saw it as a separate subsidiary enterprise and not as part of the mainstream of secondary education. Feeling this way, can we really expect parents, students, the community or industry to consider job training a vital function of the school system? Can we provide the equally important support services—adequate and accurate career counseling, work-study programs, job placement services?

In vocational education, perhaps more than in any curricular area, *we must look ahead* when we plan and execute programs. Work in America is changing dramatically and rapidly. Blue-collar jobs are dwindling in the wake of automation, and service fields are emerging strongly as an area of opportunity for employment. In these fields, communication and human relations are extremely important. We must remember this when we plan vocational curricula; and particularly as we try to relate them to the academic subjects. One could argue, for example, that English, which teaches communications skills and sharpens our awareness of human relations, has become a critical *vocational* subject.

In other aspects of the secondary school's program, too, we can apply lessons from the recent past. In teacher training, for example, we have begun to train teachers by having them actually teach. We've accepted the notion that in many ways learning to teach is like learning to play tennis. You can talk about it, analyze it, watch movies of it, but you'll never learn to do it until you actually do it under the tutelage of someone who is good at it.

Some of our best Master of Arts in Teaching programs and the Teacher Corps operating out of the Office of Education have built on this principle. Now we must apply it specifically to preparing teachers for hard-pressed urban schools as well as for the special demands of rural areas.

SOMEBODY KNOWS THEIR NAMES

From the organization of high schools, we've learned some lessons which we must apply to our mammoth central-city schools. Youngsters—particularly adolescents—must feel that the school does not submerge their personal identities. They must feel that someone knows their name. Yet in some big city high schools of 3000 to 5000 students, this is now impossible. A student may attend classes for several years and get virtually no personal recognition until graduation day when someone mispronounces his name. (In the ordinary elementary school, by contrast, the principal makes it his business to know the names of all children and their parents.) The high school student, chasing around to five classes a day, is the only person in education who suffers the indignity of being counted six times a day to ascertain if he's still there—although some colleges still perpetuate this indignity and in the process perpetuate the adolescence of their students.

Such an institution is bound to be destructive of any youngster's feeling about himself—his confidence and self esteem and desire to succeed. And with the trend toward consolidation of schools to gain efficiency and richer learning opportunities, this situation can easily worsen—if attention, energy, and money are not focused on solving it. As we have seen in the campus rebellions where students felt ignored and diminished, the results can be tragic.

The answer is not to give up the advantages of large-scale operation, but to balance those advantages with quite feasible internal reforms which can give each student a human environment in which he feels he belongs. Specifically, large high schools might be subdivided into small units with particular areas of the building (perhaps even "commons rooms"), faculty members and counselors, student government, social affairs, subprincipal, etc., associated with each one. It is better to have half a dozen student councils, each generating leadership for one "house," (or whatever the subdivisions are called) than one huge student government run by a few highly visible youngsters. Two or three orchestras, even of slightly less than professional caliber, but involving 150 youngsters, are more appropriate for a large high school than one superb performing group involving only 30.

Moreover, we must recognize that the most neglected resource for learning in the school is the resource of the students themselves. One provocative implication of the Equal Education Opportunities Survey carried out by Coleman and Campbell is the amount of knowledge students gain in school from the other students. Why not build on this evidence and plan the use of students as resources for learning and teaching more consciously than we typically do? Some students can tutor others and gain in learning while helping others to do so. And more than academic learning takes place in the school that gives students a recognized role in the purposes of the school. Students develop in such a school a sense of responsibility and a better understanding of other human beings.

School administrators and teachers still think of a school too much as a place where they are doing something to people, not enough as a place where young people do a great deal to and for each other.

NEW BUILDINGS—FOR NEW CONCEPTS

Such efforts will take time and money. They may irritate some teachers; they will certainly require changes in existing buildings and more radical changes in how we design new ones. We may even depart from the often prevailing idea, identified by Harold Gores of Educational Facilities Laboratories, that the school is the only social institution designed primarily to make it easy to clean. The school which says to the student, "I'm indestructible," is looking for trouble. On the other hand, experience has shown that children from all backgrounds respond very well to schools which, in their design and decor, treat them with respect and dignity. At the North Carolina Advancement School, for example, we hung real paintings from local collectors—and our student body of "difficult" youngsters treated them with the greatest respect. Young people know instinctively what we think of them by our provision of these amenities. If we can provide them in our funeral parlors, bars, and executive · offices, we ought to be able to provide them in our schools—or are our values such that we care less for our children than for these institutions?

Our schools, however, need more than amenities. The improvements I have described are almost impossible to achieve today in many of our big city schools. Why? Because reorganization and decentralization are at the very least difficult to execute when each day the system is faced with the immense job of herding thousands of youngsters, in two or three sessions, into and out of classes of 30 to 40. We need a massive construction program to provide the physical plant for adequate urban education. Schools were built

in our cities before they were prevalent in the country. Unfortunately, too many of these old buildings are still in use. Particularly
in the eastern cities, 50-year-old high schools are not uncommon.
And inadequate as they are, the very same schools tend to be
terribly overcrowded. In rural areas there are still many small,
inadequate schools and a need for further consolidation and
buildings to go with it.

From one perspective, this deplorable situation presents us with
a great educational opportunity. The job of reconstruction is so
enormous that, once we generate the required money (and I am
hopeful that the Federal Government will find a way to help here,
though at present no significant federal resources are available for
construction), we will have the challenge—and the chance—to build
much of our secondary school system over again from the ground
up. This, of course, could provide an opportunity to design schools
for better learning and better social relations among our youngsters.

OPTIONS FOR TOMORROW

Future building programs, for example, could be planned so that
new schools break up, rather than continue, segregation—both racial
and economic. It may take a long time to alter boundaries to bring
the suburbs into school systems that contain part of the city, but
nothing now prevents city and suburb from joint planning for
common programs or shared facilities. New York and New Jersey
surrendered state prerogatives to form the Port of New York
Authority in the interest of improved transportation. If we can
make such concessions for transportation, I suggest that we can
make them for education. Indeed we make them every day over
such matters as water supply and sewage disposal. Why not children?

Perhaps we need a system of educational parks within each inner
city. Each of these parks—centralized school complexes—could provide classes from prekindergarten through high school and even
junior college. By 1980, our cities might have educational parks
which will house 10,000 or more pupils, and will cut across all
geographic, economic, and social lines to draw students. While
such parks would deny the neighborhood school, they would express
the vitality, the imagination, and the cultural mix that every vigorous
city exemplifies. Students in such a facility would attend a genuine

city school, rather than going to school in one section untouched by the broader influences of metropolitan life—and the large complex can have subdivisions that will provide intimacy and a sense of being known.

BEYOND BUILDINGS

Construction of new urban high schools, and their proper design, are only one aspect of meeting the needs of the city's youth. We must take several further steps if we are going to revitalize secondary schooling in the big cities.

First, we must recognize that the ghetto high school does not need the same financial support as the suburban high school; it needs much more. We must realize that the ghetto school must provide special services that some people still consider educational frills. Services such as counseling, guidance, and job placement; small classes; remedial instruction; the latest teaching methods and equipment; psychological, medical, and dental aid.

We must change inner-city high schools from nine-to-three citadels where all human life vanishes with the dismissal bell, into centers that offer opportunity to parents as well as children. Inner-city high schools must create community where there is no other focal point for a common life and shared interest. We must staff our ghetto schools so that they can remain open from morning to late evening, offering adult instruction in everything from reading to making the most of the shopping dollar.

And in this newly involved institution, we must above all create the opportunity for, and the expectation of, performance by youngsters of the poor. Cultural disadvantage need not foreshadow poor academic achievement. Youngsters sense a school's lower expectations and grow to demand less of themselves because the school demands so little of them. Schools are not custodians. Children are there to learn, not just to be kept off the street. The greatest disservice we do disadvantaged youngsters is to lower our expectations of their potential. Therefore we must avoid the dangerous assumption that the children of the poor should seek a vocational focus while more fortunate children head for advanced education. Our secondary schools will be doing their job well when the same proportion of disadvantaged and fortunate children are college bound.

Beyond expressing our national need for more teachers of every description, we have done little to focus on teacher preparation needed to serve the children of the poor. In general, our colleges and universities train teachers for ideal classrooms, and although some slum schools may have excellent buildings and equipment, enveloping ghetto environment cries out for special attention.

City school systems must adopt assignment policies that will guarantee slum schools their share of experienced, able teachers. We must counteract the tendency of experienced teachers to choose more pleasant schools as soon as their years of service entitle them to transfer. We also must change the policies of schools and teacher organizations which confront slum youngsters with inexperienced, uncertificated and impermanent teachers.

Besides more and better teachers, slum high schools need volunteers and paid teacher aides to supplement the work of the fully trained teacher. Added personal attention from adults who really care can do as much as any other service to lift the slum child's performance.

I am convinced that the points I have dwelt on here will be fundamental traits of the best high schools of 1980. And this program can be acted on now. If we care to, we can apply without delay the critical-mass concept to the resources we already have; we can thereby make better use of those resources. We can invest our human and material capital where it will do the most good.

Such changes, which emphasize special attention to the mass of those who have been left out of opportunity in America, will not come about easily and smoothly. Many people will oppose them. Others will be critical because they are too slow in coming.

The question we all face is do we have the nerve and the endurance to bear the resentments, to absorb the frustrations of unmet hope and to bridle the impatience for faster progress? Can we, at the same time, absorb the criticisms that we are going too fast? Or, will we who have the responsibility to lead and the economic security, will we feel so threatened by criticism that we will tighten up, try to reverse the course of change, and so commit our nation to a tragic confrontation between the haves and the have-nots in a land where there is plenty for all?

As educators, we really have only one choice. We must accept the problems created by progress and push on for more progress. The pessimism that some cultivate can lead the rest of us to underestimate the distance we have already traveled towards a better society; just as it can provoke us into overestimating how far we still have to go.

THE FUTURE
CURRICULUM

What To Teach— And How

Ole Sand

1980 is already here. If one recalls those books written in the 1950s and their predictions of amazing changes ahead and looks at life in classrooms today, a funny thing happened on the way to the future. A useful cautionary exercise for the reader of this chapter is to remember the way teaching is as we predict what it should be.

The issues of priorities, balance, and content selection are focal points for any consideration of what to teach and how—be it 1970 or 1980. In this chapter we will discuss these issues and make some predictions. The reader with an interest in a particular content area may wish to apply the ideas stated in this chapter to the following chapters on specific aspects of the future curriculum.

When one looks at the curriculum then and now, five eras can legitimately be identified. In the 1930s, during the heyday of progressive education, the child was the primary focus. In the 1940s, when we were engaged in a world war, the curriculum was *society*-centered. In the 1950s and the 1960s the scholars have been in the saddle, and the curriculum has been primarily subject- or *discipline*-centered.* As we move into the 1970s, we will be concerned with the *total* curriculum for all youth. Hopefully, by 1980 we also will have a truly *humanistic* curriculum.

Another way to look at the reform movement of the past decade is to say that Phase One is over. It focused on academic scholarship, on the structure of separate disciplines, on comprehensive packages of instructional materials, and on in-service training of teachers. In Phase Two, there will be pedagogical scholarship comparable to the academic scholarship of Phase One—without, of course, losing the latter. In Phase Two, a theoretical framework will precede everything else. The curriculum will be viewed as a whole rather than as bits and pieces. Finally, up-to-date curricula will be designed that

---

* For more extensive discussion see Ralph W. Tyler, "The Curriculum—Then and Now," *The Elementary School Journal,* LVII, No. 2, April, 1957, pp. 364-374.

make no compromise with truth and yet prove attractive and relevant to all students.

ESTABLISHING PRIORITIES

It is not particularly difficult to achieve general agreement about the goals of education. It is generally accepted, for example, that the school has a major responsibility for preparing youth for today's society, that the student should read, write, speak, and master his numbers.

This pleasant surface agreement crumbles all too often at that crucial point in debate when priorities are discussed—when someone starts insisting that reading is more important than cheerleading. Smiles freeze in that instant when educators and laymen face decisions on what knowledge, skills, and values are needed by young people; which are best taught by the school; and which shall be left to the home, church, or to chance. That problems will arise is one of the absolutes in this uncertain world of education.

Such decisions will be sounder and easier to reach if a few reliable criteria are applied: (1) Is it learning of complex things, demanding careful organization and extended practice? (2) Is it learning in which the essential factors are not always obvious, where the principles, concepts, and meanings must be brought to the attention of the learner? (3) Is it an experience that cannot be provided directly in daily living but that is still relevant to each learner? (4) Is it learning that requires more purified experience than is commonly available in life outside the school? (5) Is it learning that requires reexamination and interpretation of experience?*

A basic assumption in this chapter is that the school is only one educational institution. Dewey's disciples sometimes confuse his sound advice about schooling the whole child with nonsense about the school taking responsibility for the child's whole education.**

The National Committee for the NEA Project on Instruction asked "the right questions" about this issue—questions as significant for 1980 as for today. To determine the school's responsibilities, answers to these questions must be found:

—What knowledge, values, and skills do children and youth in our culture need to learn?

* Based on Ralph W. Tyler, "Emphasize Tasks Appropriate for the School," *Phi Delta Kappan*, XL, No. 2, November, 1958, pp. 73-74.
** Drawn from Lawrence G. Cremin, *The Genius of American Education*, Pittsburgh: University of Pittsburgh Press, 1965, p. 8.

—Which of these goals can best be achieved by the school?
—What knowledge, skills, and values can best be taught by the home, the church, and other social institutions?
—Which learnings require the joint efforts of the school and other agencies?
—What then should be included in the school program? What should be excluded from it?

The committee then made the following recommendation:

> Priorities for the school are the teaching of skills in reading, composition, listening, speaking (both native and foreign languages), and computation . . . ways of creative and disciplined thinking, including methods of inquiry and application of knowledge . . . competence in self-instruction and independent learning . . . fundamental understanding of the humanities and the arts, the social sciences and natural sciences, and mathematics . . . appreciation of and discriminating taste in literature, music, and the visual arts . . . instruction in health education and physical education.
>
> The responsibilities best met by joint efforts of the school and other social agencies include: development of values and ideals . . . social and civic competence . . . vocational preparation. The decision to include or exclude particular school subjects or outside-of-class activities should be based on: (1) the priorities assigned to the school and to other agencies; (2) data about learners and society, and developments in the academic disciplines; (3) the human and material resources available in the school and community.*

There are no easy answers to the question of what should be included and what should be excluded in the high school program. There never will be. A complex, purposeful, human enterprise like teaching does not lend itself to easy, final answers. Each high school in America must deal with the questions cited above and base its answers on self-study and careful thought. Our plea is to avoid at all costs the creeping curriculum where never have so many learned so little about so much. Of one thing we are certain—there is an inverse relationship between the thickness of the catalog and the excellence of the program.

BALANCING THE PROGRAM

Sputnik was the good news of damnation. Fear of survival led to federal support of science, mathematics, and foreign language. Then someone asked, "Why survive if one cannot live a life of taste and

---

* National Education Association, *Schools for the Sixties: A Report of the Project on Instruction* (New York: McGraw-Hill, 1963), p. 32.

grace?" Teachers of High School 1980 will keep constantly before them the question, How can the school provide a program appropriately balanced for each individual and maintain it amidst various pressures for specialization? Note that our plea is for a balanced *program*—not for a human being so well balanced that he behaves like a machine. We still want people who are out of equilibrium enough so that they are creative.

In today's world of breathtaking technological advancement, the all-important position once attributed to the humanities has been usurped by the sciences, and we are bequeathed a disturbing imbalance that threatens to leave today's student starved in the humanities. Willy-nilly, we are the sudden beneficiaries of the TV-sputnik-computer-pushbutton-sonic-boom-mushroom-cloud era and, as Broudy points out, ". . . many of us cannot escape the feeling that if we do wholly surrender our fates to the new gods, we may be saved *from* our humanity rather than *for* it."* Northrop, in a provocative and penetrating study, echoes this sentiment:

> Ours is a paradoxical world. The achievements which are its glory threaten to destroy it. The nations with the highest standard of living, the greatest capacity to take care of their people economically, the broadest education, and the most enlightened morality and religion exhibit the least capacity to avoid mutual destruction in war. It would seem that the more civilized we become the more incapable of maintaining civilization we are.**

Ask one of your students about the sun. What will he tell you? It is 93,000,000 miles from the earth, approximately 866,500 miles in diameter, with a surface rotation of about 25 days at the equator. If he is to live in the shadow of bigger and better bombs, perhaps he must be taught all these facts. Yet, it will always be the larger purpose of education to lead him to appreciate the radiance of a sunset. And here, G. K. Chesterton has something to say to our point:

> There is a notion adrift everywhere that imagination, especially mystical imagination, is dangerous to man's mental balance. Poets are commonly spoken of as psychologically unreliable; and generally there is a vague association between wreathing laurels in your hair and sticking straws in it. Facts and history utterly contradict this view. Most of the very great poets have been not only sane, but extremely business-like; and if Shake-

* Harry S. Broudy, "Aesthetic Education in a Technological Society: The Other Excuses for Art," *The Journal of Aesthetic Education,* Inaugural Issue, I, Spring, 1966, p. 13.

** F. S. C. Northrop, *The Meeting of East and West,* New York: Collier Books, 1966, p. 1.

speare ever really held horses, it was because he was much the safest man to hold them. Imagination does not breed insanity. Exactly what does breed insanity is reason. Poets do not go mad; but chess-players do. Mathematicians go mad, and cashiers; but creative artists very seldom. . . .*

Science is not the panacea of life's problems. We must keep our debt to it in clear perspective. Its Nembutal helps us sleep; its wrinkle-resistant wash-and-wear clothes us; its climate-control protects us from the weather. But the test tube has yet to come up with a shake 'n bake formula for increasing man's ability to think, to feel, to appreciate, to understand ourselves so we can understand our fellow men, and to help us live in this valley of the dolls that science has fashioned for us.

The teacher who teaches with zest, who speaks and listens well, who helps his students interact with more than boredom or rebellion is a humanist, an artist working with humanity, and his art is the one thing in this pep-pill world of ours most likely to beget in his students a thirst, a passion for the fullness of life.

The only reason that a teacher should be a person, alive to the things that are, is that he must encourage speculation and lead it. To help a student learn about an unknown and vastly different country requires a medium, a metaphor in which the known and the unknown can meet, each taking meaning from the other and such a medium is the essence of music, of poetry, of art. Students taught by a real humanist will become real humanists, readers, listeners, men of intellectual and emotional delight, ready for a kind of intimacy with the world which will breed not contempt, but freedom of mind, a way out of the slavery of mere conformism to society. President Kennedy put it well when he spoke at Amherst in October 1963 at the memorial service for Robert Frost:

I look forward to an America which will not be afraid of grace and beauty . . . which will reward achievement in the arts as we reward achievement in business or statecraft . . . which will steadily raise the standards of artistic accomplishment . . . which will steadily enlarge cultural opportunities for all of our citizens.

We have dealt mainly with balance between the humanities and the sciences. Those who plan High School 1980 also will consider the following kinds of balance: cognitive, affective, and psychomotor; academic and vocational subjects; in-school and out-of-school experiences; curricular and extracurricular activities; and the like. High School 1980 will have many ways of achieving balance. The NEA Project on Instruction recommended:

* G. K. Chesterton, *Orthodoxy,* New York: Image Books, 1959, pp. 16–18.

The school can provide and maintain a curriculum appropriately balanced for each student by offering a comprehensive program of studies, making early and continuous assessment of individual potentialities and achievements, and providing individualized programs based on careful counseling.

To avoid the imbalance that can result from limiting financial support to certain selected subjects and services, general financial support should be provided for the total program. This applies to local, state, and federal support.*

Sir Ronald Gould sums up the issue of balance:

If men and women are to be adequately prepared to grapple with the human problems of life in the second half of the century, and also take their place in an ever-changing society, they must have some facility with *love letters* and *lab notes.***

SELECTING CONTENT

The third issue, content selection, becomes increasingly crucial with the rapid expansion of man's knowledge. Never before have the forces of change spun with such incredible speed. In the nearly 2000 years since the birth of Christ, there has been first a very slow and then a rapidly accelerating accumulation of knowledge. The first doubling of man's knowledge occurred in 1750, the second in 1900, the third in 1950, and the fourth only ten years later. How will this sentence read in 1980, and what will it mean for the curriculum then?

So much has been learned that, as the Red Queen in *Alice in Wonderland* complains, ". . . it takes all the running you can do, just to keep in the same place." Because of this explosion of knowledge, the problems of what to learn require a vastly different approach today. Memorization of facts does little to prepare students for a world which will demand increasingly imaginative solutions to problems. The Pepsi generation, nourished by sputnik and Romper Room and *Playboy*, will not settle for the old prepackaged pap. Art must spark the realization of quantity and relationship and convergence, the way Walt Disney did it. Literature must be

---

* *Schools for the Sixties, op. cit.,* p. 47.
** Sir Ronald Gould, "Curriculum Change," *New Dimensions in Curriculum Development*, Toronto: Ontario Curriculum Institute, 1966, p. 7.

the open-sesame to the dignities and depravities of man's striving, the way *21st Century* does it. Music must open the boy and release the man locked inside.

Attempts to meet this need for different approaches have resulted in a plethora of national curriculum studies. They spring from the urgent need for bringing the school curriculum up to date, incorporating the useful, discarding the obsolete. Schools considering national curriculum studies would do well to heed Heathers' six "facts of life" about educational innovations: (1) Few of the educational innovations currently being marketed have been fully developed, implemented, and evaluated. (2) Many innovations exist in a variety of forms rather than having a standard form. (3) An innovation ordinarily must be modified somewhat to adapt it to the requirements of a local situation. (4) Making effective use of an innovation always calls for a system of interrelated changes in the local situation. (5) The most crucial factor in making an innovation function at the instructional level is staff reeducation. (6) In most instances, local leadership must be relied on to plan and conduct the school system's innovative programs.*

Of the 12 basic questions studied in the project cited previously, probably the most perplexing was, How can schools make wise selections of content from the ever-growing body of available knowledge?

Three pertinent recommendations dealt with bases for selecting content, for keeping it up to date, and for using national curriculum projects:

1. The objectives of the school, with a clear statement of priorities, should give direction to all curriculum planning. This applies to adding content, eliminating content, or changing the emphases on various topics and fields of study . . .

2. Each curriculum area should be under continuous study and evaluation and should be reviewed periodically. One purpose of such reviews is to determine whether recent findings in the academic disciplines are, or should be, reflected in the instructional program. These reviews should utilize the knowledge and skills of the teacher, the school administrator, the scholar in the academic disciplines, the scholar in the profession of teaching, and the lay citizen, each contributing his special competence to the total task. . . .

3. In making selections of content, school staffs should study the

* Drawn from Glen Heathers, "Guidelines for Reorganizing the School and the Classroom," *Rational Planning in Curriculum and Instruction: Eight Essays,* Washington: Center for the Study of Instruction, National Education Association, 1967, pp. 64–65.

results and recommendations of curriculum projects sponsored by nationally oriented groups with a view to applying promising findings.

There should be a systematic procedure for studying the results of these curriculum projects. The procedure should recognize the importance of balance and continuity in the total school experience of students and include the steps prerequisite to curriculum changes.*

EVALUATION AS A BASE FOR CHANGE

If the projections in this chapter are to become a reality, rational curriculum planning is essential—with emphasis on evaluation as a base for change. Rational leadership is required with artistic application of *principles* rather than rule-of-thumb procedures.

Space permits only a quick summary of directions as far as evaluative aspects of rational planning are concerned. National assessment is a particularly controversial issue. While the hazards are well known, National Educational Indices may well be as essential to High School 1980 as Economic Indices now are to the businessman. It seems inconceivable that we would rather operate our schools on the basis of ignorance than on the basis of information. Some seem to fear that the more we know the worse we will behave. We submit that the opposite should be true.

Without perspective regarding the progress we have made and the difficult tasks we face, our citizens have an inadequate basis for making judgments. As a result, decisions are frequently made on hearsay or widely publicized assertions rather than on a reasonably clear picture of the educational situation.**

In our opinion, the only place we can stand on this issue with professional comfort is on the side of all the knowledge and all the public support we can get.

The following summarizes the directions apparent in the field of evaluation:

* *Schools for the Sixties, op. cit.*, pp. 50–55.
** Drawn from *National Assessment of Educational Progress—Some Questions and Comments*, Washington: Department of Elementary School Principals in cooperation with the NEA Center for the Study of Instruction, 1967.

FROM	TO
1. tests as punishment	evaluation as a stimulant, a humane guide to continued growth and learning
2. measurement by paper and pencil tests	a variety of evaluation techniques with emphasis on observation
3. memory of the facts	focus on creativity and inquiry
4. exams at the end of a course	cooperative and continuous evaluation
5. narrow range of behaviors measured	evaluation of cognitive, affective, and psychomotor behaviors
6. evaluation only by the teacher	self-evaluation
7. colleges setting "standards" for admission	colleges cleaning up their sterile programs and working with schools to develop valid evaluation techniques

These trends are based on the following conceptual approach. The teacher has four fundamental tasks: (1) development of objectives, (2) selection of learning opportunities, (3) organization of the learning opportunities, and (4) selection of appropriate evaluation procedures. In developing objectives, the curriculum maker looks at data from society, organized knowledge, and the learner. Then he prepares objectives that state precisely the changes in behavior required of the learner and the content to which that behavior is directed. The formulator of educational objectives then has two further tasks. First, the objectives must be delimited to correspond with a set of values and, second, they must stand the tests of feasibility and attainability in terms of what is known about learning and the learning process. Psychology and philosophy are often called validating screens when used to examine objectives in this way.

It is clear that the process of evaluation is essentially the process of determining to what extent the educational objectives—changes in human behavior—are actually being realized by the program of curriculum and instruction.* Another major purpose of evaluation is to appraise the effectiveness of the means. Assumptions basic to evaluation are: (1) education is a process which seeks to change the behavior pattern of human beings; (2) the kinds of behavioral changes sought are the objectives; (3) the program is appraised by finding out how far the objectives are being realized; (4) this involves discovering to what degree behavioral changes are actually

* Drawn from Ralph W. Tyler, *Basic Principles of Curriculum and Instruction* (Chicago: University of Chicago Press, 1950).

taking place; (5) a wide range of evaluation techniques must be utilized; (6) the participation of students, faculty, and lay people is essential.

The procedures suggested as we evaluate include: (1) formulate a statement of objectives; (2) clearly define each objective in terms of behavior and content; (3) find promising evaluation situations; (4) select and try out promising methods of obtaining evidence; (5) determine the aspects of human behavior to be summarized and the units or terms in which each aspect is to be summarized; (6) devise means for interpreting and using the results to improve the program.

The teacher concerned with the content areas in the succeeding chapters of this section will apply this conceptual approach as he plans for mathematics 1980, science 1980, English 1980, and the like.

AMAZING CHANGES AHEAD?

Will a funny thing happen on the way to the future again? Not if we apply the preceding principles of evaluation and planning and also take cognizance of appropriate processes and procedures! Schaefer warns us of the danger of a "standard 'choreography' for noting pedagogical prescriptions in each curricular area."* Those who plan the science, mathematics, English, and other content programs should beware of those who plan to devise materials which can make their desired impact upon students irrespective of the ignorance or sophistication of a particular teacher. As we look back to the 1930s and 1940s, teachers did have an influence on the curriculum even though some of their decisions may have lacked scholarship. In making his plea for the school as a center of inquiry, Schaefer gives us an important guideline for high school 1980:

The present proposals reintroduce scholarship to the life of the schools, but, with bland rudeness, only children have been recognized. . . . I am fully convinced that unless teachers are accorded full intellectual partnership in both the substance and pedagogy of what they are expected to teach, new sequences of materials, no matter how elegantly contrived,

* Robert J. Schaefer, *The School as a Center of Inquiry*, New York: Harper & Row, 1967, p. 51.

will introduce disappointingly few youngsters to the inherent pleasure of learning.*

If the future of secondary education is to be what it should be, the school will be *the* center of inquiry, and the teacher will be a live model of the inquiring scholar with whom students can identify. Goodlad's summary of where we sometimes are today is appropriate:

The past two decades have produced or extended an impressive cluster of ideas and concepts pertaining to the conduct of schooling. I believe that the evidence, logic, or reasoning behind some of them is sufficient to commend them to our attention. Depending on their implementation, we might expect today's schools to be characterized by the following: (1) rather clear statements of institutional objectives, stated in behavioral terms; (2) instructional emphasis on learning how to learn, on long-term structural elements of subject matter rather than isolated bits and pieces; (3) multi-media learning packages in every classroom, designed with concern for the integrity of the content as well as intrinsic appeal for the students; (4) extensive instructional recognition of individual differences reflected in evaluation procedures, assignments, and expectations for students; (5) considerable use of basic principles of group dynamics, human interaction, and democratic classroom leadership; (6) use of sound principles of learning pertaining to motivation, reinforcement, transfer of training, and so on; (7) little attention to age and grade as criteria for what to teach (as in nongraded, continuous progress plans); (8) flexible use of personnel resources (as in team teaching); (9) clear evidence that we are in the "golden age of instructional materials."**

These are central guidelines for 1980. One need only look at the schools in the ghetto as one example of our current failure.

The following chart is a summary of where we are and where we are headed as far as curriculum is concerned:

HIGH SCHOOL 1970	HIGH SCHOOL 1980
1. primary emphasis on academic scholarship	a curriculum relevant to all students
2. involvement of only academic scholars and teachers	involvement of all levels of decision makers in the schools, including laymen and scholars, but with special emphasis on the participation of teachers and students
3. child, society-centered, or discipline-centered curriculum	the total curriculum, the humanistic curriculum

* *Ibid.,* p. 52.
** John I. Goodlad, "Educational Change: A Strategy for Study and Action," *The National Elementary Principal,* XLVIII, January, 1969.

HIGH SCHOOL 1970	HIGH SCHOOL 1980
4. selling teacher-free prepackaged programs	truly experimental programs; pharmacies of tested educational alternatives
5. tinkering with the means of education	focus on ends, aims, objectives; the philosopher returns to the center of the stage
6. trying to teach everything	establishing priorities
7. focus on the gifted and/or the deprived student	focus on *all* students as individuals
8. bits and pieces; one course at a time	comprehensive school improvement program (nursery school through college)
9. elementary and secondary reform	higher education too (Can the colleges catch up with the high schools?)
10. in-service *training* of teachers	in-service *education* of teachers

Another continuing curricular issue relates to the ways of putting learning experiences together so as to provide for effective organization. The main structural elements in which experiences are organized include specific subjects like geography, arithmetic, history, spelling; broad fields like social studies, the language arts, the natural sciences; a core curriculum for general education combined with broad fields or with specific subjects. Over the past decades, each of these structures has received emphasis at particular times. Continuity and sequence are facilitated when the courses are organized in larger units and in a larger general framework. Integration of experiences is less difficult with the core curriculum because there are not so many boundaries between subjects. High School 1980 undoubtedly will experiment with each of these structures, keeping in mind the three criteria of continuity, sequence, and integration in the student's experience.

TEACHING 1980

In the first portion of this chapter, we have dealt primarily with what to teach. One must also consider the spirit and guiding principles of how to teach in High School 1980 if what we have said is not pure speculation. We believe the schools should move in the following directions:

HIGH SCHOOL 1970   HIGH SCHOOL 1980

1. *Memory*   *Inquiry*

   So much has been learned in so many areas of knowledge that it is even now no longer possible for students to learn even summaries of existing knowledge. Sheer bulk defeats any effort to teach knowledge as a body of facts to be learned. . . . The school problem once known as coverage is meaningless and obsolete. Coverage is no longer difficult; it is impossible.

2. *Spiritless Climate*   *Zest for Learning*

   Students will enjoy school. There will never be a substitute for a good teacher when it comes to moving a student to the edge of his seat, eyes shining, hand lifting before the question is completed. One way to decide if a high school is good is if one hears a good belly laugh coming from some "classroom" once every half hour.

3. *The Group*   *The Individual*

   Human variability and individual differences are facts of life. They cannot be ignored, nor should they be. Variability demands alternatives, milk can be homogenized, but not children. "On their own in school" is the theme for high school 1980. The student will have started school on his birthday, with a birthday party, rather than with "September madness." The mythical group can no longer control his destiny.

4. *Teaching as Telling*   *Teaching as Guiding*

   The psittacotic method of teaching will be illegal. No teacher will be permitted to conduct recitations where students give parrot-like answers—a disease worse than parrot fever.

5. *The 2 x 4 x 6 Teacher*   *The Teacher and His Staff*

   The $2 \times 4 \times 6$ teacher, as we all know, is one who is stuck between the two covers of a textbook, the four walls of a classroom, and the six periods of a school day. By 1980, the theme will be the teacher and his staff: man, media, and machines.

6. *Scheduled Classes*   *Appointments and Independent Learning*

   Rigid scheduling of classes and pigeonholing of students will be a thing of the past. Once he gets to school, the student will not encounter the cyclical ringing of the bells that makes the classroom resemble a bus depot, with arrivals and departures every 40 minutes. "No bells ring" will be the motto of 1980 along with "on their own in school."

7. *Self-Contained Classrooms*   *Community-Contained School*

   High School 1980 will be a diffused learning environment, including academic resource centers, museums, parks, business offices, public buildings, an array of guidance and computerized programming centers, and probably even homes. In Philadelphia there is a high school without walls. Students attend classes in existing cultural, business, and scientific facilities along the mile-long Benjamin Franklin Highway—art classes at the Philadelphia Museum of Art, English at the Free Library of Philadelphia, chemistry at the

Academy of Science, journalism at the *Philadelphia Inquirer.* The idea is to dramatize the fact that the schools are the community and the community the schools.

TEACHER 1980

What does all this mean for the teacher of 1980? He will not fear change. He will no longer wait for things to happen. He will make them happen. He will no longer be the victim of change. He will be an agent of change. The scope of negotiations will be increasingly broadened to enable him to become influential in all the decisions of the schools.

The teacher will use the machine; he will not be replaced by it. As Gores says:

There will be individual sound motion picture machines smaller than a breadbox, lighter than a record player, cheaper than a microscope, capable of presenting single concepts in 5 or 6 minutes of motion, color, and the simultaneous voice of the best and wisest teacher. And there will be talking books, cassetts which compress into the size of a package of cigarettes, 90 minutes of anything worth listening to, with the added advantage of being copied at the rate approaching what Xerox can do with the printed word.

When this happens . . . the teacher can rise to a higher calling. No longer burdened by the dispensing of so much information, the teacher will deal less with facts and more with values—the meaning of it all. At long last the teacher will return to his ancient trade—philosophy—what's true, what's false, what's moral, what's immoral, what's amoral, what's right, what's wrong. Technology will elevate the teacher to a higher plane of professionalism. For the competent teacher, the one who can inspire the child to understand America, love it, love it while he reshapes it, technology holds not the threat of unemployment but the promise of professionalism.*

Any teacher who can be replaced by a machine should be.

But education's potential will be realized only if today's clashing powers (student power, community power, industry power, black power, teacher power) are able to combine their efforts in cooperative leadership. Leadership is a function—not a position or person. Leadership is concerned with how people can be brought to work

* Harold B. Gores, "Whipsaw," Unpublished paper presented at AASA School Masters Rotary Club meeting, Atlantic City, February 20, 1968.

together for common ends effectively and happily. It is the ability to contribute to the achievement of those ends either through ideas or through ways of working to accomplish them. Leadership, unfortunately, is often confused with command—as the contest between the Japanese commander and the British colonel demonstrated in *The Bridge Over the River Kwai.* Command, however, is always concerned with power over people, while leadership is concerned with power over problems.*

Mary P. Follett, perhaps, expresses Herrick's ideas more simply:

When you and I decide on a course of action together and do that thing, you have no power over me nor I over you, but we have power over ourselves together. We have, however, no authority over John Smith. We could try to get "power" over him in a number of ways . . . but the only legitimate power we could have in connection with John Smith is what you and John Smith and I could develop together over our three selves. . . . Genuine power is power-with; pseudo power, power-over.**

Teacher 1980 will be more like a college professor. Instead of being an all-purpose walking-talking oracle every day all day to the 25 or 30 youngsters in his class, the teacher will become a clinical specialist diagnosing the particular needs and strengths of each individual child. He will spend more time planning the content and style of his teaching than he does in the classroom itself. He will be the prober, the needler, the catalytic agent to spur students to want to learn rather than the man-with-all-the-answers.

But this impressive array of time, facilities, and instructional aids, impressive as they may be, will not be sufficient to assure successful teaching. What more is required of the teaching process?

Aretha Franklin poses the crucial question:

Has it got soul? Man, that's the question of the hour. If it has soul, then it's tough, beautiful, out of sight. It passes the test of withitness. . . .
But what is soul? It's like electricity. "We don't really know what it is," says singer Ray Charles, "but it's a force that can light a room." The force radiates from a sense of self-hood, a sense of knowing where you've been and what it means. Soul is a way of life—but it is always the hard way. Its essence is ingrained in those who suffer and endure to laugh about it later.†

---

* Drawn from Virgil E. Herrick, "The Principal Looks at Himself," *Educational Leadership,* IV, April, 1947, pp. 442–448.
** Mary P. Follett, *Creative Experience,* New York: Longmans Green and Company, 1928, p. 199.
† *Time,* June 28, 1968, pp. 62–66.

Our motto for teacher 1980 will be "He who would kindle another must himself glow." We want teachers who fit in the left-hand column—not the right:

YES	NO
Bonnie	Clyde
Charlie Brown	Orphan Annie
Holden Caulfield	Andy Hardy
Cleopatra	Julius Caesar
Thomas Jefferson	George Washington
Jesus	St. Peter
"Mona Lisa"	"Nude Descending a Staircase"
Sitting Bull	Custer**

In conclusion, when the history of the world is written, the Greeks will be remembered for liberty, the Romans for law, the British for parliamentary government. But we in the United States will be remembered for one thing only, the only nation in the history of the world to take seriously the idea of universal public education. High School 1980 will add the words "equal" and "quality" to this dream.

Harold Gores says it well about how we accomplish the ends discussed in this chapter:

The beauty of the relevant metaphor is that it enables the person to discredit the status quo without seeming to have done it. If it is done with love and a light touch, a Neanderthal can alter his position without losing face and thus we make progress.

Everybody wants progress but nobody wants change. If we assault the status quo head-on and with spears, it closes ranks to defend itself from the ravages of progress. But if by apt metaphor the medieval mind can move to higher ground without appearing to have left his main position, something is gained. And progress is made up of little gains.*

* *Ibid.*, p. 66.
** Letter to Ole Sand from Harold B. Gores, February 5, 1968.

The Reformed Science Curriculum

Paul F. Brandwein

If only we had some verified formula for analyzing the essence of learning, and of predicting its outcome, we might write: $E = mc^2$, where E equals educability, m, the mastery of instruction, and c, creativity. Too often, we have written of instruction and learning as if we had certain knowledge, rather than hope. Too often, in our zeal for reform, because reform was necessary, we have talked of normative theory as if it were factual theory. Too often, in *science* education (where our training and experience should have taught us the essential difference between established fact and hypothesis) we have gone from *word* to *word*, rather than from *work* to *work*. Thus, we talk of "teaching through inquiry," establish certain programs (PSSC, CHEMS, BSCS, ESCP, and the like), hold vast numbers of institutes which bring teachers together, and then assume that teaching has indeed been changed, that teaching is indeed "through inquiry," that is, through the modes which nurture science. Not so. Out of observations of teaching of science, which we have carried out in the past five years (1012 school systems), we have been led to hypothesize somewhat as follows:*

If present practices in administration and instruction in the high schools persist, then instruction in the arts of investigation will be minimal. The inadequacies in practice and administration and instruction do not seem to me to be primarily the result of basic inadequacies in instruction and administration per se, but are probably the result of the incredible demands made upon the energies of administrators, supervisors, and teachers—demands which cannot be met.

To summarize the observations made:

1. Roughly 90 percent of the physics and chemistry and earth science teachers observed, lecture 90 percent of the time in the classroom.

---

* Adapted from Paul F. Brandwein, *Observations On Teaching,* Center for the Study of Instruction, November 1968.

2. Roughly 80 percent of the biology and general science teachers (seventh, eighth, and ninth grades) lecture 80 percent of the time).

3. Roughly 70 percent of teachers in the fourth, fifth, and sixth grades lecture 60 percent of the time.

4. In the vast majority of cases (about 95 to 99 percent), where the laboratory was used in instruction, the laboratory materials were prepared in advance to the end that a satisfactory conclusion would be reached within the time limit of the laboratory period (50 minutes single lab period, to 120 minutes in an extended lab period). That is to say, the laboratory "experiment" was not an "experiment" at all—but an exercise. One may postulate that in the vast majority of school systems, about 90 percent, not *one* experiment (in the sense of a strategy devised to *add* to knowledge, or to discover hitherto uncovered phenomena, or to construct new models) was planned or completed by the vast majority of high school students. In my observation, in less than 5 percent of the schools was a single student given the opportunity to experiment in the sense of the term used here. Inquiry, as the relentless pursuit of a hypothesis in proof or disproof, was generally not practiced.

However true these observations it is nevertheless clear that teachers are quite honorable in their desire to make the art of investigation central to their teaching. Even casual observation will show this aim to be impossible of attainment, generally; thus, to all practical purposes, honorable and ethical people are placed in the position of stating objectives they *cannot* reach. At least four sets of factors are responsible—factors which should be, and perhaps, will be, corrected by 1980:

1. School buildings are, in large part, not built to facilitate the arts of investigation. Experimental and inquiry techniques require the "holding over" of equipment and space beyond the single teaching period in which an investigation may be initiated. Time and space to do this are not available in the vast majority of old and new schools. That is to say, funds are not allotted for this purpose. In the years leading up to 1980, they should be made available, thus making possible the teaching of the arts of investigation as we know they should be taught.

2. The teaching schedule of an elementary or high school teacher prohibits the inclusion of procedures which would permit the uses of "the methods of intelligence"* (if you will, "inquiry"). First, to plan for the idiosyncratic modes of inquiry requires time for planning and preparation universally not available to teachers. In the

---

* Bridgeman's term encompassing the variety of idiosyncratic "methods of the scientist."

main, junior and senior high school teachers have five or more periods of instruction per day, often with three preparations per day, and sometimes incredible as it may seem, five preparations—plus school duty. The class load is often in excess of 36 students per class, often more than 180 per teacher. The situation in the elementary school is even more serious! In addition, there is the correction of papers, laboratory reports, examinations, or the like. This teaching load is an overload and, in effect, makes individualization of instruction, and instruction in the arts of investigation, almost impossible to realize. By 1980, the correction of the overload should be a primary aim of the governing boards of education.

Second, communities do not give administrators sufficient funds for the capital and perishable equipment required to press forward with the procedures characteristic of the methods of intelligence which may often include the experimental approach.

3. The overload of teachers may be postulated, at least partly, to the underlying reason why teachers lecture rather than follow the practices they approve (in speech and writing) such as individualization of instruction, questioning, and small group instruction. Most teachers understand that a "lecturer," but *not* a "teacher," can be replaced by the machine. (To digress: this is not to say, that present "programs-in-machine" aid even the lecturer. We are likely to see the same failure of machine-processed information-giving, as we saw in programmed information-giving. Innovators in both of these areas simply are not taking the time necessary in contemplation, and in the production of creative programs.)

Any observer of teachers will find that even the best of them are "fatigued" by the overload. At least, the lecturer, using brain and larynx to repeat the known, minimizes fatigue by serving habit and memory. The lecture is often routine and does not sap the faculties required in the constant interaction characteristic of the surging, unregulated thought coming out of students engaged in the brilliance of discovery rather than the calisthenics of the laboratory exercise.

If we are correct in our observations, and we believe we are, then the modes of producing change in education which we have followed in the past, need changing first. But it seems apparent that this will not be so, unless, at least, seven myths are faced, dispelled, and destroyed. We propose to state the myth, attempt to dispel it, and offer up for consideration a statement, or device, which harmonizes more closely with present considerations. Since the past is very often prologue, the year 1980 may see a more graceful view of the problems coming out of these considerations. These myths are inevitably not, for everyone, in their order of importance.

MYTH I

Equal educational opportunity requires equal exposure to identical courses, using identical instructional materials, given in identical time spans, to all students.

We know that students vary in ability, in background, in experience and in life-style. We know they vary in gifts, opportunities, and destinations. For example, certainly not *all* students can profit from PSSC (Physical Science Study Committee) physics to the same extent; in fact, with our present instructional practices, a considerable number of students cannot achieve satisfactorily in PSSC physics. The difference between those who achieve satisfactorily in physics and those who do not, seems to be based in large part on verbal and mathematical ability. (PSSC is but an example; other course work presents similar problems.)

In 1980, we shall have advanced sufficiently in our attempts to meet the variability in ability, in destination, in life-style. Two approaches may be useful:

1. *All* students will have *access* to all course work. However, due regard for variation in ability, therefore, in achievement will result in the compassionate regard for students as individuals; thus students will not be penalized for their inability to achieve up to the highest levels expected by the teacher (the honored "A") but will be honored for achieving up to the levels commensurate with their ability.

2. Or there will be a variety of courses—adapted to ability level—which will permit students to achieve at their highest level. The labels A, B, C, D, F will perhaps (though one doesn't see this by 1980) be eliminated. It will be sufficient to describe the work the student has done for those individuals or institutions (colleges, employers) who require knowledge of his schooling.

An alternative device to dispel the myth might be to institute continuous progress (nongraded instruction). By 1980, perhaps 5 to 10 percent* of high schools may have instituted continuous progress,

---

* In the writer's opinion, when 5 to 10 percent of high schools institute a form of instruction, then a strong trend has been established. When 20 percent follow a plan, it is demonstrable that it is only a matter of time before a majority of the schools follow the trend.

or a similar type of instruction, which permits the student to progress at his own pace without penalties for proceeding at a pace slower than the norm will probably be more acceptable in the 1980s. After all, progression in learning at one's own pace is at the heart of individualization of instruction.

There is considerable theory to buttress the belief that "learning is its own reward," but a satisfactory way of rewarding those who progress more slowly needs to be found. Our competitive society still rewards the higher rates of mobility towards a goal. The rapid learner is still the superior learner, but is it fair to reward accident of birth conferring on some superior DNA, and a superior home environment?

In 1980, to assist in self-pacing a variety of procedures may be employed; amongst them:

1. Learning Activity Packages (LAP). Learning activity packages are in the form of instructions addressed to the student. In essence, LAPs are a kind of syllabus in which the student carries out all the activities which feed a concept; LAPs are developed by committees of teachers out of the curriculum design accepted by the faculty and are designed for mastery by the students at a variety of levels. Thus, a vast conceptual scheme such as "The sum total of matter and energy is conserved" is broken down into a sequence of concepts such as, "Matter is particulate"; the latter is then developed into a LAP.

In the LAP the student often carries out readings in a basic text, laboratory work, readings in a variety of books, magazines, and other references, uses, records, films and filmstrips, and consults *a* teacher (his "consultant") whenever he requires help. Lectures, group discussions, and the like are orchestrated within the work of any group of students. But the essence of the approach is that each student is expected to proceed at his own pace. It appears as if this trend will be more solidly established in 1980. It is highly probable, that modified forms of *programmed instruction* will be developed as part of the LAPs—but units of programmed material will not necessarily be *the* LAP. What seemed an error in practice when programmed instruction was first instituted will probably be corrected, namely, the innovation is not *the* mode of instruction, but is rather one *part* of a *system* of instruction, made up of a variety of modes of instruction and materials.

2. Computer Assisted Instruction. In the 1980s, leading school systems will have instituted some form of computer assisted instruction. Probably the error (noted above), which halted the advance of programmed instruction, will not be repeated with CAI. To repeat, in 1980, teachers and supervisors will perhaps more generally consider orchestrating systems of instruction. Thus a text, or programmed instruction, or LAP or CAI, or a "course in film," will be considered part of the materials of *instruction,* not a *method* of instruction.

In short, to dispel the myth we have isolated, by 1980 we shall have come more nearly to accept the concept of variability in students and recognize that variability in students is a practical guarantee of their freedom to learn in a variety of ways. This should mean, in turn, that equal opportunity in education means variety in methods of instruction and consequently a variety of instructional materials orchestrated in a system of instruction. Further, students will not be compared to each other on their achievement in a single course; rather they will work to fulfill their abilities. Their work will be described, not scored. Perhaps, in 1980, this will be so.

MYTH II

The scientist is engaged in discovery; therefore, the legacy of science is to be acquired through discovery (present synonyms: inquiry, processes of the scientist).

However this myth came to be, it was probably not planted and propagated by scientists. For scientists have always stood on the "shoulders of others"; science is cumulative; a scientist inherits a legacy from those who came before him. A scientist doesn't *start* with a problem; he starts with a kind of *knowing* which came out of study. At least he "knows" as much of his field as he can muster.

This is not to derogate the uses of curiosity, but certainly, in the high school, a student should learn that scientists utilize the work of others, that they do not discover *anew* what is their legacy, what is part of their culture. They are *interdependent* with the scientists presently at work in their field and those who came before them; they *share* their knowledge. The scientist uses the skills of *independent inquiry* but always he uses the *skills of interdependence* as well; that is, he uses the library (the work of others) as well as the laboratory. This must mean that before a student begins work on a "problem," he should try to find out what has been done before— if only to probe the resources of his text, library, and community resources.

Biological evolution may be considered the *transmission* and *transmutation* of the genetic code; cultural evolution may be considered the *transmission* and *transmutation* of knowledge and values. To transmit the culture mainly through "discovery" or "inquiry," that is,

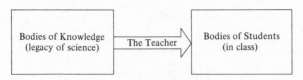

FIGURE 1. A module in which
the energies of the teacher are
central in presentation.

to have each child discover the culture for himself is the most
inefficient way of instruction known. True, the student can inquire
through reading. The massive and masterful legacy of science cannot, at all odds, be rediscovered; if each generation must rediscover
it, we perish.

Inquiry, or discovery, or problem solving in science then should
be reinterpreted as developing an environment in which the learner
is given the fullest opportunity to use his *own* energies in making
the legacy of science his own—as well as to undertake *independent
study* and true inquiry, that is to do a true experiment (as part of
an investigation). The orchestration of a system of instruction developed above (LAP within a system of instruction) serves this purpose;
the system, in effect, orchestrates the skills of interdependence and
independence.

The "model" of instruction which encourages the student to use
his own energies in learning might be diagrammed as below in
Figure 2, as compared with Figure 1 (which is presently in effect
in a majority of high schools).

The schools in Figure 2 are the building. The school—constructed
as a set of boxes within a larger box—is giving way to a device
designed for instruction in the skills of interdependence and independence. Rooms per se are giving way to individual study carrels,
flexible modules for large and small groups, for team teaching, for
discussion and the like—with flexible scheduling as basic to the flow
of students.

The trends seem to be in this direction, and by 1980 we should
begin to determine whether a "model" of instruction *similar* to that
in Figure 2 will begin to gain acceptance. Or perhaps—it should be
hoped—there will be a superior model because we shall know more
of the way children learn; that is, we shall have developed viable
factual theories of learning, not only normative ones. But if a normative one (based on such research as is presently available) is useful,
then perhaps one which will serve until a more useful one is developed may be stated as follows:

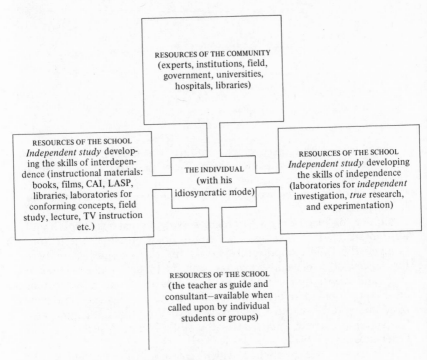

FIGURE 2. A system of instruction
in which the energies of the student
are central in inquiry.

In any specified act of teaching, a new environment is created; is *responding* to the changed environment, a learner gains capacities (enactive, iconic, symbolic, psychomotor) not achieved through prior experience, but specified in the given act of teaching.*

The emphasis in the theory is on the *response* of the learner. The lecture then is to be considered as one of the materials of instruction; it "tells," much like a film, a text, or a tape. There are few

* Modified from P. F. Brandwein, *Notes Towards a General Theory of Teaching*, Harcourt, Brace & World, 1966. (See Jerome Bruner, *Toward a Theory of Instruction* for special uses of the terms "iconic," "enactive," Harvard Press, 1966.) Unfortunately, Bruner did not state an "explicit" theory of instruction. He is, of course, much more qualified to do so than the present writer, whose attempts came out of a desperate need to define "teaching."

The theory courts obsolescence; nevertheless, it functions as theory, speaking as it does to what we conceive as *instructed learning* (that is, learning in a time-binding institution, the school, where experiences are bound in nonrandom order, in a curriculum.

trustworthy ways of knowing whether the "listener" is a "learner." A lecture, then, except in the hands of those rare individuals whose lectures are truly *new* experiences, because they are fresh analyses and rare syntheses, transcending what is textual, should be considered part of the *materials of instruction,* not as a *method of instruction.* In any event, in the 1980s, the energies of learning will increasingly come from the activities of the learner; the lecture will (no, it must) be progressively reduced until it takes less than 50 percent of scheduled time—or even less. Hopefully less.

MYTH III

Laboratory work, as presently constituted, teaches the arts of investigation.

In my observations over the country the laboratory period as it is ordinarily conducted, does not serve, in the main, the arts of investigation. The laboratory, as presently used, mainly confirms, through manipulation of apparatus, what is known. It illustrates, in effect, through self-demonstration, what is "taught" through classroom lecture, discussion, text, and workbook (or laboratory manual). This is valuable and useful in itself, for students should see that the concepts and supporting data of science have empirical validation. Students need not only recognize *what* they know, but how they know it. But the laboratory has other noble uses.

By the 1980s, school construction will have advanced to the point where space will be available so that in any given year *each* student can do at least one *original investigation* which will involve his own experimental design. Essentially, the concept of an original investigation is this: The student shall design an investigation which will yield data not hitherto available in *his* particular environment.

Simple "original" investigations:

—an investigation into the birds or small mammals (or whatever animal group) of a designated environment
—an investigation into the mosses or ferns (or whatever plant group) of a designated environment
—an investigation into the geology of an area
—an investigation into the background radiation of an area

Complex "original" investigations. The "problem" in this area might be suggested by scientists. To develop increasing skill in the arts of investigation and to participate in problem solving on the "embryo-scientists level" it is suggested that teachers consult scientists for suggestion of areas of investigation in which students may be successfully involved and in which experimental work may be done. Further, it is hoped that this approach, or a more useful one, will become more feasible in the 1980s. Moreover, genuine problems should be made available to the student and not those of a "makework" nature. For this reason (if I were a member of such a consortium), I should personally be limited to suggesting problems in the areas of investigation concerned with the physiologic races of fungi in my field of research. But a consortium of scientists coming out of all fields might well address itself to a variety of students. For example, the Biological Sciences Curriculum Study consulted hundreds of biologists in an attempt to furnish original investigations to high school students. Indeed, the Consortium of Biologists has furnished over 100 suggestions for such independent investigations. Many of them would do credit to graduate study. Yet, high school students are successfully prosecuting many of them; they are enabled to carry out *one* original inquiry, involving a variety of investigational techniques (including experimental technique) during a school year.

We may predict that *all* the students who will become scientists *will be in the high schools in 1980.* So will *all* the students who, as adults, will support scientific research, either as donors of gifts or donors of a vote in support of research.

MYTH IV

The teacher teaches individuals—not groups.

Meetings of science teachers, in national or regional conventions, seem never to adjourn without some statement on the ideal mode of instruction: individualized instruction.

In my observation, under present scheduling and present programs, teachers cannot deal *primarily* with individuals; they are forced to deal primarily with groups.

It is clear that most high school teachers teach five classes per day. In the small high schools, these sometimes require three or more preparations (e.g., chemistry, physics, and biology). With a teaching responsibility of 150 or more students, it is not possible to minister to most students individually. As stated earlier, perhaps the reason for the almost universal utilization of the lecture as a means of instruction is that it is the least fatiguing and most economical (although generally ineffective) way of meeting five classes of boys and girls.

For these and other reasons, in the 1980s a variety of devices may be employed to reduce the teaching, supervisory and administrative responsibilities of teachers. It will become, so it seems to me, necessary to introduce:

1. Team teaching (with its promise of attending to large groups, small groups, and individuals).

2. Learning Activity Packages (so that each student is partly responsible for his own instruction through individual study. See Figure 2).

3. *Development of Learning Centers.* (These are essentially areas where books, films, filmstrips, and retrieval systems are available to all students upon their call.)

4. *Conceptually Oriented Curriculums.* These make possible nongraded or continuous progress based on LAP's, or concept-oriented instructional materials (e.g., texts, unitexts with accompanying laboratory materials).

5. *Computer Assisted Instruction and Programmed Instruction.* (These may be developed primarily to teach skills, e.g., mathematical skills, classifying, dissecting, and other skills which involve nonscholastic activity.)

6. *The Employment of Non-Teaching Personnel.* (E.g., laboratory aids, clerical aids, part-time assistance of parents, to remove the burdens of non-teaching duties from teachers.)

7. Other devices, particular to a school or community, which can be developed by a staff to increase the time available for instruction of individual students and, at the same time, make minimal large group instruction. In my experience, most faculties display considerable inventiveness in devising schema which increase their potential.

All of the foregoing depend in turn on dispelling the following basic myth of American education.

MYTH V

High school begins in the ninth grade.

The child's early development conditions his future. Evidence is amassing to show that the child's development from pregnancy on is basic to the future behavior of the child. In one of the writer's studies on gifted children in high school, and Roe's studies on gifted scientists, data emerged that indicated that more than 80 percent of scientists were first born, or only children. The inference seemed clear that early training at home, prior to schooling, was of the essence, that children who were given opportunity for independent study were more effective students.

Be that as it may, in the 1980s it is probable that high school teachers will act on the simple understanding that the education of children in the earlier grades affects their work. They will then assume, even as in certain schools now, a working relation to the elementary and junior high school. (This may be in the nature of consulting, in-service, or teaching duties.) The purpose: to advance the education of children in the schools which feed the high school.

MYTH VI

The sole function of the high school is to develop competence in its students.

There was a time when critics such as Bestor and Rickover—and others who saw so very clearly that a function of the American education was to develop competent scholars and citizens—interpreted competence solely as competence in the variety of subject matters of the school. This is still, in my observation, a predominant notion of the function of schooling. Yet there is a major undercurrent of thought expressed in writing and thinking in American education not yet clearly expressed in action; it is this: Americans want their children to be as *compassionate* as they are *competent*.

Increasingly, Americans are considering the goals of education not only in terms of fitting children for vocational competence but competence in advancing civilization in its most compassionate role. This would mean that in the 1980s the development of programs in science would speak to the abilities of *all* children. Not all children can take BSCS biology, CHEMS chemistry, PSSC physics, Harvard Project physics, SMSG mathematics, but *all* of them need an understanding of the physical universe and of human behavior. Galileo, Newton, Darwin, and Mendel, Einstein, Bohr, Pasteur, and the host of others to whom we are permanently in debt did not only affect physics, chemistry, and biology—they affected life and living. Scientists have left *nothing* of the fabric of civilization untouched. Boys and girls who cannot understand de Broglie, or Planck, or Bohr, or

Feynman, or Woodward, still need to live productive and useful lives with understanding and without fear and superstition!

If we would want our children to be compassionate, the schools must be compassionate. In the 1980s a full-fledged effort in curriculum and method—using the devices of individualized instruction which we know—will be developed to meet the full spectrum of ability, including those who did not choose the appropriate DNA to enable them to understand the complexities of mathematical physics, chemistry, and biology.

Moreover, grading systems might, at last, be on their way out. To vent the sins of the fathers on children by means of grades is, in essence, immoral. By the 1980s, we shall begin to inaugurate—on a large scale—systems of reporting which describe what children do. They will not be labelled by grades for, to repeat, grades do not label, they libel.

MYTH VII

Advances in education come out of social crises.

One hears that we are a "crisis" nation in the solution of social problems, including problems in education. So it would seem. World War II precipitated a crisis—met by so-called war courses. Sputnik precipitated another, met by the curriculums devised by hyper-committees—PSSC, BSCS, CHEMS, CBA, SMSG, and the like. We seem to await succeeding crises—and then to indulge ourselves in speedy, pragmatic solutions, full of hope. Then the crisis abated, we give over to what seems to be a steadier course but which in the end spawns still another crisis.

Thus, government entered the "crisis of sputnik" with vast infusions of money, only to reduce its expenditures when the crisis seemed over. Then government gave over its functions to authors and publishers who—as they had in the past—maintained a steadier service to the schools.

By the 1980s the present social crisis may be solved but there are others coming—pollution of the air and of the waters will soon be intolerable. The cities may choke, and overpopulation will hasten famine in countries which have not yet achieved scientific agriculture or begun to control their populations; so the data seem to cast their shadows. And always the schools respond; always—even if society doesn't. But in education, at least, an overwhelming response to a crisis energizes—but also debilitates. Teachers are carried up with vast programs of summer retraining (called institutes); schools are mobilized; programs are energized with vast sums of money, but crisis after crisis debilitates. The shouting voice is soon shut off by the failure of nerve.

By the 1980s, if not sooner, devices for *continuing, sensible,* and *sensitive* review of curriculum and method should be established. One of the most promising is what we shall call a *consortium of teachers.* The consortium is designed to take in a geographical area in which a university or college has sway and influence. It consists sometimes of formal, other times, informal organization. Usually it comprises scientists from the university or college, educators from the school of education, supervisors and teachers in high school, junior high school, and elementary grades, and representatives of the community. The consortium of teachers usually takes on these functions:

1. To conduct continuing in-service programs which not only advance the competence of teachers, but inform the university scholar on the nature of instruction in the schools.
2. To review all curriculum efforts, however sponsored (i.e., by government, foundations, or publishers).
3. To conduct regular seminars and / or discussions concerned with the advancement of curriculum and method.
4. To organize funding of special programs—for disadvantaged, aggrieved, or gifted.
5. To maintain liason with the community; the aim: to retain confidence and support, moral, social, political, and financial.

By the 1980s, we shall perhaps have dispelled the myths to which we have addressed ourselves. We shall have begun to dismember the practices which still give the myths substance. In the 1980s we shall have realized that education is surely a profession, but just as surely it has greater scope: it is a mercy.

By the 1980s perhaps we shall have begun to understand that, in a sense, a school is concerned with a major discipline: *the discipline of responsible consent.* The objective of this discipline is at once simple, overreaching and overwhelming: *between impulse and action, to interpose evidence, reason, judgment, and compassion.* A discipline of responsible consent speaks to the human use of human beings.

In the 1980s we shall have come to act on the great premise of American education: each child is a supreme moral worth. In the 1980s we shall have come to know that the school must not only enable, but also ennoble. By the 1980s we shall recognize that a smaller world needs larger minds to encompass it. We shall come to know that in this world the skills of interdependence are based on the skills of independence, on the skills of the autonomous person. Perhaps by the year 2000 we shall have come to know that the school is the single place where differences are prized, where innermost feelings can be expressed, where consent and dissent are of the same coinage.

By the year 2000 we shall have come to know that above all the school must heal.

The Reformed Mathematics Curriculum

Robert B. Davis

High school mathematics is one link in a structure that strikingly resembles a chain fence: on every side there are connections to other links, with resultant stresses and limitations. We can overlook all of these influences, and design a wholly independent high school mathematics program, only at the risk of finding ourselves cast in the role of interior decorator for a new *Titanic*.

1. INFLUENCES FROM ELEMENTARY SCHOOLS

Obviously some links in our chain fence pull upon the high school and try to force it to change. Equally obviously, a good many other links tend to hold things rigidly in place, to impede or prohibit any change whatsoever.

There is no better example of this than the influences that emanate from the elementary school. Children who enter secondary schools have just "graduated" from elementary schools or middle schools, and bring this background with them when they arrive. What kind of background is it?

In far too many cases it is the same as it was a decade—or several decades—earlier. There *are*, for example, seventh graders who cannot recognize the full quota of 26 letters of the alphabet, and (since mathematics is usually limited by any weakness in reading) whose mathematics is correspondingly ill-developed.

But more effective educational programs are being created in a few elementary schools. This takes the special form of turning out a more autonomous child—and therefore one who ought to be taken more seriously by the high school. It also takes the form of more individualized programming in elementary schools.

Now more individualized elementary programs necessarily imply a greater variety in the students who enter high school. Probably there will still be some who don't know all 26 letters of the alphabet (because of transfers between schools, and other reasons, it is hard to eliminate this group entirely), but the range will be more spread out. In mathematics we already know that it is possible to graduate from grade six a sizeable percentage of children who have mastered most of "traditional" ninth grade algebra, and in addition know considerable analytic geometry, a significant piece of matrix algebra, and various applications of mathematics to other subjects (such as physics and economics). Even more importantly, these children are *in the habit* of taking an original and creative approach when they encounter a new mathematical situation. They have not been "pushed" or force-fed in elementary school; rather, they have been allowed to see that mathematics can be exciting, they have been put within sight of useful mathematical ideas (such as the mathematical concept of function), and they have been granted the freedom to pursue their own directions and to develop their own methods.

Will secondary schools be prepared to receive a much more diverse group of entering students? In at least one actual case we know about, the secondary school was in fact *not* ready for many of these children, and did not serve them well. (The problem, of course, is not limited to the area of mathematics: it will appear also in the areas of spoken foreign languages, science, music, writing, and current events, for some elementary schools are already showing great progress in these areas.)

2. INFLUENCES FROM THE UNIVERSITIES

By far the greatest pulls and pushes on high school programs are exerted by universities. College admission requirements constitute an obvious source of external pressure, but university influence is felt even more potently in other ways.

For one thing, universities set an example which high schools often unconsciously, tend to imitate. If university-level instruction takes the form of someone standing in front of a class and delivering a lecture, we can expect a great many high schools to "educate" by having someone stand in front of a class and deliver a lecture. If university instruction stresses laboratory investigation, or "ecological" studies of the local environment, these approaches are likely to appear in high school.

Universities help to establish the tone or climate of intellectual life generally. It is therefore important (and unfortunate) that at the moment universities tend to ignore, wherever possible, "practical arts" or "honorable crafts" and to rely instead upon a maximal use of verbal generalizations. This has even more consequence for the *pedagogical* side of high school mathematics than it has for the "content" or "mathematical" aspect. One university administrator has said (with regret) that "we live in the age of the musicologist." His meaning is all too clear: universities today find it easier to grant degrees in musicology (e.g., for *abstract* and *verbal* "studies" of music) than they do for skill in (say) playing the viola, or in composing string quartets. Similarly, they can offer credit and grant degrees for abstract studies of classroom behavior, but they fail to take seriously the actual *art* of teaching itself.

This has profound implications for all precollege teachers, whether in high school mathematics or anywhere else. If the school is to become, as John Gardner has hoped, a "self-renewing institution," then teachers must practice appropriate *personal* forms of growth and continuing learning. At present they are ordinarily led to pursue abstract studies in pedagogical methods that do not usually relate to their own actual teaching, or else they are cast in the role of dependent "clients" who receive instruction in more advanced mathematics. All too often they cannot approach this mathematics creatively, and may not even understand it; since they are themselves reduced to dependent client status, they turn around and treat their own high school students in this same way.

Possibly the most conspicuous aspect of the university is its nearly total fragmentation into departments that do not communicate with one another. The university usually shows little or no concern for educating a "whole" person in any sense whatsoever, but instead merely assembles, rather promiscuously, a collection of unrelated (and often unrelatable) pieces. In "student teaching," to give but one example, a prospective teacher may work under, and possibly learn from, an inadequately trained supervising teacher in a local school, where neither the supervising teacher nor the local school subscribes to the educational approach presented in the university's "methods of teaching" course. A mathematics course may be equally unrelatable to high school curricula. All of this randomness (or chaos) is sometimes justified on the grounds that it develops breadth in the student. At a more sophisticated level it is defended on grounds of "academic freedom"—nobody can tell a college professor how or what to teach. In fact, though, this incoherent randomness is a purely accidental (and very unfortunate) consequence of the internal disorganization of the university itself. One could create coherent programs with focus and emphasis, without discarding diversity and academic freedom. Present-day university management procedures have merely found this an unsolvable problem, but solutions could be developed.

The result of four years of such education is that the teacher does not become an autonomous self-renewing person, and the school therefore does not become a self-renewing institution either. When pressed (perhaps by his own desire to understand), the teacher can only once again return to the university as a dependent client of a rather menial sort.

Any significant improvement in schools must be related to some resolution of the university's approach to teacher education. Improvements can easily be imagined, and sporadic isolated efforts have occasionally even succeeded, temporarily.

Teachers can work together, as in England's "teacher study groups," to consider the improvement of mathematics learning in an integrated way. *The same people* can tackle the content and the pedagogy. Teachers can be inquirers, which can be a self-renewing role, instead of being "professionals," which usually means someone who, being afraid to show ignorance, is consequently unable to learn or to grow in any significant way. An integrated approach probably requires the recognition of teaching as an honorable craft, not to be studied by memorizing 10 basic verbal generalizations, but rather by *doing* mathematics creatively on an appropriate level, while simultaneously considering what high school students themselves can do.

What I propose for teachers has largely been achieved in most law schools. An excellent description of legal education is given in Martin Mayer's recent book *The Lawyers.* Law students get practical experience in courtrooms, and approach law via the "case-study" method. It is an interesting piece of irony that while law itself is nearly the apotheosis of attempts to deal with reality by means of verbal generalizations, the *study* of law is cast in the most practical and most active form possible. A good lawyer is in fact an inquirer, and he inquires in a quite practical fashion. In the long run, is there any other choice for the education of teachers?

3. INFLUENCES FROM THE SCHOOL COMMUNITY

Perhaps this heading is not completely accurate, for influences "close to" the school are nearly always related to the climate of opinion emanating from the universities, or else come from other specifically innovative schools, or from demands of the teachers' union, community-control parent groups, or student power advocates. But these influences at least cluster rather closely around the school itself.

Since the complete list is far too long for review here, I have made a few selections based on my personal likes and antipathies.

a) Conversations with Computers. One of my favorite innovations is the introduction of languages designed to facilitate "conversations" between human beings and computers; among these, my present favorite is *LOGO,* a language developed by Bolt, Beranek, and Newman, and now being used in grades two and three in a Newton, Massachusetts elementary school, in grade seven in a Lexington, Massachusetts junior high school, and (recently) in grade twelve in a Concord, Massachusetts senior high school. The potential importance of this can be seen by considering the quite large amount of literature (especially Joseph Featherstone's articles in *The New Republic*) that calls attention to possibly the greatest intellectual challenge met (and mastered) by all children: learning to speak their native language. Potentially LOGO, and similar computer languages, provide a second experience of comparable importance, but with significant differences, since the formal linguistic demands for man-machine communication are different from those for talk between one human and another. Control of ambiguity must be much tighter when dealing with a machine that makes little use of context, and no use whatsoever of common sense, in order to determine what you meant to say (as distinct from what you actually said).

Notice that LOGO-like "conversations with computers" do not put the child under the control of the computer (as computer-assisted instruction often does). This language approach is unique in another sense as well: it is not a matter of learning mathematics first and then employing a computer as an exercize in applications; on the contrary, one *first* learns to converse with the computer, *before* learning much mathematics, and then one gradually becomes experienced in mathematics as a result of using the computer to play games, to write letters, and to do whatever else one can think of to do with the computer. The emphasis is heavily on creativity, initiative, and originality. (The Concord twelfth graders used the computer to translate standard English into Pig Latin, and some students in Ithaca, New York programmed the computer to conduct a long conversation about who could use the car on Saturday evening.)

b) One Geometry Versus Several Geometries; One Algebra Versus Several Algebras. Traditional school mathematics has dealt with one geometry —Euclidean geometry—in a way that has strongly suggested that this is the only possible geometry. Twentieth-century mathematics, however, recognizes many different geometries. (The distinction is presented especially well in Irving Adler's book *Mathematics and Mental Growth.*) The situation in algebra parallels the situation in geometry. What raises problems for the immediate future is the fact that university teaching usually deals with many geometries (or with many algebras) at one fell swoop, by making powerful use of an abstract approach. (The word "abstract" means something different within mathematics. Within *pedagogy* the abstractions are mainly verbal generalizations, and the question is whether they are very helpful or not. By contrast, there is no question about the power and validity of abstractions *within mathematics.* After all, mathematics itself is abstract, and quite essentially so. The only question within mathematics is whether certain powerful abstractions can be understood by inexperienced students who have not previously encountered a large enough sprinkling of special cases. We may run the risk of summarizing a vast experience that these students have never had, and which they do in fact need.)

Traditional high school practice, then, deals with only one geometry, and with only one algebra. Modern university practice deals with many algebras all at once (by considering groups, rings, fields, and so on). What should the high school do in the years ahead? Will it continue the tradition of studying one single algebra and one single geometry? Should we instead adapt the university approach to the high school situation, and use powerful abstract methods, thereby dealing with *all* of the many different geometries at once (much as we add artichokes and avocados and strawberries by one single "abstract" arithmetic, and do not ordinarily develop one special arithmetic for adding

$$2 \text{ artichokes} + 3 \text{ artichokes} = 5 \text{ artichokes}$$

another special arithmetic for adding strawberries, and so on). Or shall we try to create an intermediate approach, where we study several geometries, but one at a time, using less abstract methods? (Again, a parallel question can be put for the case of algebras.)

c) Inductive Learning and Physical Embodiments. Perhaps the current emphasis on *inductive learning* (which is probably justifiably associated with three names: George Polya, David Page, and Jerome S. Bruner) is not so much something "new" as it is a recent return to something that was once commonplace, but has gradually been discarded and deserves to be reinstated. An example may best serve to explain what we mean by "inductive learning": If I wish to tell a student what "proportional variation" means, I have at least three choices of method:

(1) I might say: "The variable x will be called proportional to the variable y if $y = kx$, where $k \neq o$."

(2) I might use the following dialogue (more or less, anyhow):

TEACHER: If 1 pencil costs 3 cents, how much will 2 pencils cost?

STUDENT: 6 cents.

TEACHER: How much will three pencils cost?

STUDENT: 9 cents.

TEACHER: How much will ten cost?

STUDENT: 30 cents.

TEACHER: If I buy twice as many pencils, how much money will I spend?

STUDENT: Twice as much.

TEACHER: . . . and if I buy three times as many pencils?

STUDENT: You'll spend three times as much money.

TEACHER: [Having established an idea, he now proceeds to name it.] All right, when things work that way we say that "the cost of the pencils is proportional to the number we buy." Now suppose we go to another store [the teacher is now trying to establish the "boundaries" of the idea by considering a negative instance]. This new store wants to encourage large orders, and to discourage small orders under 25 cents, and they give a discount on large orders . . . ."

(We leave the rest of this conversation to the reader's imagination.)

(3) Finally, I might have the children study many functional relations, probably in some cases using concrete objects. For example, they might study the relation between the height of a vertical stick and the length of its shadow, by making actual measurements, working quickly so as to get done before the sun's position can change very much.

Table Showing Relation Between
Height of Stick and Length
of Shadow

HEIGHT OF STICK	LENGTH OF SHADOW
2 ft.	3 ft.
3 ft.	4½ ft.
4 ft.	6 ft.
5 ft.	7½ ft.

Similarly, they might use a graph to display the rate of growth of the perimeter (P) of one face of a cube, the area (A) of one face, and the volume (V) of the cube, plotted against the side (or "edge") of one face:

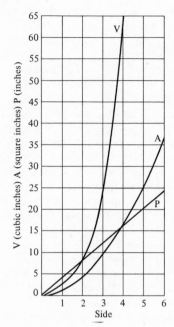

FIGURE 1.

After the children had carried out many such studies (or simultaneously, while they were doing so) we would introduce the kind of dialogue given in our second approach, and even the algebraic formulation used in the first approach.

Analysis of these Three Approaches. These three educational approaches might be described as follows: the first example is directly abstract and is couched in a symbolically-coded generalization; the second approach uses a specific instance, or several specific instances, from which the student's own mind is expected to create the appropriate generalization; and the third approach uses extensive actual experience as the point of entree, thereafter letting the child construct the generalization much as in the second approach. (Z. P. Dienes refers to this as the use of "physical embodiments" of the mathematical idea.)

From 1940 until the 1960s mathematics in the United States has been generally discarding concrete experience, and even much use of illustrative examples, and has been moving increasingly toward the abstract approach shown first above. Comparison of trigonometry, calculus, or even physics textbooks from the 1940s through the 1960s will generally confirm this. (Again, there is no question that a proper abstract formulation *at the proper time* has great value—indeed, the essence of mathematics, on the formal side at least, lies precisely in its ability to manipulate abstract statements of this sort by means of an appropriate logic.) For many students this growing tendency toward abstraction appears to have made the study of mathematics more difficult (although for some students it appears to have made it more rewarding and possibly actually easier). Individual differences in human thought processes are by no means well understood, but for many people it appears that their minds can easily perceive a few instances and from these construct an appropriate general principle, whereas their minds are not usually prepared to accept the general principle, in symbolic form, *ab initio*. (We have found this in children at least as young as four years of age, and thereafter for all ages greater than four, even throughout adult life.)

The use of the inductive method—*giving the children some instances and allowing the children to produce the generalization themselves*—has been dramatically illustrated with young children by David Page, and with high school-age children by Warwick Sawyer. It has been discussed from the point of view of a psychologist by Jerome S. Bruner, and from the point of view of a mathematician by George Polya and by W. T. Martin.

Thus, the first of our three illustrative approaches we would call the abstract symbolic approach. The second we would call the inductive approach.

What about the third approach, using sticks, cubes, etc.? This approach has been developed pedagogically by Edith Biggs and others (mainly in England), and has been conceptualized theoretically by Jean Piaget, Roger Brown, and others. It is obviously similar to the inductive approach, except that it begins by providing the child with what Roger Brown has called "massive readiness."

My own guess for the 1980s is that all three of these approaches need to be recognized, polished to a smooth finish, and put to work in our schools. This may be one important aspect of individual differences between students.

The distinction between these approaches will become especially important if we make greater use of computer-assisted instruction or programmed learning materials; indeed, a growing controversy is underway concerning the appropriateness of programmed learning of mathematics.

d) Programmed Instruction and Behavioral Objectives. Mathematicians usually view "doing mathematics" as something ranging from a human cultural tradition to an indecomposable "gestalt." Some recent psychologists and educators have developed a contrary interpretation: they break mathematics down into quite small pieces, and have the student learn these pieces carefully, one at a time, usually in some definite predetermined sequence. The hope is that the small pieces will accumulate like deposits in a bank account and will gradually emerge as a unified totality, the ability "to do mathematics." This possibility is likely to have a large impact on both high school and university mathematics.

Frequently but not necessarily related to this "atomistic" approach is the notion of beginning curriculum design by "stating explicit operationally-defined behavioral objectives" (which have come in some circles to be called BOs). Both the pedagogical approach of using the "bite-sized" pieces arranged in an inflexible sequence, and the theoretical interpretation of curriculum design in relation to a priori behavioral objectives, have become matters of pronounced disagreement. Both have devoted defenders and each has its articulate opponents, who are no less determined. The outcome can be guessed at, but what will actually ensue is (obviously) known.

Concerning "bites" versus "gestalts," my own surmise is that there are many cases where a murkiness in mathematics can be clarified, and difficulties eliminated, by judicious use of the procedure of breaking things down into small pieces and carefully sequencing these small pieces.

Concerning the stating of explicit behavioral objectives, I am also cautiously optimistic:

(1) BOs have been used so badly so often that one tends to suspect they are hopeless. More likely they are not. As has occasionally happened to the great religions, BOs often become an article of faith, and thereafter a ritualistic fetish, so that in some educational practice their actual value was lost sight of. If they are reconsidered, and once again regarded as *tools* (which they are) and not as tokens of acceptable orthodoxy (which seems everywhere to be but one step removed from sterility, then BOs can turn out, occasionally, to be *helpful,* not to identify the faithful, but to assist us in getting on with the job.

(2) The dogma that one *begins* by stating BOs is clearly wrong. The infant has not selected his career, the explorer has not at the outset seen his new world, and the investigator does not know a priori the phenomena he may encounter. *After* initial explorations, as many new directions begin to open up, an explicit consideration of objectives may concentrate effort, and may help us to measure *one aspect* of our progress. Of course, the price we pay for so tight

a focus is an inability to see the broader picture, and we are always in danger of building a castle in an area that the tide will soon sweep clean, a very real danger nowadays in education.

(3) There may well be valuable—indeed, priceless—educational experiences for which we cannot state behavioral objectives, and which must be taken whole (and without a priori prescriptive analysis) or else not at all. For me, visiting Westminster Abbey or Coventry Cathedral is in this category, and so is listening to any of Beethoven's last five string quartets. We must be very careful to see that such experiences are not neglected merely because we have no explicit "operationally-defined" behavioral objectives for them—and we must not destroy the value of a visit to Westminster Abbey by formulating behavioral objectives for it. . . .

Put together, the notion of programmed instruction and the notion of wisely-chosen behavioral objectives can, if they are used, completely remake high school and university mathematics. The traditional lecture might disappear, or almost disappear. Everything, from libraries and publishing houses to school architecture, stands a chance of being altered in quite fundamental ways.

The culture or gestalt notion of "doing mathematics" may or may not be irreconcilable with a minutely analytical approach. Probably we shall have to wait and see. But we might remember Gresham's law for education: a cheap and easy method may tend to drive out a subtle one that is not widely valued, irrespective of their relative merits in any profound sense. Here, too, we need to be careful. We may be losing something we have not yet even learned to value—like fresh air or clean water.

e) Advanced Placement Calculus. I value this not only because of what it offers to students—namely, a chance to roll up your sleeves and do some real mathematics—but even more because of what it offers to teachers. It is possibly our best available example, this side of the Atlantic, of what *teacher study groups* can mean. Around Boston, for instance, a group of teachers have been meeting for several years to study calculus, advanced calculus, and effective ways of helping high school students to learn calculus. This is the kind of autonomous, relevant, integrated study by professional people that is absolutely essential if schools are ever in fact to become self-renewing institutions.

f) Really Advanced Programs. By this title I do not mean to disparage twelfth grade calculus, but after all, learning in grade twelve what you would otherwise have learned in your freshman year at college is nice, but hardly very revolutionary. Very much more is possible, as the Madison Project demonstrated some years ago in Weston,

Connecticut, and as the Kaufman group (now at Carbondale, Illinois) demonstrated more recently at Florida's famed Nova School. Quite a large number of children can reach today's university-level mathematics *at least as early as grade eight.* This *is* remarkable. Even more remarkable is the fact that adults have largely ignored both experiments. The thought of ninth graders who know more than you or I may is possibly disquieting—indeed, *all* high-level achievement is disquieting. We invariably suspect some sort of foul play: keeping the poor kids up all night with homework, or rewarding them with candy pellets, at the very least. In point of actual fact, both the Weston experiment and the Nova experiment showed above all else *how very easy* it is for children to advance at this rate. It is probably a far better indication of their *natural* rate of progress than the present school program offers.

The conventional wisdom of educational research is hard pressed to analyze these experiments. You cannot do it by merely allowing the child to move through traditional material as quickly as he is able. The traditional material gets in his way, slows him down, limits him, turns him off. A jet is not merely a DC-3 where the pistons go up and down faster and the propellers rotate with unprecedented angular velocity. It is absolutely something else.

g) Changes in School Structure. In the summer of 1967 a group of professionals met on the campus of Pine Manor College in Wellesley, Massachusetts. A few were educators, but most were biologists, physicists, chemists, or mathematicians. Their task (under the Cambridge Conference for School Mathematics) was to outline a school curriculum that would relate mathematics and science as closely as possible—perhaps often even obliterating the distinction between "math" and "science."

I think it especially significant that small groups kept straying from this task, and found themselves irresistibly drawn to the job of designing quite different experiences from which children could learn—quite different experiences that were intended to occur in quite different settings. One group, for example, argued that high school is basically an imitation of the lecture-hall model of university education. But why should the high school borrow its form from the university? Might schools not look elsewhere for models? For example, how about a model based on common forms of industrial practice?

Incoming students would be interviewed, perhaps, by a "personnel" man—himself, of course a "student" in this form of "school." He might then proceed to meet with a "program planning group" that planned next week's activities, or possibly even today's lunch. Or he might work with a "purchasing office"—that bought materials for next week's program, or for today's lunch. He might work with a "production" group that *made* today's lunch, or operated this week's program. He might work with an "operations analysis" group that studied effectiveness and efficiency; or a "department of education" (I.B.M. has one) that instructs students in specific skills (notice that our student might be *teaching* for the department of education, or he might be studying there). He might be carrying out community service projects, or working on the "company in-house journal," or using a computer, or supervising a playground of younger children, or helping to write a history of the local community.

How would mathematics fit into this kind of social setting? The whole suggestion is hypothetical, so you may as well use your own imagination. I am impressed by the fact that professional biologists and professional mathematicians think that this could be an exciting setting for the effective study of science and mathematics.

4. THE WAY-OUT VIEW

In the preceding remarks I have deliberately restricted myself to a rather pedestrian projection of what we see right now. It is of course true that we live in an age where pedestrian projections may concern themselves with such matters as the instantaneous nuclear annihilation of 100 million United States citizens, the construction of an anti-ballistic missile system costing perhaps 400 billion dollars, and the venture of landing man and laboratories on the surface of the moon. All of this we seem able to accept in a prosaic and quite off-hand fashion.

In projections of high school education one might ask for more imaginative conceptions of future possibilities than any that I have mentioned thus far. To those of us within the profession whose daily work is aimed at freeing the immovable links in our metaphorical wire fence, even the most modest of plans sound utopian when we turn to the task of implementation. The prospects for change are nearly always bearish, almost never bullish.

But reading a recent essay by Paul Goodman ("The Present Moment in Education," *The New York Review*, April 10, 1969) convinces me—if I did not in fact believe it already—that I am wrong in considering only what other things we could do inside today's high school, or else what alternative forms of high schools might be built. There is, after all, at least one further possibility: we can search for alternatives to the high school itself. Is it in fact inevitable that young people can only grow and learn within the confines of a high school? Such a proposition seems highly unlikely and becomes more unlikely the more closely we examine it. Name anyone of great accomplishment and the odds are considerable, I think, that his formal education either terminated early, or at least suffered occasional interruptions. Why do we want all of our young people in school—for their sake, or for ours? Or is it because, despite films, television, and remote-access computers, we can still devise no other way in which young people can learn what they need to know? Or— and this is the sorriest reason of all—is it merely because we have come to do it in this way, and this, therefore, is the way we feel we must do it? Does our single educational approach exist because it exists, or because we are really unable to create any promising and viable alternatives?

I would argue that the most exciting prospects of all lie in the direction of devising a variety of alternative approaches for young people to move into effective adulthood. I believe we can do it.

The Reformed English Curriculum

Neil Postman

Not long ago, I attended a conference of courageous educators who met to discuss the theme "Teaching English in the 1970s and 1980s." I thought them courageous because they were willing to proceed with their discussions in spite of the possibility that (1) the planet will not be fit for human life in the seventies and eighties, (2) even if it is, there might not be "schools" as we normally think of them, and (3) such schools might not require "teachers." My main contribution was to suggest still another possibility: that there will be no such subject as "English" by 1980. What is called "English" is not a very old subject, in American schools at least, and it seemed worth remarking that there is no one who can safely predict what subjects the future will require. After all, the ancient Greeks could never have guessed what the high school curriculum of today would consist of. Neither could the Medievalists, the Elizabethans, nor the Pilgrims. Sixty years ago, Latin would have looked like a sure thing.

Perhaps what I meant to say at the conference was that there *ought not* to be such a subject as English by 1980; that English, as it is commonly taught, is shallow and precious, is not very interesting to most children, and, above all, has very little *survival value* for people who are going to live most of their lives in the seventies, eighties, nineties, and beyond.

I will not take time here to catalog the shortcomings of English. If you have not already noticed that English is withering away, being consumed by its own irrelevance, the chances are slim that I can make you see that this is, in fact, the case. I do want to point out, however, that what happens in school *should* have survival value (or what's an education for?) and that the soundest reason for having such a subject as English has always been that children *need* to be competent in using and understanding the dominant communication media of their own culture. When these media were largely limited to such forms as novels, poems, and essays, the content of English made some sense. My purpose here is to suggest an alternative to

English for the high school of 1980 when we will be so deeply immersed in the nuclear space age.

I call the alternative "media ecology." Its intention is to study the interaction between people and their communications technology. More particularly, media ecology looks into the matter of how media of communication affect human perception, understanding, feeling, and value; and how our interaction with media facilitates or impedes our chances of survival. The word ecology implies the study of environments: their structure, content, and impact on people.

An environment is, after all, a complex message system which imposes on human beings certain ways of thinking, feeling, and behaving. It structures what we can see and say and, therefore, do. It assigns roles to us and insists on our playing them. It specifies what we are permitted to do and what we are not. Sometimes, as in the case of a courtroom, or classroom, or business office, the specifications are explicit and formal. In the case of media environments (e.g., books, radio, film, television, etc.), the specifications are more often implicit and informal, half concealed by our assumption that what we are dealing with is not an environment but merely a machine. Media ecology tries to make these specifications explicit. It tries to find out what roles media force us to play, how media structure what we are seeing, why media make us feel and act as we do.

Media ecology is the study of media as environments.

Now, the first thing to be said about media ecology is that I am not inventing it. I am only naming it. There are more than a score of living media ecologists and another dozen or so who are no longer living. Among the latter are Edward Bellamey, Harold Innis, George Orwell, Aldous Huxley, Norbert Wiener, and Alfred North Whitehead. Among those who are currently doing important thinking in the field are Buckminster Fuller, Jacques Ellul, Marshall McLuhan, Peter Drucker, Herman Kahn, David Riesman, Ray Bradbury, Harold Lasswell, Don Fabun, Walter Ong, Edward Hall, Paul Goodman, Lyon White, Ruell Denney, Ronald Gross, Ashley Montague, and Edmund Carpenter. In one way or another, each of these men is asking the kinds of questions that are characteristic of media ecology. For example, their questions have to do with the present and the future. Mostly the future. Their questions also have to do with our chances of survival, and how to prepare ourselves intellectually and emotionally for media environments most of us do not quite believe in, and which we may not be able to control. (That we are all suffering even now, in some degree, from "future shock" can simply be taken for granted.)

One media ecologist, Edmund Farrell, is reflecting at present on the effects of medicine, space, and other technologies on our seminal metaphors for love, mystery, and wonder. When heart transplants or plastic hearts become commonplace, what will become of the "heart" as the symbolic source of human compassion? When the moon is found to be a desert of dust, where will lovers gaze? Have jet aircraft already "disappeared" the mystery and wonder of the sea? TWA has recently run an ad that stresses the fact that at 600 miles per hour the Atlantic Ocean is no more formidable to cross than the Mississippi. Where will we find our symbols of love and wonder? Is it important that we do? If we do, what changes will the new symbols make in our ritual life and in the structure of our symbology? Speaking of seminal metaphors, media ecologists are even now looking into the implications of semen banks. Should we have them? If so, who should run them? Will they enhance or degrade our concepts of "the dignity of man" and "the sanctity of life"?

Strange questions? They are the stuff of media ecology. Here is a spray of other questions. They are at different levels of conjecture, but of almost equal interest to media ecologists: What effects are television, film, LP record, transistor radio, etc., having on youth? To what extent are such media environments responsible for the generation gap? for student rebellion? for the search for self through drugs? What kinds of revolutions does TV cause? Are books obsolete? If so, when will we find out? If not, what useful purposes will they serve? Why, indeed, can't Johnny read? Will he ever? Why should he? What will be the long-range effects of the information explosion? Will it destroy hierarchies? Will it mean the end of organized religion? of the industrial state? Who will program the computers? What should we use them for? What will they use us for? Who should be forbidden to use them? Are schools obsolete? What uses shall we make of bugging devices? of the television-telephone? Do we need privacy? What will the pill do to our concepts of sex and marriage? of children? of religion? Will the electric car save our cities? At what cost? Are cities obsolete? Have mass media "repealed" the Bill of Rights? Have they made politics an offshoot of show business? If so, what should we do about it? What new kinds of politics will we require? What will be our new literary forms? Of what use will "tradition" be? What ideas will we need to forget? To what extent is technology remaking our language? Have the mass media polluted our language environment? To what extent is our language impeding our understanding of technology?

Politics. Literature. Art. Sex. Love. Education. Law. Death. Language. All of these have been and will be changed further by the new communications technology. And the worst and best part of it all is that no one knows for sure how, or when, or exactly why. That is why, when talking about the activities of media ecologists, one must use such verbs as "reflecting on," "looking into," "wondering about." In other words, media ecology has not yet developed firm methods of inquiry. At the moment, there are only fragments of methods available. Some media ecologists have popularized the use of language itself as an instrument of inquiry, in a manner somewhat akin to what I. A. Richards calls "feed forward." One makes discoveries about the world by inquiring into language, inventing new words, playing with metaphors, and in general searching for ambiguities and partially concealed meanings. Many media ecologists have used history as a "counter-environment" from which they can view contemporary happenings. Others have borrowed heavily from the methods of anthropologists in an effort to achieve some distance from what they wish to look at. Still others have relied upon their interpretations of art as a means of discovery, on the assumption that artists intuitively reveal what is happening in their own time. At this point, it is by no means clear that media ecology will turn out to be a science. Perhaps it will be an art form. Or some synthesis of both, in the manner of psychoanalysis. Certainly, no one has as yet come even close to inventing a thorough, or very useful, taxonomy of media ecology. Included in its current lexicon is everything from the language of jazz (hot media and cool media) to the language of science (entropy, feedback).

It goes without saying that media ecology has so far produced very few established facts and not even a handful of plausible theories. And that is exactly why media ecology lends itself so perfectly to the school curriculum of 1980: it is not yet a subject and may not be one for many years. Media ecology is a field of inquiry. Fields of inquiry imply the active pursuit of knowledge. Discoveries. Explorations. Uncertainty. Change. New questions. New methods. New terms. New definitions. A "subject" implies replicating, memorizing, ventriloquizing someone else's well-established answers to someone else's well-formed questions. A field of inquiry implies "a finding out." A subject implies "a parcelling out." That is why, in the school of the future, subjects (as we usually think of them) will have very little value. The school is no longer a viable medium for communicating what is already known, and hasn't been for at least a quarter of a century.

In the first place, there are too many already-knowns (subjects) to be encompassed by a "curriculum." There are dozens of subjects that are arbitrarily excluded from school: cybernetics, psychocybernetics, non-Euclidean geometries, astrophysics, psycholinguistics, archaeology, anthropology, linguistic philosophy, sociology, psychology, and so on. In short, most everything that's happened in the past 50 years. In the second place, the school cannot compete with other media as a means of information dissemination. What the book, magazine, newspaper, film, television, radio, and the rest started, the computer is certain to finish. The fact is that the amount of information that the school can make available to the young is so small in relation to the total and informal effort of the other media that it is, literally, not worth talking about. In the third place, what is already known is changing so rapidly that even well-established subjects have lost their stability. And the idea of a school subject is based on the notion of a stable content. One of the unpublicized scandals of our schools is that their present course divisions (English, history, chemistry, art, etc.) have about as much meaning as would a curriculum divided into such courses as phlogiston, earth, fire, water, and air. (Phlogiston would be an elective, of course.)

Thus, the curriculum of the future is most likely to consist of fields of inquiry from which students learn how to learn about that which is unknown. This means, of course, the end of instruction as the dominant means of structuring the classroom environment. It also means the introduction of many new fields of inquiry, of which media ecology may well be the most important.

How rapidly media ecology, or something like it, will replace the nineteenth century concept of English instruction is difficult to predict. "Subjects" die hard (which is another reason, in the nuclear space age, why they are inappropriate metaphors on which to base an educational program). Subjects generate specialists with vested interests. Specialists reproduce themselves wantonly. Establishments result from the whole process. But media ecology has some important things going for it: It is, first and foremost, *relevant* to what is happening in the world, and no farfetched and precious philosophies need be invoked to justify it. Media ecology is *necessary*. If the questions it asks are not asked, we may all lose our perspective, our sanity, and then our lives. Because media ecology deals with the unknown and the future, it is an invaluable instrument for helping the young to learn how to know the unknown and to prepare for change.

Then, too, the irrelevance of English (as grammar, print-literature, and composition) is becoming increasingly noticeable. Teachers are beginning to realize that the "newest" development in English, linguistics, turns out to be a new system for diagramming sentences. Even diehards are finding it something of a strain to "teach" English, and everyone seems to be asking, What is English, anyway? Finally, there is the irrevocable, uncompromising fact of the media themselves and the magnitude of the cultural transformations they are bringing. It is inconceivable that the schools of the future will be indifferent to all that.

Let us assume, then, that the schools will not be indifferent to all that. What might a 1980 high school class in media ecology be like? To begin with, the teacher will be quite different from his 1960 predecessor. Most likely, he will not regard himself as a specialist in a subject whose content he is committed to impart. Instead, he will be something of an expert in how to find things out, especially things whose answers cannot be found in libraries; that is to say, he will be oriented toward the future and its problems. He will think of a syllabus roughly in the way modern physicians think of blood letting: that is, he will understand why teachers of the past used a syllabus (or a textbook or a standardized test), but he will regard such procedures as wholly inappropriate to his own work.

But most of all, he will differ from today's teachers in his understanding of the role of a "teacher." He will not be much of a talker; rather a listener. Not much of an answerer; rather a questioner. Not much of a tester; rather a rewarder. Not much of a restricter; rather an opener. His work will consist largely of designing an environment in which high school students can learn how to ask questions, to distinguish between relevant and irrelevant questions, to invent methods of finding answers to their questions, to develop the capacity to conduct inquiries with rigor, and to apply the results of their work to some vital aspect of their lives.

His students would also have to learn how to be competent in the uses of all modern communication technologies. Thus, their learning environment would include the presence of tape recorders, TV cameras, photo-offset equipment, movie cameras, radio transmitters, telephones, television-telephones, still cameras, computers, etc. Such an environment implies that his students will be activists in the way that, at the moment, only student revolutionaries are. For example, it would be part of the study of media ecology for students to produce a regularly published newspaper, their own radio programs, their own TV programs, their own movies, their own architectural designs for cities, homes, schools, churches, and hospitals. The media ecology "class" may not even meet in a classroom because the answers to the questions the students would be asking would have to be found in the process of their *doing* something and, in such circumstances, who would have time to attend class?

Below are several examples of inquiries and projects that a high school group in 1980 could conduct as a part of their media ecology "course:"

1. What are the language and other symbol differences that exist among the various people in their community?

Obviously, one result of such a study might be the publication of a glossary, or dictionary, or even a linguistic atlas. The point is that this information is largely unknown and is, in any case, constantly changing. But such an inquiry would also lead to studies of the form, meaning, and impact of verbal and nonverbal symbols. Media ecologists are, of course, greatly interested in symbology, and any inquiry into language moves quickly to such questions as: How do symbols "start?" How do symbols change? How can people be made to "forget" important symbols? What are some dangerous symbols? Some good ones? How can you tell?

2. In what ways are the perspectives and attitudes of young people different from those of older people in relation to sex, drugs, politics, work, leisure?

The important questions here are: What kinds of evidence would be acceptable? What methods can be used to obtain such evidence? In what practical ways can communication among young and old be facilitated?

Such inquiries might lead to the production of a series of TV or radio programs produced, written, directed, performed by students; studies of differences in language, clothing, manners, fears, rituals, etc. Obviously, in this inquiry (as well as most others in media ecology) conventional subject matter lines are crossed and recrossed. For example, what we presently call psychology, sociology, anthropology, and aesthetics would be involved in getting at these questions.

3. In what ways will new technologies affect various institutions, beliefs, and definitions in the society, e.g., churches, schools, marriage, voting, patriotism, justice, etc.?

Since the students may be the only significant group in the culture examining these questions systematically, they might produce for the rest of us a series of articles, monographs, even books, as well as film documentaries on this subject. Again the key questions are: What evidence is acceptable? How and where can it be found? What, if anything, can be done to avoid disorder? How does one make predictions about the future? The students might write, draw, film, photograph (whichever is appropriate) projections of the future of various institutions: What will our schools be like? Will we have schools? Will people marry? Will they vote? Pray? Will nations exist? Will there be world law? Who will administer it?

4. What should be the characteristics of those in leadership roles in the year 2000?

This question presupposes that the students will spend time considering which values and symbols need to be preserved, and which ones need to be "forgotten." Perhaps the students could design a whole school system that would help to reinforce those attitudes and behaviors that they believe the future will require. I would not be surprised if their inquiries led to some serious work in "sensitivity training" or some similar method of increasing self-knowledge.

5. In what ways do the mass media inform or misinform the public on vital issues?

This question could lead to the production of films, pamphlets, newsletters, etc. that would monitor the information environment created by the mass media. For instance, one group of students might engage in trying to verify the accuracy of statements made on news broadcasts. Another group of students might engage in designing alternative methods of electing representatives and of increasing the viability of participatory democracy. For this purpose, a media ecology group might wish to plan a constitutional convention whose purpose it would be to restructure our system of government to fit the communications technology of the twenty-first century. It would be easy to imagine the students corresponding with lawyers, engineers, artists, philosophers, etc. from all over the world to solicit their opinions on this problem. Moreover, it would be highly desirable for the students to govern their own school: to establish criteria for judging performance, to arrange for the purchase and use of media within the school, and to determine ways in which the school can serve the community. This last point is a particularly important one. Every media ecology group ought to be deeply involved in finding ways to relate to the community that surrounds the school. For example, media ecology classes could inform communities on all laws relating to media and technology. Students could produce a weekly journal of media criticism, in which films and radio and TV programs are evaluated. Students could also publish a newsletter which would comment on community problems, especially emphasizing those that are perpetuated through semantic misunderstanding.

6. What can be learned of future problems through the study of communications history?

In this inquiry, students would immerse themselves in the study of the history of communications with a view toward understanding how new media change society. Fortunately, there is relatively little known about this process, and students will have an authentic opportunity to contribute to scholarship in the "social sciences." It may even be possible for students to discover some as yet unformulated principles of social change.

7. What are the characteristic art forms of today? What might be the art forms of the future?

Here the students would be engaged in the production of art forms, as much as analyses of them. The class would produce a steady stream of folk songs, comic strips, cartoons, advertisements, comedy routines, photographic essays, collages, pop, concrete and found poetry, radio plays, etc. The only time an art form becomes something to "appreciate" (in the school sense) is when it is dead: that is, when it no longer has any impact on the culture. It is not so difficult to imagine a time when some of the best contemporary art will come from high school students, *if* art is thought of as inseparable from contemporary technology.

No one knows, of course, what all of this would mean to the schools of 1980. You would have a situation where the students knew more than their teachers, where state departments of education would be unable to use conventional standards of teacher certification, where commercial textbooks would be practically useless, where guidance counsellors would be extraneous, where conventional school administration would be impossible, where the schooling process would be indistinguishable from the educative process, where the usual method for selecting and training teachers would have practically no value, where ordinary high schools would be one of the richest sources of research and idea production in the community, where universities would be forced to organize themselves on some other basis than majors, minors, subjects, courses, departments, divisions, credits, grades, etc. (No self-respecting media ecologist would accept such arbitrary, even bizarre, categories.)

As puzzling as all of this may sound, one must understand that the world of 1980 and beyond will make very severe demands on the schooling process. No serious English teacher can believe that the future will be accommodated by reforms in methods of diagramming sentences, or by replacing old book lists with new ones, or by adding units in logic and the history of language. No serious English teacher can believe that the future cries out for improved methods of teaching composition. The future, quite simply, will require the pursuit of relevance; and this, in turn, will require a new subject, a new teacher, and a new student. Toward this end, I offer media ecology.

The Reformed Social Studies Curriculum

Charles R. Keller

The purpose of education in general and of the social studies in particular should be to help young people come to grips with, and begin to find answers to, that most basic of all questions, Who am I? Such is the case in 1970; it will be even more true in 1980. For who among us believes that life a decade hence will be any less difficult than it is today, that it will be any less fragmented, that there will be any less need for self-identity, inner resources, and inner unity? In 1970 the poet, William Butler Yeats, seems prophetic in his 1920 poem "The Second Coming." The first verse goes:

Turning and turning in the widening gyre
The falcon cannot hear the falconer;
Things fall apart; the centre cannot hold;
Mere anarchy is loosed upon the world,
The blood-dimmed tide is loosed, and everywhere
The ceremony of innocence is drowned;
The best lack all conviction, while the worst
Are full of passionate intensity.

In 1980 the "falcon" will be hearing the "falconer" and the "centre" will be holding only if, among other things, we have education concerned with the Who am I question. Young people will be living in a world they did not make; they will need an education that will help them to live effectively and responsibly in this world—and perhaps to change it.

So, what needs to be done in the field of the social studies? Change there has been during the past decade but not the revolution that some people—I have been one—have been calling for. What should be the ingredients in a real revolution, insofar as a revolution is possible? I am prepared to dream, but I insist on dreaming realistically.

I begin not with organization, not with content, not with schedule, not with technology and media, but with people—with teachers. Much change is in order. Teachers will have to forget *their* version of "It's what's up front that counts." They will need to belong to the "draw it out" rather to the "pour it in" and the "pour it on" school of teaching and to become associates-in-learning with the students. They must have such confidence in young people that they will give them ample opportunities to do real independent work. One characteristic of a good teacher is his willingness on some occasions to give a student an hour to find out something for himself that he the teacher could have told him in five minutes.

A great teacher once said, "A teacher is first of all a very, very careful listener." She was right. Teachers must learn how to listen. Young people not only want to be listened to but are worth listening to.

Teachers will have to side with Henry Adams who wrote in *The Education of Henry Adams*, "Nothing is so astonishing in education as the amount of ignorance it accumulates in the form of inert facts." The emphasis should be on problem-finding not problem-solving as is advocated today—although I must say that the latter is an improvement on what I have often called the new three Rs of education —restraint, rote memory, and regurgitation. Here we have made a start. Two students in an interdisciplinary humanities course recently set themselves the problem of finding out just what kind of president John F. Kennedy had really been. One was violently pro-Kennedy, the other violently anti-Kennedy. They realized that they had been very young when Mr. Kennedy was assassinated and that they felt as they did on the basis of prejudice; they set themselves their own problem. Two other students in this same humanities course were stirred by Lawrence Ferlinghetti's poem, "I Am Waiting," which concludes:

and I am awaiting
perpetually and forever
a renaissance of wonder

They expressed their feelings in a colorful, skillfully-made mosaic. And another student in another humanities course, bothered by the drug problem, made a movie to show his attitude. I could go on.

It is clear that revolutionary changes in teacher education must take place. Teachers will have to learn to meet young people where they are. That sometimes overused word "relevance" will need to have real meaning for teachers, for students in 1980 will respond only to education that has a significant and recognizable bearing upon their lives. "Relevance," by the way, does not mean "presentism" and does not refer only to the contemporary. Socrates and Sir Thomas More can be very relevant if approached in the proper manner. In 1980 when an older person shakes his finger at a young person and says, "When I was your age . . . ," the young person will say, "But you never were my age." Indeed, this reply should be given in 1970.

Teachers will have to know their subjects and—equally important —must either be acquainted with other subjects or have real respect for them. They will need to become used to working with other teachers. Class-centered, course-centered, subject-centered, teacher-centered education, punctuated by bells, hopefully will be on the decline in 1980, and what I call "humanities education"—man-centered, idea-centered, experience-centered, interdisciplinary—will be on the rise. Groups of students will be working with groups of teachers for blocks of time, and students will have considerable *un*scheduled time, with teachers available for consultation. A whole new approach to teaching will need to be developed—less lecturing, less "telling," less asking of questions to which teachers already know the answers. There should also be less textbook-learning and less concern about grades. Education should be "becoming." Students must really be involved in what they are doing.

Much learning will be done outside what is now called the class-room—in other parts of the school or outside the school. One April day a group of ninth graders had an exciting experience at Williams College and in the Francine and Sterling Clark Art Institute in Williamstown, Massachusetts. In the college library they learned something about rare books and saw and heard about the Paul Whiteman Collection. After lunch a Williams College professor gave a talk, "Two Ways of Looking at Things: the Utilitarian and the Aesthetic"—using a fork, a Robert Francis poem "The Base Stealer," and a photograph of a Renoir painting *Onions*, in the Clark Art Institute. Later the young people visited the Art Institute —an art teacher was with them—and looked at paintings, pieces of sculpture, and silver in a new way. That night when the students were getting out of the bus, one young man said, "Hey, that was better than school, wasn't it?" And another young man replied, "Today that *was* school, and that's the way school ought to be. We should take the classroom into the world more than we do." How right he was—for 1970 and for 1980! Such expeditions will be com-mon in 1980; in addition students from many schools will be having a variety of experiences in their communities.

There will have to be changes in teaching, teacher education, and learning by 1980. Furthermore, teaching loads should be drastically reduced and teachers should have fewer of the onerous duties that have nothing to do with teaching. Administrators and school boards must take new looks at teaching and learning and must encourage and initiate not mere innovations but revolutionary changes in the structure and the spirit of education.

During the next decade much new material and many new teaching aids will appear. Textbooks will be relegated to the kind of use dictionaries receive. In their place will be materials that make possible real inquiry and discovery. Technology will be playing an important role in education, what with computers and information retrieval, TV programs that can be put on when wanted, films, slides, videotaped programs, etc. But men must be telling technology what they want and when. It should not be a case of robot-like teachers—and students—in computer land.

What about courses? What will the social studies curriculum look like? Will there be courses? Certainly there should be even less of a national pattern than at present. With the purpose of the social studies changed—not to make good citizens, not to fill students with facts, but to help them understand who they are—the emphasis will be less on specific content and coverage and more on comprehending the past and present and developing ways of living in a confusing world. I talk about an inner space program. We have an outer space program and have spent billions of dollars to put men on the moon. The inner space program will put men into their own hearts and minds.

Current attempts to race through world history will be abandoned. Instead, post-holing will be in style, the consideration of selected periods, areas, events, ideas, and persons in some depth with needed wires strung between the posts in the form of reading and lectures. The aim will be to tie in the "Where have I come from?" with the "Who am I?" In the years preceding this experience there should be an introduction to the social sciences that will acquaint students with economics, political science, geography, anthropology, and sociology and with the methods of social scientists. Throughout the social studies program the social sciences will play an important role.

The isolation of one country's history from that of other countries will be questioned. One day in an advanced placement class in European history the unification of Italy was being discussed. A student wondered why the unification took place when it did rather than earlier or later. We thought of other developments during the two decades 1850–1870, and we found not only the unification of Italy but also—the unification of Germany, a new Japan, a new United States, a new Canada, a new Austria-Hungary, a new France, the freeing of the serfs in Russia, the Taiping Revolution, trouble in

India, the discovery of oil in the United States, the publication of Darwin's *Origin of Species* and the first volume of Karl Marx's *Das Kapital,* and the appearance of new forms in art and in music. "It was a renaissance," said one young man. The term *"renaissance"* was questioned; we decided that the period should be called the "naissance." The "naissance" of what? Of the world we live in. We hoped that some day in some single course all the events and developments mentioned would be studied. This kind of course should be quite common in 1980.

Hopefully many courses will begin with the present and will then take looks at the past in ways that throw light on how we got where we are. Not long ago, a group of not-go-to-college students were questioned about their American studies course (more on this subject later). I asked, "How much do you know about the Spanish-American War?" and received the answer that I expected, "Not much." "That's too bad," I continued. "You should know quite a bit about that war." When a young man asked, "Why?" I was taken aback, hemmed and hawed, and finally said, "Well—then you might understand a little better why we are in Vietnam." The student countered, "I have read about Vietnam, but I have never seen any mention of the Spanish-American War." And he went on, "Why not start with Vietnam? Then someone may ask how we got there, and the Spanish-American War can be brought in in a meaningful way."

The present repetition of American history—frequently in grades five, eight, and eleven—will, I hope, be eliminated. A friend with three children, one in each of the grades just mentioned, recently said to me, "Come over to our house some evening when the young people are studying American history. It's gruesome." Such repetition is bad for students and teachers. By 1980 American studies should be the eleventh grade course, with no standardization of the course and no textbooks.

Let me illustrate what I mean by American studies. The Puritans can be studied through their writings, a play, novels and short stories, and architecture. The search for American independence can be considered through politics, economics, military developments, expansion, literature, art, architecture, and music. Attention should be given to selections from Alexis de Tocqueville's *Democracy in America,* published in the 1830s but still relevant in 1970 and 1980. (I am intrigued by two voyages that began in 1831, that of de Tocqueville and that of Charles Darwin in the *Beagle.* Perhaps somebody would take time out, as I would, to study these two men, where they went and why, what they did, and what they wrote.)

In some schools the period from the Civil War to World War I will come alive by beginning with a consideration of Charles Ives the musician, Louis Sullivan the architect, Theodore Dreiser the novelist, Walt Whitman the poet, and William James the philosopher. The values of the people of this era will be revealed by their attitudes toward these men; and a study of the causes and the result of these values will throw light on the political activities and the economic developments of the times—and *vice versa*. Change in the twentieth century can be considered in the fields of politics, economics, science, cities, music, art, literature, civil rights, attitudes toward war, etc.

The whole curricular pattern in the social studies need overhauling. Courses with such titles as "Cities," "Protest Movements," "Revolutions," "The American Dream," "Elections," "Utopias," and "Russia (or China) in the Twentieth Century" should be introduced —that is, if there are still courses. Or studies of individuals at different times and in different parts of the world. I have long wanted to try using four documents as points of departure: the Mayflower Compact, the Declaration of Independence, the Constitution, and William Golding's *Lord of the Flies.* When Upton Sinclair, Norman Thomas, and John Steinbeck died almost simultaneously, I asked, "Why not a study of these three men and their times?" Possibilities are and will be unlimited. These courses—I hope they will be interdisciplinary "experiences"—should be man-centered, as I have said, and they do not have to have the all-too-common semester and year "time tags." Why not break the familiar time patterns and limitations?

Courses in Afro-American history? I hope not in high schools. I want blacks and whites to be considered as *Americans.* American history—or American studies—should be thoroughly rethought with a view to doing justice to all groups. It seems to me that blacks and whites should be treated as immigrants—different kinds of immigrants—into this country and studied as such. Where did they come from? Certainly Africa should be studied not just as such but as the homeland of more than 20,000,000 Americans. I recall that a friend of mine says, "The real 'dark' continents are Europe and America. The people there know so little about Africa." Where did these immigrants come from, I repeat. Why? What happened to the different groups? Why? What about their cultures? Where are we today? Where do we go from here? Relevant? Nothing could be more relevant.

What about advanced placement courses in 1980? They may still be necessary, but I hope not. We used to say that we liked the advanced placement program because it would be most successful when it was no longer needed. In 1970 advanced placement courses and examinations in history are only beginning to reflect as much as they should new developments in the social sciences, history, and other aspects of the humanities. In 1970 it sometimes seems in order to wish for a few school-level courses in colleges. In 1980 let's hope that schools and colleges will be working together in such ways that colleges will pick up students where they are and give them exciting experiences. Then the advanced placement program will have fulfilled its purposes.

At this point I turn to one of the most important and interesting developments in American education that may well be the key to education in general and to the social studies in particular in 1980. I refer to the interdisciplinary humanities courses that have appeared in schools around the country. These courses provide a needed challenge to the separate-subject-dominated curricula that we find in most schools. They get at the fragmentation in education that is so much with us—fragmentation in time (note the school day), fragmentation in space (note too many school buildings), fragmentation in subjects (we have too much "academic segregation"), and fragmentation in teachers (most students identify with one teacher and one subject rather than with an intellectual experience). I have become an ardent antifragmentationist.

In these courses young people find the relevance and the relationships that they are seeking. That question, Who am I? is at the heart of humanities courses. They are concerned with ideas and values rather than just with facts. Learning takes place in a new context. Humanities courses can be parts of an inner space program with emphasis on inner resources. What good is a collection of facts without inner resources? By inner resources I mean an identification with the past and with one's neighbors, an acquaintance with the decisions people have made in the past and are making now, a knowledge of the bases on which decisions have been made and are being made; the development of the powers of judgment, sensitivity, taste, compassion, wisdom, imagination, and delight; a willingness to face up to things as they are—without illusions; an awareness of the fact that acts have consequences; a variety of interests; and a desire to be creative in one way or another. When I think of inner resources, I think of the humanities.

In humanities courses, as I have indicated, there is problem-finding. Much independent work is possible; students spend less time confined to classrooms. Education can really be discovery, and among the things that young people discover are themselves.

Art, music, and the dance get new positions in the curriculum and add new dimensions to education and to life. A not-go-to-college student recently said of his American studies-humanities course, "It's about time that history included literature, art, music, and the dance." "The work of the painter, the musician, and the poet," John Herman Randall has written, "teaches us how to use our eyes, our ears, our minds, and our feelings with greater power and skill." In these courses can be what William James liked—"knowledge by aquaintance"—rather than what he disliked—"knowledge by description." Ralph Waldo Emerson was once boasting that Harvard offered all branches of knowledge. "Yes," said his friend Henry David Thoreau, "all the branches and none of the roots." The humanities provide the roots.

Humanities courses are for both go-to-college and not-go-to-college students; most of them at present are for twelfth graders. They have, and should have, no pattern in content or organization. They should grow out of the interests and talents of teachers and students. One course began last year with the art, music, and literature of the present, went back to the Greeks, moved forward to the Renaissance, dealt with the eighteenth and nineteenth centuries, and returned to the present. On one occasion the students were listening to "July 4" by Charles Ives. The young man sitting next to me began to thumb through his notebook. Soon he pointed to a poem by e.e. cummings that goes in part, "Next to of course God Amerca I love you." "Mr. Ives is saying in his music, "the student exclaimed," the same thing that Mr. Cummings is saying in his poem." "Never forget this moment of discovery, relevance, and relationship," I said.

Another course is concerned with the humanities in three cities—fifth century B.C. Athens, renaissance Florence, and modern New York. Here is a student comment:

The humanities course seems to pull things together so well, and in this unity I find an emotional stability. But humanities to me is not a security but a chance to grow.

In a third course, taught by one teacher, students read important books and become acquainted with the community through talks by people in the community and by visits to museums, concerts, and the theater. After reading John Milton's *Paradise Lost* and Robert Bolt's *A Man For All Seasons* in this course and learning about Adam and Eve and their expulsion from the Garden of Eden and about Sir Thomas More, a young lady wrote:

My humanities course has provided me with the beginning of answers not only to the "Who am I" question, but also to the "Why am I" question. . . . Maybe some day the Sir Thomas More in me will overcome the Adam in me.

I like the statement about a course for the so-called "disadvantaged." The approach is described as follows:

> Providing students with vital, dramatic experiences relevant to their own lives, . . . providing them with these experiences through the arts, then provoking and guiding discussion. . . . The method is inductive or Socratic, proceeding from an immediate experience which the class has in common—a painting, film, symphony—to generalizations they can make about that experience. . . .

And ninth graders in a humanities course in an inner-city school considered ancient Greece, western Africa, Civil War America 1840–1875, and modern America 1920–1968. In addition, each student considered another culture and prepared a paper and a visual project. The aim of this course was "to make more relevant the various disciplines by integrating history, literature, art, music, drama, foods, clothing, science, philosophy, and economics into one course."

Numerous other varieties of humanities courses have appeared, most of them taught by teachers working together. Many are allotted more than one period; many include "taking the classroom into the world"; some meet in special humanities centers. Testing is at a minimum, and the traditional type of testing is frequently nonexistent. Students keep journals. There is lessened emphasis on grades. One of the goals is to help young people read and really understand, look and really see, listen and really hear, feel and really be involved.

In 1980 there will be many more, and many new kinds of, humanities courses. Indeed, we may have "humanities education" and a real revolution in the social studies and in education in general.

By "humanities education" I mean man-centered, idea-centered, experience-centered, interdisciplinary education that includes not only the humanities but also the social sciences and the sciences. We are moving in this direction in the humanities and the social sciences. In science we find exciting ecological stirrings, and by 1980 great strides forward should have been taken in the study of man in relation to all the elements in his environment. I am now thinking and talking about—in C. P. Snow's terms—"an education for the third culture." Only man who has studied man can live as man. Mrs. Esther Raushenbush, former president of Sarah Lawrence

College, was saying what she wanted in *college* education when she wrote:

The chance to discover the important questions, to discuss ideas, to explore humanistic studies, not as academic subjects but as a way of being, serves students' search for a value system as well as for knowledge.

I want the same for *high school* education.

The fragmentation in time, space, subjects, and teachers that I have mentioned will be lessened in "humanities education." By-the-bell, by-the-course, by-the-subject, by-the-teacher-in-the-usual-sense-of-the-word education will be eliminated. Not long ago in a social studies class a film strip on Russia was shown, part of which had to do with Pavlov's dogs. Believe it or not, just after Pavlov's dogs went off the screen, the bell rang and the students sprang out of their seats. I was the only person who thought it was funny. Whether the students were salivating or not, I do not know. I suspect not. Certainly bells should be silenced by 1980—not merely by turning them off as is now done in a few schools but as a result of radically restructured education.

In "humanities education" more learning than we can now envisage will occur outside the classroom in 1980. The museums and performing arts centers are already on the move and will be important associates with schools in new ways a decade hence. As I write, a Metropolitan Museum of Art publication is on my desk, together with reports of the activities of the Lincoln Center for the Performing Arts and the Saratoga Performing Arts Center. These institutions and others like them throughout the country are prepared to work with the schools—with both students and teachers—in really effective ways. And the communities themselves will be laboratories in which young people will do much learning.

"Poetry," Robert Frost once said, "begins in delight and ends in wisdom." "Humanities education" will begin in delight and continue on into wisdom. In Mr. Frost's poem, "What Fifty Said," are these lines:

When I was young my teachers were the old.
I gave up fire for form till I was cold.

"Humanities education" will combine "fire" *and* "form."

In *King Lear* Lear says to the blinded Gloucester on the heath, "You see how this world goes," and Gloucester replies, "I see it feelingly." Humanities education will help young people to "see feelingly" and to "feel seeingly."

In a few places around the country partial humanities education is under way in 1970. In one high school, for instance, seniors have a humanities experience for half of each day, with so-called regular classes during the other half in foreign languages, mathematics, and science. Students together with teachers of history and the social sciences, English, music, art, and the dance are deeply involved as "The Public Man," "The Private Man," "Man and Woman," and "Man and Society" are considered. A speaker talked with the seniors and then wrote:

What I didn't expect was the lack of tension, the freedom, the gaiety, silliness, and ease the students seemed to have. It was all so natural and joyful. And the pride and enthusiasm of the teachers I met both in their program and their students. . . .

More visitors to more schools should be making such comments in 1980.

A real revolution in the social studies by 1980? Perhaps not, but we may be well on the road. Young people deserve and must have nothing less—young people who ask "Who am I?"

In a high school one day some students gave me their version of the Robert Frost (I keep coming back to him) line, "I had a lover's quarrel with the world." Their version was, "We have a lover's *query* with the world." Many things must be done if we are to keep it "a lover's query."

The Reformed Foreign Language Curriculum

A. Bruce Gaarder

In the brief span of 10 years before 1980 nothing is likely to happen to make high school foreign language teaching and learning entirely different from these activities today. Nevertheless, certain trends—some of them discernible in the schools today —will likely be strong features of 1980 and in the final two decades of the century should completely revolutionize foreign language work for both teacher and learner. The prognosis of marked improvement for both is clear.

Much of what I have read and heard lately—both before and after Marshall McLuhan—indicates that we are heading toward one or more super-ethnic cultures of some kind, super cultures going beyond the bounds of any present nation, or region, or ethnic group. Knowledgeable prognosticators are saying, for example, that by 1980 or close to it all unrestricted information, all cf what libraries now contain and most of what schools now transmit will be immediately, almost instantaneously, available to anyone—thanks to digital computer technology—anywhere that there is an information outlet. Already there are such access stations (to lesser collections of data, be it said) in some schools and some homes. They are saying that the learner's problem will no longer be to acquire facts and store them in the mind, because anyone who wants that kind of knowledge will be able to satisfy himself effortlessly. Learning, even more important then than now, will begin to have a new focus, on information classification and retrieval and on the skills and strategies of analysis and synthesis and the perception of relationships. In support of this forecast they are estimating that the present total number of "bits" of nonredundant information in all the libraries of the world would come to about 10 to the 15th power bits.* That is something like a quad-

---

* "Prospective Changes in Society by 1980," Edited by Edgar L. Morphet and Charles O. Ryan, Reports Prepared for the First Area Conference, Designing Education for the Future—An Eight-State Project, Denver: 1362 Lincoln Street, Denver, Colo. 80203, 1966.

rillion. Already there is on the market a computer with a direct access memory capacity of 10 to the 12th power bits. Perhaps knowledge will double quantitatively by 1980, but the capacity of the computer probably will too. In other words, we would be close to the point where all of the "facts" could be available immediately to anyone. Therefore, why learn them?

This, together with the omnipresent spying eye of television, is the basis for McLuhan's assertion that we will become like one tribe again, a tribe in which everyone has all the facts that matter—including all the facts about you—immediately at hand.

In a world which seems on its way toward the homogenization of all peoples, toward imposing a gray oneness on humankind, what will be the need and the chance for learning and teaching foreign languages? What the changes? I see more need and more chance than ever before. And I see some changes.

World-wide egalitarianism, usually thought of as a levelling, blurring force, really has two antithetical or complementary manifestations. One tends indeed to make us all alike. The other, strangely enough, finds every group demanding equality for its own unique way of being human. In terms of language usage, we find ever-increasing efforts worldwide to acquire English (or French, and eventually Russian or Chinese) as a second language of science and world affairs. Those professional grammarians, our scientific, English-as-a-second-language linguistic brethren, are in demand everywhere, catering to the world's death-wish campaign to anglicize itself. (Never underestimate the power of grammar.) At the same time each group wants, above all, the right to be human in its own ways and in its own language. Examples of this latter contradictory manifestation of egalitarianism abound. We see it in Quebec in the movement to give the French language and its speakers preeminence. We see it increasingly among the Mexican-Americans in our Southwest and among Puerto Ricans wherever they may be. The American Indians too are beginning to ask why they should be required to abandon their own tongues in order to be first class humans in this country. India provides numerous capital examples. The Welsh have not given up their language. Nor have the Irish. Speakers of Cakchiquel and Quiché in Central America want schooling in their own tongues. It is not unreasonable to predict that speakers of Quechua in Peru will one day reopen the question of the conquest of New Spain. During the student unrest and rioting in France in 1968 one question that was asked forcefully in southern France concerned Provençal, the *langue d'oc:* Why should it not be a medium of instruction in some schools, along with French? Donald Walsh has observed that in our own country, in Alaska, about 20 percent of the people were until recently first-class people—in Eskimo and Aleut. With the coming of statehood and the political and economic dominance of English they are relegated to second-class status and they resent the change.

In the American civil rights movement the Negro wants education equal to that given to children of the dominant group, which would supposedly mean control of a standard variety of English. Yet it has already strongly occurred to him that maybe his speech is the "real language" and he should not abandon it. When I was a lad there were hordes of heathens to be served and saved. In my town the ladies' aid society met one afternoon a month mending old clothes for their missionaries to distribute to the heathen. What has become of the heathen? It seems they are no more. The people who used to get the old garments and the word now come to Washington, D.C. dressed in Brooks Brothers clothes. This is homogenization. But they also erect a beautiful "heathen" temple on a main avenue of the dismayed nation's capital and demand respect for their own language. They are all right already. No one expects them to change, and it has become embarrassing even to use the word "heathen."

What this means is that although in the year 1980 the whole world will be a step closer to speaking Chinese or English or Russian as second languages, there is going to be an ever greater need for warmly empathic whispering in the other person's ear in her own language.

Unless ways are found to speed up or replace the process which we call memory (I am taking note of the recent work with magnesium pemoline and ribonucleic acid) we may safely assume three constants of foreign language learning in 1980, and no less in the year 2000. The first I have already stated: the need to communicate with each man in his own tongue.

The second constant is the language itself—any language—that though a continuously evolving system cannot be expected in 12 or 32 or 132 years to have altered significantly its relationship to the learner's tongue.

The third constant is that foreign (or second) languages are learned in one of two ways or in a combination of these ways: either by "natural" learning between ages 3 and perhaps 12, which occurs when the child is totally involved—at home, school, or play—in situations where the language is an unstressed but inescapable means to life's other more meaningful ends; or by "structured" learning through a systematic presentation making formal demands on the learner's analytical and analogical faculties. ("Natural" learning before age 3 is not considered here because it too closely approaches native or mother tongue acquisition.)

All other factors bearing upon foreign language learning are modifiable or dispensable: the difficulty of access to native speakers and the native environment, all methods and materials, the "motivation," the times and places for learning, the entire pupil-teacher-school relationship.

NATURAL FOREIGN LANGUAGE LEARNING

Thanks to a nation-wide movement, now only incipient, in support of bilingual schooling (the use of two languages as media of instruction for any part or all of the school curriculum) it can be expected—if all goes well—that by the year 1980 a good deal of all foreign language learning by American children will be a special kind of "natural" learning, chiefly through bilingual education in the elementary and high schools but supplemented by extensive travel and study abroad. Thirty and more mother tongues will be taught—along with English—to thousands of the millions of our children whose mother tongue is not English. This is to say that a very significant proportion of all "foreign language" learning will be accounted for by American youngsters learning—becoming fully literate in—their own non-English mother tongues. Today, it should be noted, these children, with minor exceptions, find that the schools either deplore or ignore, and invariably neglect, this linguistic resource, and enroll these pupils arbitrarily along with our monolinguals, in French, German, or Spanish. In the same schools many monolingual children whose mother tongue is English will share the bilingual schooling of their bilingual classmates.

In most schools, as today, there will either be no non-English mother tongue children or their number will be too small to warrant the choice of their mother tongue as a school language. In these schools the most common second languages offered to our monolingual pupils will be Chinese, Russian, and Spanish. The choice of these three will be dictated by considerations of geography, population, and power. Brazilian Portuguese will begin to occupy a major place in the language curriculum. German, Italian, French, and all the others now offered in our schools will continue to attract students. If Quebec becomes a stronger neighbor and in some measure independent, French, like Portuguese, will gain in importance.

The wide spread of bilingual schooling in the elementary schools, beginning in grade one or even preschool, will bring radical changes in foreign language programs at all levels of instruction. FLES (Foreign Language Teaching in the Elementary Schools) as now conceived and administered will disappear. It will be replaced by schooling in which children will have their formal school experience twice each day through the mother tongue (in most cases English) and also through the other tongue. This will continue for most foreign language learners through grade six, and for many through the remaining school years. FLES, which conceives of the other tongue as a school subject and commonly devotes 15 to 30 minutes to it daily will not be able to withstand comparison with true bilingual schooling. The latter is not only much less expensive, requires no special teaching methodology, and can claim fully half of the child's school day without any lessening of the child's achievement in English and the school curriculum, but it also offers the immense advantage of using the other language as a medium, a means to other ends, rather than as an end in itself. Thus, bilingual schooling, unlike FLES, is a form of "natural" language learning, and unlike FLES it draws on the young child's mysterious, miraculous ability to learn a second language without giving conscious attention to the language per se.

The Coral Way two-way bilingual school in Miami (one of three such full-time schools there in 1969 along with 55 part-time ones) provides data from the administration of standardized tests to indicate the achievement that can be expected in such schools. At Coral Way, in its fourth year of operation in 1967–1968, approximately half the children began as monolingual speakers of English, half as monolingual speakers of Spanish, and all received the entire school curriculum both through Spanish from regular native Spanish medium teachers and through English from regular English medium teachers. At each annual administration of standardized reading texts to determine the extent to which each pupil was able to learn through each of his two languages, the difference between scores in the two languages grew smaller. On reaching the fifth grade the Cuban children were found to learn equally well through English and Spanish. At the time of the fourth test administration (1967) there was still a slight, but statistically significant difference favoring English as the learning medium for the English mother tongue children. Nevertheless, they were strong enough in Spanish to warrant giving them instruction in some subjects for weeks at a time *exclusively through Spanish*. This is a level of achievement that cannot be expected in even our best college-level foreign language programs.

In the Coral Way experience there are some disturbing facts, and some strong implications for foreign language teaching and learning in 1980:

1. The same kind of schooling could be provided in English combined with any other language.

2. Bilingual schooling as in Coral Way is equally effective for children who are unavoidably bilingual and for monolinguals whose parents wish them to become bilingual.

3. The effectiveness of bilingual schooling does not depend on the presence of non-English mother tongue children in the school. The Coral Way school would be equally effective if all its children were Spanish-speaking Cubans, or if all were monolingual speakers of English.

4. The other-tongue teachers in bilingual schools must be highly literate and fluent and must have learned through that tongue the subject matter they are teaching. They will not be *foreign language teachers* at all in our present sense of the term, but rather teachers of the social studies, the sciences, mathematics, music, etc., who happen to be fluent, scholarly speakers of that other tongue. Most will be native speakers, many foreign born and educated.

5. Since bilingual schooling as described is much easier, much cheaper, much more effective and, paradoxically, takes less school time than ordinary foreign language teaching, it seems reasonable to suppose that when parents learn about it they will not be satisfied with our present-day offerings. (The paradox lies in the fact that although during half of the school day the other tongue is the *medium* of instruction, the pupils' attention is devoted to the *object* of instruction: the social studies, the sciences, mathematics, music, etc., even as today.)

6. The implications for "high school 1980" are obvious: Children who have experienced bilingual schooling in grades 1 through 6 (whether or not their mother tongue is English) reach the seventh grade able to study history or arithmetic or whatever through the medium of the other tongue. Therefore, we can predict a gradual shift in the junior high and high schools from teaching the foreign language to teaching regular school subjects through the medium of the foreign language. This is in keeping with a movement already perceptible in some high schools today, where instead of a senior class level (fourth, fifth, or sixth year) course in "advanced" French or Spanish, seniors are permitted to study for example, European history or Latin American history entirely in French or in Spanish.

STRUCTURED FOREIGN LANGUAGE LEARNING

Not all children will learn a foreign language "naturally," in bilingual schools, if only because of the difficulty of securing sufficient teachers. There will be reasons to change languages during one's school career. There will be need for third languages. For many reasons there will be continued demand for *structured* learning opportunities, which in the terms of this paper means acquiring the language at any age when it is no longer possible or feasible to learn by more natural methods.

While it is true today that programmed learning as applied to foreign language has not fulfilled the promises made for it ten years ago, everything still points to its eventual success. Foreign language learning is remarkably compatible with step-increment learning. A language (and performance in that language) comprise a finite corpus which can be stated precisely as "target behavior." A language, insofar as structured learning to perform in it is concerned, is a set of interrelated systems (call them its phonology, morphology, syntax, and lexicon) which from the beginning until the end of the learner's task are reducible to a series of patterns-plus-lexical-items that must be mastered by habituation both singly and in endless recombinations. Unlike learning history or philosophy, language learning requires nothing of the learner except that he do it exactly as its native speakers do.

This model of language and learning corresponds so completely to the capabilities of the teaching machine as it already exists (the tape recorder plus a visual display) that the ultimate success and widespread use of programmed, machine-mediated teaching seems inevitable. Even without the highly desirable error-recognition capability (referred to below) the machine can already assure native-like mastery of pronunciation, as Rand Morton has demonstrated through his experiments with Spanish at the University of Michigan.

Although any discussion of structured language learning must eventually center on programmed learning (Skinner's pigeon on Crowder's branch) and its related presentation devices (the tape recorder, the film, and particularly the computer) this piece will deal with neither programming nor the devices except as it seems pertinent to state criteria and predict developments in the year 1980.

The essential criteria are two: (1) optimum (rather than maximum) capability of adjusting to the individual learning characteristics of each student (optimum rather than maximum in view of the interpersonal nature of language), and (2) unlimited access by the learner to the learning materials.

Both criteria impose the use of teaching materials that are self-instructional to the maximum degree. This may well eliminate human teachers (in our present sense) from structured learning courses. It will not dispense with course writers, organizers and managers, nor with examiners and hand-holders. Indeed, hand-holding may be a major need of young learners in the year 1980 and thereafter. Above all it will not change the interpersonal nature of normal language learning and use. The interpersonal requirements can easily be fulfilled by programming into the course sequences of close, satisfying, pupil-to-pupil relationship. For instance, instead of having only the machine as a speech partner, the learner will sit with another pupil, or two, and the program will guide their interaction—as we would say today, "directing the dialogue."

It is the view of this speculator that the program should be designed originally on the supposition that one-trial learning might occur at every step of the course. The exact amount of experience with any single linguistic feature or combination of features required for mastery by a given student can never be known in advance. This seems to dictate a requirement of maximum intrinsic programming beyond the compulsory first trial.

The criterion of individualization of the teaching materials will call for a wide range of variants corresponding to age levels, vocational and other interests, sex differences, and even to regional language variants. That is to say, the course materials will take fully into account the fact that one learner is a 19-year-old girl from a little town near Birmingham who hasn't made up her mind yet about much of anything, and that another is a 45-year-old cab driver from Marseilles (not Paris) who knows exactly what he wants. These variants can easily be keyed into the program at will by the learner himself. A specific instance: if the student wishes to work in the informal *tu* form instead of the formal *yous* form he will merely press a button.

Perhaps Martin Joos's levels of style (the entire gamut, from the most intimate and folksy to the super-pedantic) can be incorporated in the program as alternative choices available to the advanced learner for selection at the beginning of a study session, enabling him to practice any or all of them. Of course they can.

THE PRESENTATION DEVICE

Present-day language laboratories will disappear, not at all because they have failed to fulfill the promises and claims made for them, but because their limitations of place and time make them necessarily inadequate to meet the criterion of access. They are never near enough, large enough, or open long enough. They will be replaced by course presentation devices with the following characteristics, all of which are now possible:

1. central permanent storage of all learning materials
2. Instantaneous random access to the store by wire or wireless for any number of learners, individually, wherever those learners may be; this means separate, miniaturized, portable equipment for each student
3. decision or branching logic enabling the device to keep a record of all student responses and utilize the continuous analysis of that record to determine each new step in each student's program, in effect to design each student's course for him alone, while he is learning
4. output (to the learner) capability which would include the presentation of visual stimuli (print, manuscript, film) and acoustic stimuli (spoken natural language)
5. input (from the learner) capability which would include the recognition of phonetic and grammatical features of spoken natural language, as well as written and button press student responses
6. error specification embracing all of the input noted above

The computer is the only presentation device now capable of providing the required storage, instantaneous random access to the store or memory, branching logic and feedback (1, 2, and 3, above). The output (4) and the required self-pacing by the learner are technically simple today. Computer engineering is still inadequate at the interface between pupil and machine with respect to the recognition and evaluation of student responses in spoken natural language (5), but the solution of the related problems is clearly within the bounds of feasibility and 10 more years.

OTHER AIDS TO LEARNING

McLuhan reminds us that the use of microwave channels and communications satellites and high-capacity cables erases all distinction *at one point* among media of communication. All—voice, TV, telephone, books, magazines and newspapers, pictures—pass through the same relays in the form of electronic impulses. Theoretically, they could each therefore be reconverted to any other medium.

This seems to indicate the likelihood of person-to-person photo-telephony (or TV) on a scale and with such ease as to permit a disembodied intimacy across oceans and national boundaries which would be strongly conducive to developing and maintaining foreign language skills. The successors of today's pen pals will in the year 1980 or soon thereafter look deeply and privately into each other's eyes via the cathode ray tube, begin with the standard *Permita Vd. que me presente a sus órdenes*, shift in time to *tu*, and eventually in thousands of cases, I would hope, embody the cross-cultural relationship and reinforce it through the strongest motivation known to man.

Person-to-person phototelephony may provide several adjunct functions beyond the one noted above. Even today TV might be able to teach more effectively simply through the adoption of techniques which increase the degree of personal involvement with each learner. One such technique calls for limiting the class seated before any TV receiver to, say, six or ten or maybe twelve pupils, each seated on a chair placed in a predetermined, fixed relationship to the tube face. Each chair corresponds to a given name in the target culture, some boy names, some girl names. Each pupil in each group of pupils assumes the name corresponding to his chair.

The TV teacher knows the chair names and their exact location and conducts the lesson as if the class were present in front of him, looking at individuals and dealing with each on a personal basis. He can then direct class activities of many kinds which involve the pupils as individuals: choral work, row drills, half-class drills, songs, games, directed dialog, and (somewhat structured) individual responses.

The motion picture film—largely unexploited heretofore as an aid to foreign language learning—offers some extraordinary possibilities. Imagine, for example, a grade school foreign language classroom one entire side of which is the screen, floor to ceiling. The projector is invisible and silent behind the screen. The pupils watch while others their age in the foreign country play or work or sing. Then it is the Americans' turn, and they try it while the young Spaniards or Chinese stand watching them and applauding their performance. With a little attention to timing, many activities could be synchronized to give the effect of the two groups working together.

Other forms of support to foreign language learning are not hard to envisage. On the pattern of military reserve officers training programs, there could and should be a "national foreign language reserve corps," made up of those persons with certain levels of competence in certain languages and who are highly knowledgeable in at least one other critical area related to the foreign people.

On the pattern of our Red Cross swimming and life-saving programs there might well be a national foreign language youth corps for students who can demonstrate competence in one or more languages, with progressive stages of advancement and appropriate public recognition.

There will be travel and sojourns abroad in every country, more easily arranged than the visit of today's Frenchman to England. Foreign language and area specialists will most commonly work and teach abroad as the most authentic representatives of their own people.

The basic and overriding weakness of today's formal, structured foreign language teaching-learning arrangements in the United States is that the circumstances of time and place and learner's age make it virtually impossible for a monolingual English-speaking student to become a first class language teacher by school and college study alone. By "first class" I mean having such competence in the language as to be able to deal—in both speech and writing—with scholarly matters in a scholarly way. The few remarkable exceptions to this dictum are so few they can be called miracles. Most "first class" teachers who began as monolinguals in the schools have relied heavily on foreign travel and residence. Thus (apart from the constant influx of foreign born and trained persons) our foreign language teaching profession is not self-sustaining at the level of its own claims and demands. Our foreign language teachers at all levels of instruction are asked to perform miracles, and they bravely attempt to do so. Miracle-making, despite its long and honorable tradition both among the Christians and among the heathen, is a shaky basis for a profession. Fortunately, the prospect is clear that by 1980, forced and reinforced by the ever-increasing movement toward bilingual education in the schools and utilization of our own native-born bilinguals, today's basic weakness in the profession could to a considerable extent be overcome.

It is to be hoped that other anomalies in our present teaching-learning arrangements (or should I say mythology?) will have disappeared by 1980. How is one to reconcile, for example, equating one year of college study with two years of high school study, in the face of our insistence that younger persons learn faster and more effectively than older ones? How explain the fact that FLES programs, even those beginning as early as grade three, do not produce by the end of grade six the clear equivalent of one "level" or year of high school learning? There is still another, even more disconcerting question: If the classroom activities engaged in by pupils and teachers are designed specifically to produce competent foreign language performance—and bearing in mind that the teacher engages in these same learning activities for several hours daily and year after year—why don't the teachers become, perforce, superbly competent performers?

In 1980 it can be expected that linguistics will continue to be a fascinating and important science and that its relevance to foreign language teaching and learning will be, even as today, significant but minimal. Then, as today, linguistics' main contributions will be its clarification of the nature of language and its systematization of the contrastive structural analysis. However eagerly language teachers await the scientific linguists' further discoveries of language universals, however eagerly they, as scholars, welcome new grammars and approaches to grammar, nothing can be expected by 1980 to lessen the learner's need to cope with the long series of patterns-plus-lexical-items and master them by habituation singly and in endless recombinations.

What I have said about the complementary forms of egalitarianism and the prospect of bilingual schooling carry an implication that may prove to be the most shocking of all. Both strongly imply a measure of cultural pluralism and a reinforcement of folk bilingualism in our country and elsewhere. Both involve recognition of the messy welter of people speaking two languages in their homes and in the streets. They involve the real world of other language speakers and folk bilingualism which foreign language teachers in the United States have ignored and which in turn has ignored the foreign language teachers. The questions are, Will the foreign language teacher—whose work has been the creation of a limited measure of elitist bilingualism for academic, scholarly, unworldly purposes—will the foreign language teacher care to involve himself in that messy confusion of folk bilingualism? Will he espouse the cultural pluralism which is inseparable from stable sustained bilingualism? Will he take over or share the task of language maintenance, of sociolinguistic planning without which our national resource of over 30 different non-English mother tongues—in addition to the scores still spoken by our American Indian tribes—will, except for the Spanish speakers and the Indians, virtually disappear by the year 2000? Will he organize himself to guard the door to his professional house, to support the able ones and rule out the incompetence?

Let me conclude with brief references to the Mexicans and to the French speakers of Canada. Both references underline the ever-stronger inclination of peoples everywhere to offset the egalitarianism which makes everyone identical by stressing the equal right of all peoples to be human in their own way and in their own language.

October 12, celebrated all over Spanish America as "el día de la raza," is a day when people are proud of themselves for being what they are. Although related to Columbus's famous voyage it is not at all the same as Columbus Day in the United States. Columbus Day is when the Italians stand tall because they know his name was really Cristoforo Colombo, when Spaniards are haughtily silent because they know who paid for the voyage of Cristóbal Colón, and both judge the recent findings about the Scandinavian Leif Ericson to be in very poor taste. But the Mexicans, when they hear talk of the discovery of America and later of Mexico say, "Discovery! What do they mean "discovered us"? We were here all along and we dammed well knew it!" People want to be accepted for what they are.

And the French Canadians: At one of the hearings held by the Royal Commission on Bilingualism and Biculturalism, one old man, a speaker of French, said apropos of the great resurgence of loyalty to the French language as a symbol of the Quebeckers' will to be human in their own way, " . . . chez un peuple où l'on marchait un peu courbé, deux cent mille, cinq cent mille individus ont tout à coup décidé de se redresser. . . . " (" . . . among a people who had been walking somewhat bent over, two hundred thousand, five hundred thousand individuals had suddenly decided to pull themselves erect. . . .")

These are affairs, as Toynbee would say, of the heart. Will foreign language teachers have the heart to expand their small academia of elitist bilingualism and embrace the real life concerns of other language speakers everywhere? All signs point to those concerns as one of the dynamic moving forces of the decades immediately ahead.

The Reformed Curriculum in Vocational Education

Marvin J. Feldman

Most American public school education is geared to the college-oriented student. This does not make sense when only two out of ten public school children will eventually graduate from college. It makes less sense when you realize that as a consequence, public schools tend to rely for results on the incentives that motivate only the most successful pupils: recognition of academic achievement, teacher and parent approval, and the like. Underlying these incentives is the principle of deferred gratification. Increased earning power, prestige and status, the system preaches, will ultimately accrue to those who learn to postpone satisfactions and to be diligent, even in the face of tedium, difficulty, or drudgery. But not all students are willing or able—financially or otherwise—to translate the attainment of future goals into the necessity for present application.

Some mark time in school because they see no other alternative. Others accept the long-range objectives as suitable, but have difficulty in relating them to daily tasks and decisions. Still others simply turn their backs on school and walk away.

We are all too ready to assume that the difference between the facile learners and the others resides in native intelligence. Actually the real difference probably lies in differing ability to verbalize—the best-rewarded skill in our educational system. The ability to verbalize is an important ingredient in one type of learning style. But there are other learning styles, which can be equally rewarding and would lead to a greater ability to communicate if only they can be matched by appropriate teaching procedures.

Underlying the teaching techniques that I will describe is the concept that intelligence is not fixed, as was once supposed, and that, furthermore, it can be developed by providing the child with enough favorable informational interaction with the environment, or as J. M. Hunt puts it, interaction that is "relevant to the role of early experience and psychological development."

R. W. White provides a clue to how best to achieve this. The human organism, says White, is motivated to "interact effectively with his environment," as manifested in his exploratory, manipulative, and activity behaviors. The exploratory behavior, he says, is best seen in "the organism's intense and persistent drive to respond to all kinds of stimuli—auditory, tactile, visual, esthetic, and so forth." If this is true, and I believe it is, it seems probable that situations which restrict or otherwise deprive youngsters of meaningful interaction with the environment would tend to inhibit the development of intelligence. Failure to match teaching procedures to learning style, it would then seem, could have just such an inhibitory effect on learning.

Some children are graphic learners. Others learn best through manipulation. Still others are affective. Most of these children could be engaged in good general educational programs if we borrowed the vocational processes themselves with which to engage them. All of these youngsters bear out what James and Dewey and Whitehead were saying: that youngsters do have different styles of learning, and everything possible must be provided to allow the learner to interact with his environment. Vocational education, conceived of as a tool for comprehensive education, rather than an end in itself, lends itself readily to the purpose of matching styles.

In some school systems, "comprehensive" describes any high school program that offers industrial arts, typewriting, and homemaking courses in addition to the usual academic subjects. Other high schools, once academic, now call themselves "comprehensive" because they encourage pupils to seek a "work experience." Still others ship students by bus to spend half of each school day in a shared workshop center for vocational activities. Lastly, there are comprehensive schools that would be more aptly described as simply multipurpose; administered by a single principal, they house under one roof three sociologically and educationally discrete schools —academic, vocational, and "general."

Industrial arts and homemaking courses are certainly relevant to education, but they hardly make a school comprehensive. Work experience outside the school program, often on the pupil's own time, unsupervised and unrelated to academic instruction, scarcely earns the right to be called cooperative or comprehensive education.

The bussing of pupils to a vocational education center that functions independently of its feeder schools is undoubtedly a convenience for school administrations that are plagued by overcrowding and underachieving students, but it does not furnish comprehensive education.

The most common type of so-called comprehensive school is the multipurpose, or tracked, school. It carries some of its students, on the first and main track, to college, but it shunts off the rest either to the vocational track, where not vocations but trades are taught, or to the so-called general track, a watered-down version of "education" which prepares its students neither for a vocation nor for the pursuit of higher education.

The track system tends to freeze students within the confines of their class, race, and social groups, denying all the groups the benefits of interaction and shared experiences. At least half the college-bound students in the tracked school are as ill-served as the students on the vocational and general tracks. It is the group that will begin but will not complete their college studies. Not only do the so-called comprehensive high schools fail to teach these youngsters skills, or give them a glimpse of the technological understanding of the society but the setup also denies them the opportunity to rub elbows with the social class and life-style with which they may well have to come to terms in the long run. The tracked school also limits the vocational student's exposure to courses that might enrich his curriculum, his capacity to function well in his chosen vocation or, for that matter, to choose other options as opportunities emerge.

The cultural isolation of such tracking system serves in the long run to deny the very bases of experiences necessary to meet the future goals of liberal education. In fact, it promotes negative interaction among the students and is an affront to the very democratic processes in which we so strongly believe.

It is impossible to study vocational education in the United States without realizing that, in fact, there is no "system" of vocational education; there are schools of all kinds, at all educational levels, but there is no system with a logical progression from school to school and from level to level. For 60 years vocational education has been confused with practical training required for a job, and has been regarded as separate and distinct from "education" as such. It is offered at the end of a process of compulsory general education and is concerned with only a fraction of the labor force. It is associated with manual occupations and is thought of as inherently inconsistent with the ideal prospect of higher education for its pupils.

The United States public education system strives to give the student every opportunity to develop his talents at the highest possible level. But the highest possible level is always the highest formal verbal educational level. The student is urged and perhaps rightly so, under the current conditions of American higher education, to prepare for college and to do nothing that might impair his ability to go there. The statement for vocational education is more often than not made in a negative fashion. We say we want vocational education for students who do not have the ability for college, yet even they are told not to take vocational courses because these might make college admission more difficult. Since vocational education as it is now thought of is not truly education at all, and is not thought of as being preparatory for the liberal arts, only the student who is determined to become a craftsman, or *who has been given up by the educational system,* takes vocational education.

Urban children particularly need the kind of opportunity that was offered on the rural farm—to take things apart and put them together, to handle, feel, discover for themselves how things work. These opportunities were the very bases for many farm children later succeeding in college. Often in serving children whose styles are not verbal we lose sight of the fact that "doing" is only the beginning. Thinking follows, feeling follows. Doing is the specific from which later generalizations will follow, and vocational education can contain a high proportion of doing.

Reaching right down into the grade school, vocational education can, for example, be employed to help the child with reading difficulties. It can provide the experiential base we so readily assume in elementary education.

The traditional school system supplies children having reading difficulties with another text, a special teacher, and in effect, intensifies the application of the same techniques and materials which have already given him trouble. A truly comprehensive school, taking advantage of the possibilities that are inherent in vocational education, would on the other hand allow the child to work in a workshop with type and simple printing presses. Instead of reading page after page of printed material, he would actually print one.

Education need not be painful and should not be passive, especially for the children who resist traditional methods. The moment of learning should be active, intense, and spontaneous, as when Maria Montessori's four- and five-year-old pupils "burst spontaneously into writing," without having been "taught" to do so. Matching teaching procedures to learning styles can help keep it that way, and this can be done through the judicious use of selected vocational processes as pedagogical vehicles. They will require the student's active participation and will greatly enhance his motivation to learn. They will help to relate his education experience to any number of adult roles as well without diminishing the quality or rigor of the educational program.

At present, however, the most important vocational processes and resources are tragically misused in the public schools of the United States. The very structure of the public school framework serves to box in vocational education and vocational educators, denying them the possibility of making their maximum contribution. The situation will be perpetuated unless we recognize that the school can do justice to its constituency only if it integrates the vocational processes in the continuum of education, beginning early in elementary school and continuing through at least 14 years of schooling.

The need, it should be noted, is to relate the vocational processes to the academic disciplines and not the other way around. There is no need for related math, as it is now taught to vocational students, only for math; no need for related science, but for science; none for related English, only for English. We *do* need—and need badly—related shops, labs, drama departments, and graphic arts, to name just a few examples.

The idea is not simply to fit vocational education into the existing system but to make it the principal feature of a new system. The plan depends upon an extensive redesign of the secondary-school curriculum, but it is a practicable plan. Aspects of it have been tried by the Ford Foundation in 30 schools in 20 cities, and early indications are that they work. These pilot curriculum experiments in all grade levels from kindergarten through college and fall into two principal categories.

The first is designed to make vocational-technical education more relevant to the needs of a modern technological society. The second seeks to end the traditional separation between vocational and academic education and make both more meaningful—and accessible—to a broader range of students. The oldest experiment is six years old; the newest was initiated in 1967.

The education envisioned by these grants is one that opens rather than closes doors; that prepares students for work in broad career fields (and perhaps more than one), not for a narrow range of specific jobs; that does not cut students off from higher education at some point in their education but allows them to proceed after high school either to good jobs or to further education; that does not separate subjects into rigid compartments but is strongly interdisciplinary and seeks ways in which interconnections can be made between vocational and academic work; that rejects a system of academic *apartheid* wherein the presumed sheep and goats follow wholly different paths and instead creates a broad highway upon which all may travel as far as their talents and desire will permit.

What has come through loud and clear from the studies is the reaffirmation of oft-repeated principles: learning is a process of engaging people in the processes and education is relevant experience coupled with purposeful activity. It has also become clear that a coordinated comprehensive program offers ample opportunity for a variety of teaching methods and of learning styles and so is more congenial to academic achievement by the nonverbal pupil than traditional, abstract-verbal programs.

The results thus far lend support to my thesis that by 1980 we must create in our elementary and secondary schools a coordinated curriculum where vocational and general education will reinforce each other; where carefully designed programs will prepare youth for advanced training for such new career fields as are developing in medical technology, the graphic arts, and a host of paraprofessional occupations; and where students will be taught general work skills transferable from one occupation to another.

Under such a system, no student will be rejected outright at any stage of his education—though he might be directed at least temporarily to more modest objectives when there was reason to believe his career choice offered little probability of success. In such a system, all students will be considered potential candidates for postsecondary education and training and all will have several options at the time of graduation from high school. They will be prepared to work at simple trades and occupations, to go to a two-year community or junior college or technical school, or move right into a four-year college. Even the choice of a two-year college or technical school will not cut off options. At the time of graduation from one such school, the student will be prepared to work at a technical level or to transfer to a four-year college in order further to develop his skills and enrich his liberal education.

An effective comprehensive program will begin in elementary school where youngsters will be introduced to the concept of choice between achievement through verbal or abstract performance and achievement through manipulation and demonstration of real objects. Both processes will be designed to arrive at the same learning goals. Each unit of work in the language arts, for example, will begin with a self-directed experience matched to individual readiness levels. Eventually all the children will reach the same goal, verbalizing or otherwise demonstrating what they have learned—responding in different ways, at different times, in accordance with individual abilities and talents. Throughout the elementary grades, there will be a continuing examination of how man uses work for self-support, how major occupations employ knowledge, and how productivity is related to a variety of abilities. A major objective of elementary education in 1980 will be to discover the talents of each child and demonstrate their relationship to the work world.

At the junior and high school levels in 1980, academic and vocational teachers will be teamed for the purpose of reinforcing each other's aims by coordinating the curriculum that they will both work to promote.

Vocational guidance will be introduced early in the middle-school years by 1980. Its aim will be to acquaint the students with the workings of industry and commerce toward the end of matching their talents with their career objectives. The vocational guidance department will, for example, provide an annual career-objective analysis for each student, based on the diagnosis, discussions, predictions, and evaluations of teachers, examinations, and computers. These analyses—really employment plans that are revised annually—will enable the student to appreciate the relevance of his school performance to his career possibilities. Like the college-bound student who even now is familiar with the ins and outs of college opportunities, the vocationally oriented student will be encouraged to know where jobs of interest to him are to be found, the types of advanced training that are available, the requirements for admission at appropriate schools, and whatever peculiarities attach to his field of interest.

Such a system will depend on a complete and continuing inventory of the composition of the work force and employment market, descriptions of requisite skills for specific occupations, and pertinent information about performance criteria in each.

This new input is particularly appropriate for the middle-school years, considering what we now know about early adolescence. Research experiments done by Taba and others have shown it is possible to teach a good deal more mathematics, physical and biological sciences, and foreign languages earlier in the elementary grades, and later in the high school, than we now even attempt to offer in the middle-school grades. If ever there was a time in a continuing curriculum for the student to be encouraged to look inward to identify his talent, to take stock of his assets, to test himself for future decisions, it is in early adolescence. Art, music, literature, guidance, and the like, belong to the middle school, and yet paradoxically, it is during these years of emotional and physical change that we offer the child mathematics, foreign languages, and the physical sciences. Most middle-school youngsters will easily tell us all the subjects they dislike, all the activities they are poor in, but very few know what it is they do like to do or what their talents are with which they are able to perform well.

To fully implement the idea, cooperating community colleges and technical institutes will be needed to offer programs that articulate with the secondary school experience. Occupational training in such schools will lead to an associate degree or to a certificate of achievement in a broad range of subjects. Cooperating technical schools will also serve to bridge the gap between the secondary schools and state colleges and universities, plotting avenues toward still further education for all those who are eager and able.

The most likely immediate beneficiaries of a comprehensive system for secondary education in 1980 will be culturally and economically deprived American students. A serious shortage of qualified non-white manpower at the technical level has been dramatically illuminated by an avalanche of materials and reports on the manpower needs in engineering, science, medicine, and the social sciences. These same reports and others have documented the fact that Negro manpower, above all other, has been largely untapped by contemporary educational techniques. Trapped by the traditional view that the central purpose of higher education is satisfied by the production of liberally educated men and women, Negro colleges have been among the most delinquent in overlooking the necessity for career training, but they are by no means the only offenders.

But what I want to emphasize will be comprehensive education of value to students whose primary interest may be the liberal arts.

Let me try an example of what I mean. A youngster who is provided with an opportunity to design, to fabricate, test, and report on an item goes through a number of behavioral changes not unlike the processes within the liberal arts. Surely few would say that the mere use of the workshop rather than an art classroom particularly would change the purpose of an opportunity to express oneself at least artistically. Whatever the medium—paint, metal, wood, music, ceramics, paper—knowledge of the properties of the materials, the mathematics of design, the esthetic experience, the bases of the social and humanistic message could all be present. The degree of creativity, of course, would depend on the particular task assigned, but on this level at least the vocational processes surely could be used as a great tool in liberating the mind for self-expression.

We might probe still deeper. A basic fault in our present theory and practice of education in the United States is the idea that vocational education not only stands apart from humanistic studies but is also a dull body of specific, technical facts and manipulative functions, and that only. Some educators are inclined to emphasize specific vocations or skills in preparation for life in the work world, leaving the acquisition of more general principles to induction from experience. Others tend to emphasize general education, leaving specific skills to be acquired on the job. Both means command supporters at all levels of schooling. The problem is further complicated in our confusion of the concepts of "training," "education," and "experience." If we agree with Garth Mangum's definition of training as an instructional function, education as a learning process, and experience dictating the mixture of training and education, the liberating role of vocational education becomes clearer. The processes themselves are introduced as necessary to meet any assumed prerequisite for liberal education. That is to say, the psychological, sociological, philosophical, and operational questions of to what extent the processes of education can be generalized for all students, becomes clearer.

To say that vocational education must become the principal core of a modern curriculum by 1980 is to say only that the remainder of the curriculum must be more fully and more consciously related to the place of individual talent in human life.

Vocational processes as pedagogical vehicles are not only relevant to the physical and natural sciences but also as a basis for the liberal arts. Beyond the self-liberating qualities of the processes themselves and their powerful stimulus for greater understanding, vocational skills are clearly the education which transmits from one generation to the next the heritage of the past and the seeds of new ideas yet to be. It surely does reflect the central reality of modern life and a real basis of intergenerational communication. If we agree that "life adjustment" is still the goal of education, then paramount in such adjustment must be the reckoning with the school's responsibility to identify the student's work-world talents so that the liberal arts have a greater meaning in his identified life-style.

Liberal education as we conceive it should be more than an education for intellectual pursuits and could embrace technical education. An educational program can and should at one and the same time and at all levels furnish its students with the wherewithal for fuller lives and for fulfilling, productive careers.

Alfred North Whitehead said this so clearly:

". . . culture is activity of thought, and receptiveness to beauty and human feelings. Scraps of information have nothing to do with it. A merely well-informed man is the most useless bore on God's earth. What we should aim at producing is men who possess both culture and expert knowledge in some special direction. Their expert knowledge will give them the ground to start from, and their culture will lead them as deep as philosophy and as high as art."

By 1980, high school graduates who prefer to terminate schooling after high school—a declining number we would hope under this system—will be invited to participate in cooperative work-study programs during the last year or two of school to prepare them for full-time employment upon graduation. An increasing number, however, would go on to higher education. Until now two-year colleges that are part of a unified secondary system or a state or county university system have had the best results in relating their vocational programs to those of feeder high schools. It is to be hoped that by 1980 more two-year colleges will take steps to achieve similar results.

Even now American four-year colleges have begun to appreciate that a larger portion of the population can profit from study at the college level than had been earlier assumed. The new aspirants for a college education, however, will by 1970 be more diversified than previous generations of college students, and many among them will have had very limited success in high school.

Nevertheless, many will argue from a narrow definition of higher education, bolstered by a rigid and simplistic notion of its function, that opening the sluice gates to admit as many newcomers as possible must be accompanied by deterioration in the quality of education. Flexibility, alternate programs, and multilevel goals, implicit in the educational system I have described for 1980, can give the lie to such arguments. For comprehensive education multiplies and broadens the pathways to higher achievement, offering promise of better lives and ultimately of a better society in which quality of all kinds can flourish.

It should be clear that to achieve our purposes for 1980, the highest priority should be given to the training and developing of a new breed of educator, vocationally competent and academically accomplished. There is no single problem of greater urgency, particularly in the field of urban education.

Much has been written about the qualities, skills, and commitments essential to good teaching. An additional attribute was proposed some years ago by Douglas McGregor. In his capacity as president of Antioch College, he advocated that college faculty should alternate between teaching and other work. Being on "intimate terms with business and industry, government agencies, unions, social and professional agencies," he said, would make for sounder teachers. "Not only would they be in a better position to relate theory to practice," he mentioned, "but they would soon begin to overhaul some theories. . . ."

If school teachers had a visceral appreciation of the world in which their pupils lived, they would have a better conception of their teaching roles. Such appreciation can be gained by living experience. Cooperative industrial education for teachers is, therefore, critical for the new breed of educator who will be needed in the comprehensive school.

The comprehensive school of 1980 will demand a continuing dialogue between academic and vocational teachers. A common set of experiences must be considered a prerequisite for such a dialogue. As matters stand now, the preparatory experiences of academic and vocational teachers are worlds apart. Beyond his undergraduate studies which include a prescribed number of courses in education and some practice teaching, the high school teacher of academic subjects in New York City, for example, is required to have a master's degree, nothing more, as preparation for his vocation.

The vocational teacher, presumably to compensate for the shop experience required of him, is excused from studying for his master's degree and even from acquiring a bachelor's degree if he is willing to sacrifice some salary increments. Two years of college work is all he needs in addition to seven to nine years of work experience to acquire a teaching license in New York, the nation's largest city. After acquiring seven to nine years of work experience, most workers who become teachers are too far removed from the spirit of school and too tired to acquire more than the minimum two years of college.

There is no doubt that the work experience the vocational teacher brings to his job is indispensable to his performance in the classroom both for the exposure it has given him to the worker's milieu and the skill it has imparted. Nevertheless it seems likely that the mission of education rather than trade instruction would be better accomplished with a different mixture of college and work experience by 1980.

For the teacher of academic subjects, school experience should be supplemented by some work experience, continually renewed throughout his teaching career. An intimate knowledge of today's industrial and business complex, proficiency in dealing with the man-made environment, and an understanding of the problems of the work world are necessary skills for all, especially urban teachers. Such competence can be acquired only through actual experience, and, therefore, work experience would be a basic element of all teacher-preparation programs. I want to differentiate here between work experience related to educational processes and work experience to meet economic needs.

Without prescribing a teacher-training program, it is appropriate to take note of the deep prejudice harbored both by the vocational teacher, who feels his industrial experience compares favorably with the academic teacher's more extensive schooling, and by the academic teacher, who is often contemptuous of manual skills. The academic-vocational gap will close when teachers of all subjects, working in reconstructed schools, are prepared to adopt alternative means of inspiring learning and to come to appreciate the genuine values that can be derived from both vocational and academic education and from first-hand acquaintanceship with the world of their students.

SPECIAL EMERGING PROBLEMS AND OPPORTUNITIES

Better
Utilization
of Resources

J. Lloyd Trump

My crystal ball is hazy. I don't *know* how the secondary school of 1980 will look. But I do know how we can make our schools of today better. Simply, the answer is better use of available resources. And I believe that the degree to which this basic rule of reform is followed will reflect a fairly accurate image of High School 1980.

What *are* "available resources"? They're people, educational materials, time, numbers, space and money. All are interrelated. Changing one and ignoring the rest would doom high school 1980 to the status of many present, inadequately conceived educational innovations. Although we categorize the resources here, a school system, of course, cannot; they are tightly meshed in the system's daily life.

THE PEOPLE

First, there are the human resources—the students, teachers, principals, parents, and other interested adults—in the school, the immediate community and society at large. Of course, students are the crucial people in schools.

Students. The talents of high school students are the most important and most underused human resource in the school. "Gifted underachievers," "dropouts," and "reluctant learners"—all these labels reflect the problem.

Actually, almost all students fall short of developing most of their potential. Why? What can we do to use these resources more fully?

School personnel need to know each student better than they do today. Available data is inadequate. Even though the intelligence and achievement tests, the interest inventories, the grades, the class-book notes, the cursory physical examination, and the notes from a once-a-semester counseling interview all sound like a penetrating dossier, they scarcely suffice. Equally disturbing, no one in the school really knows each student as a total human being. Certainly the professional counselors do not know the students; a counseling load of even 250 to 300 is too many for that purpose; all they have is a file on each one. A teacher with 5 classes of 25 to 30 students per day knows something about their achievements in the subject he teaches and can call each one by name. But he does not really know each student.

By 1980, the school will have redeployed its staff so that each teacher has the time, the preparation, and the assignment to serve as a teacher-counselor for 35 to 40 students. The teacher will collect information about these students from other teachers. She will consolidate test information and other data about them from a variety of sources. She will help them plan their programs and, in fact, help them schedule their independent study. If necessary, the teacher-counselor will refer students to professional counselors. Thus, every student in 1980 will be known as a total human being by someone in a position to help him gain the most from the school. By 1980, it will be easier for the teacher-counselors to do this because greatly increased amounts of data will be stored in readily accessible computers. Also, relationships among the facts will be clarified by studies that computer storage makes possible.

The 1970s will see tremendous progress in improving the student's productivity. Biochemistry research doubtless will produce drugs that can be prescribed to improve a student's performance. Mental and physical maladjustments caused by chemical imbalances may be remedied. Physical health will be enhanced by still further improvements in nutrition. Better counseling will help the individual's social and emotional adjustments. Also, the gains made in the 1960s to reduce racial, ethnic, and religious strife will produce better relations in the 1970s; individuals will be less inhibited by their environments—good or bad.

Several educational changes emphasized in the 1950s and 1960s will bear fruit in the 1970s. For example, factors in the school that work against the student's motivation will be reduced. Through continuous progress programs, the school will be able to place each student in a learning situation which neither bores him because he already knows the concept, skill or information, nor frustrates him because it is too advanced. Continuous progress and individual scheduling together will have eliminated failure as schools define that term today. Too, fear of failure no longer will be a prime motivating factor for success. Independent study programs will place students in learning situations in the community as well as in the schools. Stimulating to the students and aligned with their special talents, these programs will enhance motivation. So will the provisions for a student's relating to a well-liked teacher in independent study. And the student being in contact with specially selected teachers for large-group instruction. Evaluation will gauge changes in a student's performance, not his skill in memorization.

Along this line, too much of today's teaching and learning is at the stimulus-response level or at the memoriter level. Emphasis in 1980 will be on cultivating the higher mental processes: generalization, concept development, creative thinking. Data-processing equipment will retrieve details. Curriculum developers will identify what the student must know and be able to do. Reduction in memorization will allow students more and more time to follow their own interests and talents to greater degrees.

Another change in the use of human resources will be a combination—rather than the present dichotomy—of cooperation and competition. Today's schools place major emphasis on competition. An individual is evaluated in relation to his standing in the group. Public displays of grade point averages, class ranks, aptitude and achievement scores—all these pit a student against his peers.

Our alternative has been to propose group learning, teacher-student planning, and other cooperative ventures. An individual's major competitive effort must relate to what he has already achieved —he must exceed that. But cooperation also is necessary. So, while the learning process in 1980 will stress cooperation among individuals, the evaluation will stress both the individual's competition with himself and ultimate goals.

Today's students must rely too much on printed pages and the voices of physically present teachers. Schools in 1980 also will enhance human resources by familiarizing students with the outside world through the use of technical devices. Dial access, computer retrieval, video telephones, and other technical devices, unknown today, will broaden students horizons with multisensory approaches.

Teachers. Three decades of changing teacher roles will produce, by 1980, what truly may be called professional teachers. In the past, teachers' time and energy has been spent in secretarial and "baby-sitting" activities—essential to the teaching-learning process, but surely better done by persons specially trained for the jobs. Although there will be fewer teachers in relation to the total number of students in a school, the total school staff will be larger. The professional organizations will have dropped the fetish they held so long that reductions in teacher-student ratios were essential. They will have learned that only through increasing the ratio of students to teachers is it possible to improve teaching and learning.

Three kinds of assistants will be found in schools:

1. Instruction assistants: Housewives, upperclassmen in teacher education programs, and retired teachers, each with the equivalent of about two years of college training in the subject field in which they help. These assistants will supervise independent study areas, help prepare materials and evaluate student progress. They are part-time workers, usually 10 to 30 hours per week. The hours-per-week total equals 20 times the school's professional teachers. (For example, in a school with 36 teachers, instruction assistants work a total of 720 hours per week.)

2. Clerks: High school graduates with such skills as typing, duplicating, record keeping, who will be assigned full time to the teachers. The hours per week: 10 times the professional teachers. (A school with 36 teachers would have 360 clerk-hours per week.)

3. General aides: Housewives lacking training in a subject field or clerical skills will be employed to get things out, put them away, sell tickets, supervise nonstudy areas. They work part time. Hours per week: five times the professional teachers. (Example: 36 teachers have 180 hours per week of help from general aides.)

These three kinds of paid assistants are occasionally supplemented by community consultants who volunteer without pay for a specific assignment: a presentation to a student group; service as a chaperone; preparation of an exhibit.

Assistants will free teachers to carry out those school activities for which they have particular talents and interests. High School 1980 will recognize differences among teachers and capitalize on each one's resources; it will not force everyone into one mold.

A typical teacher in an innovative program will have only one or two preparations per week. These are for large-group presentations of information, not readily available elsewhere, which will awaken motivating interest and help students learn their materials. Oral assignments are complemented by printed materials that tell students of diverse talents and interests what they are expected to know and how to go about learning it. Each presentation should last about 35 minutes. The teacher's schedule will also include sitting in with students (in groups of 15 or less) who are learning how to talk to each other, how to listen, how to discuss, and to respect each other in the process. There will be 14 to 16 of these groups, each scheduled for about 35 minutes.

The teacher spends the rest of her time seeing students who need special help. They are referred to her by the supervisor of the independent-study centers. Each teacher also serves as a teacher-counselor for about 35 students. She knows these students as total human beings, collects information about them from their various teachers and from standardized tests and inventories given by the school, and learns about their home situations.

People Outside the School. The flexible school program of 1980 will capitalize on human resources both in and beyond the school's immediate neighborhood. The augmented staff I described earlier will bring to the school a carefully selected group of persons who have not been used before. In addition, data-processing equipment will contain information about talented community people whom students can contact to discuss their special projects.

THE THINGS: AV, EDP, TIME, SPACE, AND MONEY

The help that upcoming technical developments will give to students is difficult to estimate. Computers in 1980 will outnumber many times today's total. Today's computer speeds, fantastic as they seem, doubtless will increase to the point where, in comparison, the two will seem like a horse and buggy versus a jet plane. Today's electronics revolution, which may already surpass the industrial revolution in significance, will produce tremendous benefits to students. The new world of oceanography, aided by further developments in nuclear energy, will produce by 1980 material resources far beyond what most of us imagine today. Laser beams and other new forms of energy will open up material resources to students that are universe wide instead of earth bound. Conversely, books and other printed materials will become less important as other forms of information storage grow in value because they are easier to use. Students can submit questions and problems to computers and get immediate answers that today take hours of concentrated study and even then may not produce the desired data.

Material, as well as human, resources in the community will be more accessible to students. The school building itself will be much smaller than today, and will serve largely as a dock for buses that shuttle students between it and community resources. For example, students will study and work in museums, art galleries, libraries, offices, social agencies, government installations, and a variety of shops and manufacturing establishments. Field trips of an earlier day, where masses of students were taken on conducted tours, will be replaced by flexible schedules in the school enabling students to work variable times in places they and their teacher-counselors select. The school's independent study program will occupy from two-thirds to three-fourths of the conventional school week, with students covering required content mostly in school resource centers, while using community resources for most depth studies and creative efforts.

Continuous progress programs will permit and encourage students to travel around the nation—indeed, the world, in some cases—with their parents, using learning sources far removed from the local environment. Of course, worldwide transportation will be faster and cheaper in 1980, making this "international education" more feasible for more students.

Time. It's available to everyone in equal amounts. The only difference is how an individual uses his 24 hours. Conventional school programs made too many time decisions for the student. He sat in class for 50 minutes, whether he had heard the message before or whether the subject seemed important to him.

In 1980, time will be constantly controlled by students and teachers rather than a program clock in the principal's office or a computer-based schedule.

Each student will attend 16 group meetings per week, two in each of these eight areas: English language arts, fine arts, health-fitness-recreation, language arts of another country, mathematics, practical arts, sciences, and social sciences. In a weekly, 30-minute presentation, the teacher will attempt to motivate the student to engage in independent study, and provide information not readily available elsewhere. She also will suggest activities. Once a week, each student will gather with 12 to 14 others to learn how to communicate orally and to develop better relationships with other students as he engages in discussions related to the eight knowledge areas. A student may be excused from required activities by his teacher-counselor, but not often. The student will spend the remainder of his 30-hour school week following his special interests and talents, according to the schedule he and his teacher-counselor worked out.

Numbers. High school administrators in 1980 will not emphasize "magic numbers." They no longer will have confidence in 250 minutes per week, 30 students per class, 18 semester hours of professional education courses, $12 per student for library books, 750 square feet in a classroom, 18 units of credit, 7-8-9 versus 6-7-8 years experience plus 30 hours beyond an M.A. equals $9,372.00, 20 acres of ground, a 3.57 grade average—on and on, in endless succession. Apparently, the administrator's goal was to define all educational aspects in precise quantitative terms so secretaries could make decisions, or at least so that administrators could make them without thinking. The goal in 1980 will be to replace clerical decisions with professional decisions. None of the foregoing measures will be considered adequate for educational planning and evaluation. In their place will come variable decisions based on continuing goal analyses; recognition of individual differences; intuitive judgments; and the concept that decisions evolve and are subject to change as conditions change.

In 1980, numbers will serve different purposes. Educational goals will be defined in terms of performance objectives or anticipated behavior. The goal will be described numerically and so serve as one basis for analyzing the need for further changes. Above all, numbers will result from an analysis of programs rather than serve as determiners of programs—as they have in the past.

Space. We have alluded to the spaces inside and away from the school that the student uses in independent study. The conventional school of an earlier day used space inefficiently because of the multi-purpose concept. A conventional classroom was an auditorium, a place for small-group discussion, an independent study room. Actually, it was not effective for any of those activities. Special spaces in 1980 will enable each student to see and hear better than previously, making it easier to benefit from large-group instruction. Group-discussion rooms will be no larger than needed—about 250 square feet, with acoustical privacy. In the old, conventional classroom the discussion of one group interfered with other groups' discussions in the same room. The 1980 school will house independent study in specially designed spaces. Each subject will have its own resource center with materials to view, hear, read, and handle. They will not be mixed up with other subjects' materials. The library will contain advanced materials for special study. It will not be cluttered up with materials that all students use. Separate rooms will be available for conferences and socializing. Resources which the community can provide better than the school will be used on site rather than attempting to simulate them in the school.

Money. Funds available for education are an essential resource that schools have not used most efficiently. They seldom carefully measured the relationship between financial input and educational output. Although learning in classes of 25 was not superior to classes of 30 or 35, teachers, administrators and parents urged, and got, small classes at considerable added cost. Multipurpose facilities also were unnecessarily expensive. Twice the capacity of a conventional classroom can be accommodated in the same space for large-group instruction and 50 percent more for small-group discussion. These changes, plus those suggested for independent study, can cut a school's size in half, saving money needed for technical teaching and learning devices, and transportation to and from community resources. Using a variety of assistants saves money on teachers' salaries—reducing the teachers to about one for each 35 to 40 students and makes better use of teachers' talents.

WHO IS RESPONSIBLE?

Many persons will determine whether high school 1980 makes better use of its resources. No one will be more influential in a school than its principal. Superintendents, supervisors, teachers, researchers and consultants, parents, legislators, board of education members, and others will contribute to change, but the principal is in charge. He is there all the time; he can lead, support, or impede. And in the final analysis he can make the crucial difference. We need to look critically at this particular resource—the secondary school principal —to see how his position may change.

In 1980 the principal will have abandoned his traditional office near the school's front entrance where he was greeter, guard, counselor, and confidante. Instead, he will place his highest priority where he has long known it belonged—on the improvement of teaching and learning. Appropriately, his office will be associated with the teachers' offices. He will have solved two basic clusters of problems that bothered him especially during the 1960s: (1) How does he find time to improve instruction? How does he go about doing it? How does he know whether he is successful? (2) How does he manage discipline, attendance, student activities, guidance and testing, plant management, transportation, office management, cafeteria operation, public relations, teacher militancy, and opposition to higher taxes—effectively and simultaneously?

Aided by the eight contributing groups I mentioned earlier, the principal has developed a different staff organization that enables him to solve both clusters of problems. First, how does he handle the second cluster of problems—the ones to which he should devote one-fourth of his time (13 hours per week)? The principal of a large school has a variety of specially trained assistants, most of whom supervise specially trained subordinates. They give the principal the information he needs and handle most situations for him.

One assistant is the building administrator responsible for supervising the school plant, cafeteria, transportation systems, and office; for seeing most visitors and salesmen; and for deciding if they need to see someone else. This person has specific training for these assignments, including their role within the framework of school objectives. He has authority for final decisions and makes them so effectively that seldom does anyone feel the need to talk with the school principal.

The external relations director is the second assistant. He is responsible for developing the school's financial needs into written proposals to the central office, all levels of government agencies, and foundations. Financial proposals and the expenditure of monies translate the school's goals into practice. This assistant, therefore, also plans and conducts the school's two-way public relations program.

A third assistant is the personnel administrator, responsible for supervising attendance, discipline, guidance, and for developing liaison with other community youth-serving agencies. His contacts include police and other juvenile authorities. He also works with teachers on their welfare problems. Parents and other persons having difficulties with students can see him.

The fourth man is activities director, responsible for student and faculty extraclass activities, including supervising athletic and non-athletic programs and faculty social activities. Community groups and individuals see him about using school facilities and other cooperative activities.

No assistant needs the training given to principals or even assistant principals. Rather, each assistant's position requires specialized training and experience. An assistant's professional movement is to larger schools, central office, or state supervision of similar activities; it is not to the principalship.

How many assistants there are varies with the school's size. A 300-student school combines all assistants in one person. A 2000-student school has four assistants, each with full-time assignments. Larger schools provide helpers for each assistant.

However, in any size school, the principal spends no more than 13 hours per week supervising these assistants, receiving their reports, attending events, or dealing with appeals from their decisions. He firmly replaces any assistant who is so unsuccessful in his area that the principal must spend a good deal of his own time on it.

Now, let's look at the principal's major, 37-hour a week task—the three-fourths of his time he works with teachers and others to improve teaching and learning. The instruction staff is distinct from the staff I have just described.

While the large-school principal may spend 75 percent of his time with teachers, he may still lack time to complete the job on instruction. This principal needs highly trained persons to help with curriculum instruction. These persons, called assistant principals, are educated as the principal himself is for those particular responsibilities. Some of these assistants may become principals.

The number of assistant principals rises with the school's size: none up to 500 students; one for each 1000 students or major fraction of 1000. A school with 1200 students has one assistant principal; a school with 2100 students, two.

For further illustration, the following chart shows the differences between the principal's staff in the 1960s and in High School 1980:

HIGH SCHOOL 1969—1250 STUDENTS

Principal

Assistant Principal (business and/or attendance and discipline)	Assistant Principal (instruction and/or attendance and discipline)
Custodians Cafeteria Workers Transportation Workers	Director of Guidance (counselor) Health Personnel Special Teachers (reading, etc.) Librarians (visual aids, etc.)

Department Chairmen

Teachers (organized into departments)

HIGH SCHOOL 1980—1250 STUDENTS

Principal

Assistant Principal	Building Adminis- trator and External Rela- tions Director	Personnel Administrator and Activities Director

Teachers (working in teams)

High School 1980 has four full-time administrator-supervisors compared to the earlier high school's three—and the responsibilities are delineated better. The principal now gives 75 percent of his time, and the assistant principal 100 percent, to improving instruction.

New roles for teachers, described earlier, make it unnecessary to appoint department chairmen and provide teachers with released time to spend on administration and supervision. Actually, the costs of administration-supervision are little, if any, more than in the past. However, the use of resources is enhanced.

What 1980s principal and assistant principal do to improve instruction is quite different than what they did a decade earlier. Gone are the conventional faculty meetings, the routine classroom visits, the principal's bulletin, the committees, and the relatively unused professional library. The principal practices the same rules of teaching that the teachers follow with their students. He uses large-group instruction for only three purposes: to motivate, to provide information not readily available elsewhere, and to raise questions and suggest learning activities.

The continuous-progress philosophy guides teachers' independent study. They meet for small-group discussions. The principal works constantly with them to develop plans for self-appraisal in line with stated goals. As the school's organization makes better use of the leadership resources in administration-supervision, the total use of all other resources improves.

Better use of resources is the crucial factor in High School 1980. A school teems with human beings, all with varying talents and interests. How those resources, human and material, are used determines more than anything else how effective organized education becomes.

The Future in Guidance, Psychological Services, and Testing

Douglas D. Dillenbeck

Educational and social reforms that will occur in the 1970s are going to dictate major changes in guidance methods and responsibilities in high school 1980.

Elementary education will become more effective, particularly for those it has helped least—the poor and the slow learners. Secondary schools will adopt instruction programs and methods far more responsive to all individuals' interests and needs. Added to this, increased levels of employment, better housing, and a general drop in poverty will bring about an almost universal completion of high school and will greatly increase education beyond high school. These last two results are the chief factors that will affect high school guidance.

The most important change in guidance will be its movement toward a central position in the school's educational program. Originally an auxiliary service, concerned primarily with occupational choice and job placement, school guidance has gradually acquired other generally recognized responsibilities, especially during the last two decades. These duties include students' personal and social adjustment, college choice and admission, choice of high school program, and underachievement. Guidance has won recognition as an essential high school service, even though this status is still challenged occasionally by school districts that "economize" and drop their guidance services, along with cafeteria and bus services, as an unnecessary frill.

RETREADING FOR A HEAVIER LOAD

However, as the high school curriculum grows more diverse and individualized, the student will need continuous guidance simply to keep up and get the most from this diversity. Instead of choosing his course (college preparatory, commercial, etc.) on entry, or his subjects each year, the student will face frequent curriculum choices any day—whenever completion of one learning task leads to more advanced tasks. Coming changes in curriculum and teaching methods will accelerate the trend to more choice, more frequently. Because of these changes, the school's help for the student in making these choices—that is, the guidance—will be vital in determining his education's value for him.

To meet these duties, guidance, like teaching, will take on some new characteristics. Counseling interviews, historically the principal guidance technique, will still be the apex of professional guidance, but the vast bulk of daily service must, and will be, much more economical, while remaining at least equally effective.

Much of guidance interviewing is expository and highly repetitive from student to student. It is teaching which, in a traditional subject, would be done with groups rather than individuals. Increasingly, counselors are questioning the tenet that guidance "teaching" must be tutorial even though it is not always personalized for individuals.

Much of interviewing is simply transmittal of information. Many media do this better than a counselor can. If the rationale for interviews has been that information on occupations and education did not exist in any organized form outside of counselors, this is no longer true. It *is* true that great gaps still exist in the published guidance information. However, existing information is still far too voluminous for even the best-informed counselor to grasp completely.

We have here three high-priority jobs—to organize this information in a more usable way, to keep it current, and to fill its gaps. When it does this, guidance will relieve its counselors of collecting, processing, and reporting information and, simultaneously, get the jobs done better by communications and data-processing men and machines.

FOR ROUTINE PROBLEMS, PRESS BUTTON MARKED "R"

Communications and data-processing technology also will be harnessed to give students help in some problem solving and decision making, now done entirely in interviews. Many students share certain problems—curriculum choices, for example. These problems lend themselves to a limited number of routine solutions. Expert counselors can develop such routines; or, they might be created through the consensus of many experienced counselors, or, perhaps by empirical methods. Then, they can be recorded in computer programs and made available to students everywhere. Thus, in problems that one can handle well this way, all students can have excellent guidance—even in schools where conventional counseling services are scarce or poor. We already have the technology and methods for these procedures—in primitive form—and it seems clear that a decade of refinement and program development will bring them into widespread use. These programs not only will free counselors from handling many routine problem cases, but they also will identify students whose needs the computer program does not completely satisfy. Counselors can give these individuals more, personal help.

SWITCH TO MENTAL HEALTH, SOCIAL GROWTH

The shift from remediation and problem solving to promotion of mental health and social growth—a long overdue development in guidance (and in education, generally)—may well gain impetus from the changes I have discussed. Counselors and teachers will be able to contribute more effectively to an emotionally hygienic school environment. Improved instruction programs, with responsiveness to individual differences, will eliminate many school-centered circumstances that today cause alienation, insecurity, learning difficulties, and other manifestations of emotional disturbance.

The same technology that will revolutionize elementary and secondary teaching and learning also will be applied to the training of teachers and counselors. It will provide them, by means of simulated problem situations, with the equivalent of extensive, expertly supervised experience. Teachers and counselors trained in the modern programs will be far more sophisticated and perceptive than even most of the best teachers and counselors are today.

One change sure to occur by 1980 is already being demanded by those who have been systematically denied it. That is the abandonment of the notion that you control failure by denying students access to programs they seem likely to fail. Instead, students will be encouraged to take risks, and failure will be a failure to try. Improved methods of teaching and recording student progress will make obsolete present concepts of passing and failing. They also will neutralize even the supposed—but unproven advantages—of grouping pupils according to their ability and achievements. Because much teaching will be individualized, a student will take as long as he needs to master a concept that he finds difficult. Situations that too regularly spell failure in the present lock-step pattern will, in the 1980s, be occasions for students to feel great success in conquering the difficult. Moreover, by no longer denying students experiences judged too difficult for them, the school also will cease to turn out large numbers of citizens who go through life believing correctly or incorrectly, that they would have been more successful if their schools only had given them the opportunity.

Similarily, there will be a decline in the mentality that brands prospective college students and their parents as chronically over-ambitious. People who think this maintain that the counselor's highest duty is to get these parents and students to accept "more realistic" goals. Instead, 1980 will bring a general recognition of each person's right to pursue a lofty ambition even in the face of long odds. Moreover, the ambition itself will be recognized as a powerful predictor of success—often more powerful than more conventional ability indicators. Consequently, counselors and teachers will encourage students more often to believe the best about themselves and to choose goals in that light. If this is Couéism, it also is the conclusion drawn from a large and growing body of empirical research on self concept and vocational development.

TESTING FOR STRENGTHS, NOT SCORES

Testing's role in guidance will continue to be significant—with some differences. Instead of measuring and comparing all students on a few mental abilities, tests will become a means for individuals to explore and assess their strengths in a wide range of abilities. Tests will help students discover strengths or abilities which they themselves may not have known of, rather than tell how they compare with others on one or two conventionally measured abilities—all possibly having little significance for them.

Another change in testing will be a shift toward simpler, more direct participation by the person being tested. Emphasis on positive interpretation of tests will reduce the need for psychologically trained interpreters—who help students cope with the shock of poor scores.

Tests will be used more to help students make their own decisions and less to help counselors, teachers, and school administrators make decisions about them. Provided that he understands what they mean, no one except the student himself need know his test scores.

Other foreseeable changes in testing will result from use of data-processing and communications technology. To a great extent, group paper-and-pencil tests will yield to individual, self-taken tests—computer programs, available to the student on demand. Items will be presented to the eye by picture tube and to the ear by head-sets. Responses will be evaluated instantly. Some tests will be "branched" so that the student's response to one item will determine which item will be presented to him next. This kind of program will span a much wider range of the trait it measures than most paper-and-pencil tests. These must usually be designed for populations that are relatively homogeneous, in age and grade at least.

Also, videotape will make it possible to incorporate action and sound, making the tests both more realistic and more interesting than today's usual paper-and-pencil test. Students will interpret not just the lifeless, printed version of "Hamlet's" graveyard scene but, rather, or also, a well-performed excerpt as it was intended to be seen and heard.

Sound also will be used in some tests. This way, the mastery of speaking and hearing in a foreign language, already measured in some tests by spoken-words with written responses, will be gauged by two-way vocal communication. This will be made even more realistic by the visual depiction of the scene related to the test item. Hence, an item based on conversation in a French market-place will confront the student with the sights and sounds of a French market-place. He will converse aloud, in French, with the pro-grammed voice of the test. Depending upon the test's purpose, the student may be evaluated and his errors corrected as the test pro-ceeds, or he may be evaluated when he completes the test.

THE SCENE AT MODERN HIGH SCHOOL

The following scene illustrates many changes—in both method and purpose—that I have described.

Sam Sophomore sits at a communications station in the learning laboratory at Modern High School. One of several three-sided cubicles in the room, it is equipped with a picture tube, a type-writer-like keyboard, and a microphone-earphone headset, besides reference books and writing space. Sam is just completing a unit in the programmed mathematics curriculum. He now will decide whether or not to continue in mathematics at this time. If yes, he must decide which unit he'll take next.

As soon as he completes the mathematics unit, a voice speaks through his headset. It congratulates him on his achievement and then asks if he would like to consider what to do next. Sam answers, "Yes," speaking into his microphone. His reply starts a program of interaction between Sam and a centralized data bank and computer, serving the whole county in which Modern High School is located. A recorded voice begins the dialogue with Sam:

VOICE: "Good. Look at your picture screen and tell me which statement there is closest to what you want."

The picture tube shows:

1. I want to discontinue mathematics at this time and study some other subject.
2. I want to continue the study of mathematics.
3. I'm not sure whether or not to continue studying mathematics.

SAM: "B. I want to continue the study of mathematics."

VOICE: "Good. *Your progress in mathematics has been excellent, so you can surely succeed in further study of this subject.* Do you know which unit you want to study next? Please answer 'Yes' or 'No.'"

(The italicized statement is one the computer program selects from several recorded statements coordinated with all levels of mathematical achievement. The data bank, of course, includes a complete file of Sam's previous work; the computer program specifies the rules by which his file is evaluated to select this statement.)

SAM: "No."

VOICE: "All right. Look at the screen. This is a list of the units that you might study next. Do you know what each is about? If you want to know more about any one, tell me their letters."

(Picture tube shows list of mathematical unit topics.)

SAM: "Do." (The unit on sampling statistics.)

VOICE: "All right. Let's look into that unit. We have a program that will take you about ten minutes. It explains what sampling statistics is about and how it can be used in various fields. It also will let you test your aptitude for this kind of study and your interest in it. Watch the screen and use the keyboard to record your responses according to the directions."

(For the next ten minutes Sam listens, looks, and ocassionally responds, as the program exposes him to the pertinent information about the subject of sampling statistics and its uses. This includes simulated problems by which Sam can test his ability and interest.)

VOICE: "Good. Your solutions to the problems and your answers to the questions about your interest in them both compare favorably with other students who have completed this unit successfully. You probably would be able to complete it in 15 to 20 hours. The average time is 25 hours. Do you have any questions about this unit? Please answer 'Yes' or 'No.' "

SAM: "No."

VOICE: "All right. Now look again at the unit list on your screen. Are there any others you want more information about? Please say the appropriate letter."

SAM: "K." (No information wanted on any unit.)

VOICE: "Very well. Do you want to make a decision now, or would you prefer to postpone it? Please answer 'Now' or 'Later.' "

SAM: "Later."

VOICE: "Very well. Do you want to discuss this with a counselor before deciding? Please answer 'Yes' or 'No.' "

SAM: "No."

VOICE: "Very well. We can proceed with the decision about mathematics whenever you are ready. Meanwhile, you can apply the freed time to other subjects and to planning your program further.

At this point, Sam may call up another computer program, perhaps to resume his study in another subject. Or, he may leave the laboratory for some other school activity. Later, he will return to the laboratory, recall the interrupted decision-making program, and proceed with his selection of a mathematics unit.

NEEDED: COMPUTER PROGRAMS, DATA BANKS

Nothing in the scene I just described will require any major new scientific invention. All the technology exists now—at least in the engineering laboratories of the communications industry. Much exists in our everyday world. For example, the precursors of the spoken program (which selects taped lines from hundreds of others on the basis of the student's spoken cue) are talking dolls, books, and other toy-store items, as well as talking elevators that announce floors and, when necessary, direct passengers to step back and let the doors close.

However, two things are needed to make the scene a reality by 1980. The first is the computer programs and the data banks. These are an enormous undertaking, but even more awesome when one realizes that the programs will require constant updating to be attuned to world and education changes. Both affect the kind of guidance valid for high school students. On the other hand, it seems probable that these programs and systems, produced centrally for service on a national, regional or state scale, would consume no more money and manpower than what is regularly expended by the thousands of individual high schools, with uneven, often poor results.

The other need—and by far the more important one—is for a growth of belief, not only among counselors and teachers, but among all people, in the dignity and worth of human life. Without such conviction pervading our society, there will be resistance to, and delays in, the effort to provide enough sensitive guidance.

I have made some bold assertions that certain changes will occur in the next ten or so years. I have done this simply because any alternative is both repugnant and dangerous. Optimism, in this case, is not only attractive, it is absolutely necessary.

The Secondary-School Building of Tomorrow

Harold B. Gores

People are more important than bricks. Indeed, in descending order of importance, a high school is a student body, a faculty, a curriculum, and, only last, a place. If we can agree on these matters there is then a congenial basis for discussing what difference it makes that secondary education be conducted in a good place.

To those who are uncomfortable unless everything is quantified, one can only say that judging from studies made of the relation of environment to the productivity of office workers, environment makes a difference of about 15 percent. There are some thoughtful people who believe that the tone and feeling of the place where students and teachers meet are more important, but there are others, particularly the intellectuals, who are forever citing Mark Hopkins, Arthur Garfield, and their log as proof that people are all and environment is nothing. So let's settle for a 15 percent difference, which is good interest on your money and worth talking about.

The question is: What kind of high school, circa 1980, will maximize the contribution that design, construction, and furnishing can make to the fulfillment of the institution's purposes?

Historians agree that from the first secondary school—Boston Latin in 1635, a year before Harvard's founding—until the last decade of the nineteenth century, secondary schools were mostly college preparatory.

Not until the turn of the present century did the American high school broaden its offerings and its attitudes, the better to serve and to hold all the children of all the people. Even so, many a high school was still failing to attract, serve, and hold a majority of its community's youth as late as the 1960s.

In the 1950s, the American high school was the liveliest sector of education from nursery to graduate school. Thanks to the Advanced Placement Program and the reorganization of subject matter, many high schools were turning out students in the 1960s too hot for unreconstructed colleges. Indeed National Merit Scholars were able to shop among the colleges and universities of the nation, and their choices were revealing—one fifth elected to study in Cambridge, Massachusetts.

Yet the essential thrust of the American high school remained through the 1960s to prepare for college and to prepare for work in about equal parts. By 1980, though, the school's mission will have come full cycle—preparation for a higher institution. By 1980, very few graduates will go to work; they will "go on" to college, community college, or other agencies capable of continuing their education and training.

Given all the youth, ages 13 to 17, what may be the shape and the silhouette of the place in which he spends his "high school" years? It depends.

It depends on whether the setting is rural, suburban, or urban— for each will reflect and be like the constrains of their subcultures. Back where the creeks fork, the local high school will still be a place of gathering for midadolescent youth, different from today's cross-road school in that it is connected electronically with the outer world of the state university, the Library of Congress, other higher schools, and a satellite or two. Though indigenous to the local subculture, it will nevertheless be connected to the mainstream of education at the most sophisticated of urban centers. There will be no more isolated enclaves preparing some students to go to the city, never to return, and the rest to stay home as workers in the local economy. Everyone will be connected to everything and therefore they must be prepared for everything, even though they live in the hills.

To predict the suburban high school, circa 1980, is more difficult. So much depends on whether the eventual resolution of racial conflict is toward integration or separatism. Assuming the former, suburban high schools will be built for enrollments exceeding the sum of local students if the suburb bears its share of educating the children of the central city. It is not too soon now to plan with the expectation of state and federal aid for buildings if provision is made for nonresident children.

It is in the central city with its variety of subcultures that we will find the greatest variety of schools. The predominant city high school in 1980 will be today's high school still in use and staffed for the most part by today's teachers. To be sure, the interiors of these buildings will have been rearranged to accommodate the changes in program and instructional technology which occurred in the 1970s, but essentially the 1980 high school built in the 1960s or before will be not vastly different from what it is today.

Because it is easier to start a new institution than to change an old one, it will be the schools newly built in the 1980s which will exhibit the greatest variety and the highest state of the art.

But whether the new 1980 high school is in a small town, a posh suburb, or the inner city, it will have certain characteristics not generally possessed by schools today:

1. By 1980, the school will be designed for *people*, not just for children. Operating 4000 hours a year rather than 1000, the building will be designed to serve the children well when they are in it but also persons of all ages who at other times will be gathering there. The materials and surfaces will not be chosen for their durability but for their appropriateness to the task. Interiors will be high-quality space calculated to strengthen the morale of the occupant and nourish his spirit. And such high-quality space will prove to be a prudent public investment against the possibility that some-day the premises may be used for a different purpose. A community can recapture its equity in a school building if the space is flexible and humane; whereas the indestructible, procrustean, egg-crate schoolhouse has no market value in its later years.

2. By 1980, the self-contained classrooms, lining interior corridors like the coaches of a train (or arranged back-to-back in milder climates), will have given way to large zones of air conditioned, acoustically-dampened space capable of being subdivided at will by the rearrangement of portable furniture and equipment. Indeed, by 1980 most high schools will have embraced the open plan characteristic of the new elementary schools of the late 1960s, and the trend of corporate office space toward open plan. This means that only rarely will interior partitions rise to the ceiling and that the academic sections will take on the physical appearance of the "interior landscape" which alert corporations began to provide in the 1970s for their corporate headquarters.

Quite aside from what pulling down the walls of Jericho does to the human spirit, the economy is clear; whereas it costs approximately $7.50 per square foot to remodel and rearrange conventional office spaces, the cost approximates 50¢ a square foot if the space is open plan from the beginning. Presumably such economy will apply in substantial measure to the alteration of schools through their half-century lives. Even if the savings achieved by business are not totally transferable to the schoolhouse—and this is quite possible since education is not noted for frequent change—the fact that the 1980 schools will be easily convertible to other uses guarantees that the building will hold its value until the day it may be sold.

There will still be classrooms but they will look more like living rooms than like kitchens. They will not be hard, reverberative, ceramic vaults bounded by four cement-block walls and filled with slippery plastic furniture. Just as education's undergirding psychology has progressed from stimulus-response to organismic, the classroom cum living room will suggest to its occupants that they gather in the round to discuss important matters among themselves, and in the presence of a wise teacher. (Incidentally, important matters tend to be more round than linear.) This classroom, this forum, this pit, this living room is most likely to be located on the perimeter of a library. Of the library we shall have more to say later.

3. By 1980, the American high school will have learned how to track the academic progress of individual students. Schools will then be not for groups and classes but for individuals. Thanks to computer-managed instruction no child will get lost or be relegated to anonymity. By 1980, the industrial-educational complex will have developed the tools enabling each child to have easy access to vivid presentations of fact. Less dependent now on the teacher as principal dispenser of information, the student, having acquired the "facts" from inanimate objects, is prepared to enter the forum—the classroom—to discuss the meaning of it all. Students thus prepared will obsolete the teacher who knows the name of everything but the meaning of nothing.

4. By 1980, the design and construction of new schools will have embraced the industrial revolution. Just as in Canada in 1969, and gradually in the United States since 1965, schools will be built of preengineered components—modular parts and pieces designed to fit each other exactly when assembled on site. Though "systems" building was introduced to the United States through the schoolhouse—one of the few times that education ever led its society—the general adoption of systems building in education will have to await the general adoption of systems design and construction by government and industry. This will come fast, and by 1980 even education, directed by 21,000 School Boards and 2,300 degree-granting institutions of higher learning, will have gotten the message of its own invention.

5. By 1980, many of the functions now performed by "school administration" will be contracted out to the private sector. Three examples:

a) The design of the buildings and their construction will be "commissioned" to the private sector. Schools will no longer have architects and planners in residence, firmly implanted on Civil Service and grinding out the same old buildings, year after year.

Instead, alert and energetic corporations will perform for a fee the planning of schools. The notion that school districts should employ people to perform all its services will be obsolete by 1980.

b) Student bodies have to be taught, exercised, and, alas, fed. As long as the subculture served by a particular school is reasonably homogenous, and as long as student bodies consent to being herded, the conventional gorge-and-go school cafeteria, shining white in enameled antisepsis, seems to work. Lines of students passing Indian-file along steel counters to receive their municipal rations in neat compartments on a plastic tray, only to be confronted in the end by a cashier, is efficient, quick (28 minutes from bell to bell), and nobody gets sick.

In the simpler days of the 1960s this was the scene for the kids who had money. Others, lacking either the cash or the stomach, were seen furtively to open a paper bag off in the corner, there to partake of a sandwich supplemented sometimes by a half pint of federally-assisted milk, the assistance inspired less by the nutritive needs of children than the financial needs of farmers.

By 1980, though, the feeding of children will have come into more sensitive arrangements. Dining will replace feeding. The great cavernous space called the cafeteria will have been replaced by smaller spaces in which children will dine together without regard to ability to pay and in surroundings which suggest that eating can be a cultural experience. Indeed, in the central city, the cafeteria, where the fights used to start in the late 1960s, will have given way to subspaces of amenity and grace, where students—and hopefully their teachers—will dine together on meals that may be prepared many miles away but served on the spot.

In some cities there will be breakfast for some. And after the children are fed at noon, the aged of the community will congregate there to eat and to socialize. And dinner in the evening at one's friendly school cafeteria will not be beyond the reach of any lonely person. Thus the school's facilities for feeding will come alive and work for all of the people, not just children, all of the time.

School districts will increasingly employ entrepreneurs, operating for profit, to supply and serve esthetically pleasing and nutritionally adequate meals for all. New York City's experiment in the late 1960s with frozen foods may well key the conduct of city school cafeterias in the decade ahead.

By 1980, the high schools will have found a politically acceptable way of seeing to it that all children get fed. The meal will look good and taste good, and the place of eating will be less institutional, smaller—maybe even at the place where the student is working when hunger strikes. As the schoolhouse comes alive, as it uses its capital equipment more hours a year for more people, as it becomes a service center for children first, but also for persons of all ages and conditions, school bond issues will have better luck at the polls.

c) Much instructional technology will be contracted out to the private sector. No longer will it be thought reasonable that a school district purchase all the instruments of instruction. Rather, the schools will hire a service to be performed and not buy hardware and software soon obsoleted. By 1980, major corporations will offer "learning services" which include the devices and related materials to produce the contracted result. Just as in food service, so in technological support, schools will come to rely on rented rather than purchased services, and the notion that schools should be staffed to do everything for themselves will prove to have been but vestigial remains of our primitive past. Such companies as RCA, CBS, Westinghouse, and scores of others, will have demonstrated their capability, by 1980, to teach the children through services which no one school system can economically assemble. This will decimate the ranks of tenured supervisors of various subject fields, each rediscovering the wheel, school district by school district, but the end result will not be fatal to those who perform their jobs with imagination.

6. By 1980, high schools in the inner city will not be great fortresses in sullen confrontation with their neighborhoods. Rather, many will be like Harlem Prep, a converted supermarket which nonetheless provides a supportive environment for learning. Harlem Prep doesn't look like a school, smell like a school, or feel like a school. It is a dignified place for late adolescents to gather and to learn. Its furnishings and appointments are mature, not juvenile. It provides an environment which buoys the spirit and self-image. Nothing about it suggests that its occupants are naturally destructive, that the place is designed to defend the taxpayer from the natural ravages of youth. The environment of Harlem Prep says: we respect you; we expect you to rise to our expectations of you; we bet you will because, you see, we trust you.

The fact that the school is a converted supermarket is irrelevant; it is a good place for good people to be—and environmentally, is a more humane place than municipalities ordinarily provide.

Let us now turn to three major spaces to be found in high school 1980: the library, the gymnasium, and the science laboratories.

1. The Library. Traditionally, school libraries have been dreary places. Indeed, in many schools until quite recently they weren't *places* at all. They simply didn't exist. As recently as 1963 there were over 10 million students going to schools that had no library whatever. In those schools where libraries did exist, the majority were absurdly inadequate: a converted classroom or two in a remote corner of the schoolhouse with a few hundred—sometimes a few thousand—books lining the walls, a current periodical rack consisting largely of house organs and gift periodicals from the American Legion or Rotary Club, and seats at tables for 20 or 30 readers sent there as a captive group to study from textbooks. The library was open from 8:00 A.M. to 4:00 P.M., leaving students with five or six classes per day little time to use it. The budget, if there was one, was tight, and much of the librarian's time was spent dashing from some back storage room, where she processed books, to the charging desk.

There were exceptions of course, particularly in a few large city schools, the private schools, and some of the university laboratory schools. But by and large, this was it. It remained so until the early sixties when this type of library began to go out of fashion.

Pressure for the development of better school libraries had been growing slowly for over a quarter of a century, finally reaching a peak in the current decade. Came the sixties, the motive force for change was the heightened demands on the schools by a society itself undergoing profound transition. The response of the education community to these demands was expressed in the concepts of instruction tailored to individual ability, team teaching, independent study programs, flexible scheduling, revised curricula, and an emphasis on higher academic quality.

To realize these goals, however, every student needed access to ample collections of resource materials, to professionals trained in organizing and providing information services, and to physical housing conducive to their effective use. These were, in fact, the sine qua non upon which rested any restructuring of the house of education.

It followed then, that new types of libraries would have to emerge. And they began to do so, moved along by such programs as the Knapp Foundation grant to the American Library Association of over a million dollars and, within the last three years, by the availability of federal funds for the purchase of books, audiovisual equipment and materials, and for physical facilities.

In some cases, as in those underdeveloped countries where social change is a leap from feudalism into the jet age, the new libraries are so different from their predecessors in philosophy and appearance, their very name seems no longer to express their reality. The old library has become the new learning resource center.

Witness this transformation at the Weston High School near

Boston, Massachusetts, a noteworthy example of one type of school library of the future.

Until 1967 Weston's library, like most, had been located within a classroom building. In the fall of that year the library moved into new quarters—an independent structure of architectural distinction that proclaims its central role in the life of the school. What had formerly occupied the space of three classrooms, or some 2,300 square feet, is now a three-story building of 23,000 square feet. A collection of 6,000 volumes is now to be a collection of 33,000, ultimately 50,000 volumes. Integrated into it is an additional body, modest but growing, of 2,500 filmstrips, 8mm and 16mm films, slides, tapes, records, and microfilms, with lightweight portable equipment, including television receivers, and headsets for individual or group use. Periodical subscriptions number 175. Production facilities for duplicating newspaper articles, magazine pages, reference materials and the like, speed multiple copies to classrooms and single pages to individuals without cost. A former staff of one librarian assisted by a clerk is now a staff of five; included among them, a trained cataloguer, reference librarian, and a specialist in audio-visual materials. The highest priorities of professional staff time are for work with students in their quest for learning materials, and with teachers on the evaluation and selection of materials for instruction purposes. The annual operating budget for the library— $20,000 in 1966—has more than tripled: $72,000 for the current fiscal year or 8.6 percent of the school's total operating expenditures.

Places are provided for viewing, listening, reading, and typing. There are seats for 250 students (35 percent of the total student body). Fifty percent of these are for youngsters who wish to work alone: 100 in the form of individual carrels where students can enjoy visual privacy, using print, and nonprint media on equipment plugged into the carrels. Working comfort within the carrel extends even to the option of writing surfaces which may be set in a sloping position, and book racks for holding open atlases and large books. Lounge chairs are provided for the sprawling that goes with sustained periods of relaxed reading. For those who don't like to work alone or those engaged in group projects, there are small conference spaces. These do double duty as rooms for teaching seminars. Teachers themselves use the library heavily. Among other reasons for the library serving as their home base, that is where their offices are located. This deliberately planned proximity of faculty and students makes for casual informal contact and guidance.

The building itself is a modular loft type, a sweep of open spaces unencumbered by fixed partitions so the interior may be rearranged as the life within it changes. A conduit system provides for future hook-up with outside information sources. Floors are a grid with cables laced through them checkerboard fashion, thus making wiring available for the use of electronic learning equipment almost everywhere and anywhere within the building. Air-conditioning makes possible year-round use. Functions are zoned so that distracting, noise creating elements are separated from reading facilities. Carpeting, which helps to absorb sound, also provides amenity. Natural textures in the structural materials and furnishings, the skylights, the ceiling heights that soar in some places and swoop intimately low in others, and nooks that are private juxtaposed against larger extroverted areas, offer an environment comfortable, inviting, respectful of the differences between the individuals who are its clients.

In this 800 student school, where youngsters may choose to spend their unscheduled time in a quiet study hall, or a lounge, or in any of the shops or labs for work on their own, the place they are choosing is the library. Each day it clocks roughly 1200 student visits. It is in operation 12 months a year and evenings until 9:00 P.M.; this fall its doors will be open on Sunday afternoons as well.

Another example of an evolving life style of the future school library is the Oak Park and River Forest High School, in a suburb of Chicago. The recipient of over a million and a half dollars in Federal Title III funds and $135,000 in Knapp grants, it serves as a center for experimentation and demonstration of the effect of a first-rate library on the total functioning of a school. This one embodies a sophisticated and complex network of spaces and services so organically intertwined with the entire school, it is difficult to fix where one ends and the other begins.

A brief overview of its vital statistics and some of the noteworthy aspects of its program conveys the magnitude of its role.

Space: The central library covers two floors of a building wing, totaling almost 40,000 square feet. This includes three adjoining suites that serve as specialized resource centers for math-science, for world history, for foreign languages. Three additional resource centers for art, business education, and music—soon to be added in locations near their departmental headquarters—will increase the total square footage under the purview of the library.

Collections: Over 47,000 books; 270 periodicals; a body of almost 10,000 filmstrips, 8mm and 16mm films, disc and tape recordings, transparencies, slides, microreels, and tapes for a central retrieval system.

Staff: A total of 26: 13 full-time, 13 half-time. These include four and one half full-time professional librarians, two full-time A-V specialists, a director for the dial access retrieval program, an instructional materials designer, library aides, and secretaries.

Reader stations: Approximately 500, with 70 percent as individual study carrels.

Enrollment: 3300.

Noteworthy aspects: (a) An electronic information retrieval system for the transmission of audio and, soon, video programs. This one, specifically designed with the help of the Ampex Corporation, is one of the first to overcome the major deficiency of the average dial retrieval system, i.e., the inability to retrieve a program already in use by another student without coming into it at midpoint or waiting until the first user is through with it. The system here is engineered so that, in response to a command from a carrel, a master-tape deck records a program at high speed on a duplicate tape. Within a few seconds any student in a carrel can dial a program and have the master tape subrecorded. He then uses the duplicate tape at normal speed, releasing the master tape in a matter of seconds to another individual who may then order another subtape.

Thus far, 25 live carrels have been installed from which any one of 224 programs can be dialed. Ultimately, there will be 175 such carrels, some with random access video capabilities as well, and dial reception stations will extend to 200 classrooms.

A final stage of this project will connect the library's resources with 26 public and private elementary and secondary schools in the region, and with nearby teachers colleges with whom Oak Park and River Forest has a cooperative student-teacher training program.

It is already possible for any student in the district who has a touch-tone telephone in his home to dial the school library for an audio lesson without cost to himself.

Teachers are released to produce audio programs for the storage bank, and thus far some 900 programs have been prepared. Each week the library prepares a catalog of the programs in the bank for that week, for distribution to students and faculty to keep them informed of what is available.

(b) Each resource center is staffed with a full-time librarian with a background in the appropriate subject area, and/or a teacher of the subject whose presence is scheduled, so guidance and assistance is available to students throughout the day.

All materials deposited in resource centers are acquired, processed, and catalogued in the central library. In addition to software, the centers house the portable equipment for their use, and such other hardware as microscopes, calculators, dice, cards, and the like.

The math-science center contains, in addition, two teletypewriters on which students can "call" problems directly into a computer located at the Illinois Institute of Technology on the other side of the city, receiving print-out solutions in return.

(c) Teachers are free to structure their courses as they like, dispensing with class periods and conducting some units in the resource centers where students work on their own projects. In the math-science center, for example, the library staff may set up carrels with microscopes and other science paraphernalia and the student, using audio tapes and 8mm single concept films to direct him, studies independently.

(d) Current operating budget: $180,000 exclusive of monies for the retrieval system. Electronic retrieval funds for this year, with the inclusion of a $446,000 capital investment derived from Title III, will add more than a half million dollars more to the library's operating expenditures.

In sum, the evidence presented by the frontrunners, the schools such as Weston, Oak Park and River Forest, as well as others, points to libraries in the future that will be consuming more and more space within the school, with a corresponding decrease in the proportion of traditional classroom space. Increasingly, the emphasis will be on the individual and his quest for information, with greater options allowing him to choose when, where, and by what means to study, in accordance with his personal style. The use of non-print media will equal the book and magazine, transmitted in some places through fixed electronic installations, in others by lightweight portable equipment the student may take home with him; and in some places, by a combination of both types. Most schools will be spending greater portions of their capital budget on library facilities, more of their annual budget on library operations, and the library will become central in the thinking of architects and educators planning facilities and programs.

Indeed, of all the spaces devoted to a specific function, the library will be the most dramatic. Not only will it be the single largest academic space in the American high school, it may eventually be mostly what a school is—a great repository for all the carriers of information to which the avid scholar has quick access. Thanks to miniaturization, portability, and the inexpensive and quick copying of paper, audio and video tapes, and films, materials to learn from will be available increasingly where the learner is and not in a one-copy control depository.

2. *The Gymnasium.* At the Chicago World's Fair of 1893, European gymnasts stole the show. The rhythmic exercises of such superb physical specimens, swinging their wands and dumbbells, promptly set off in American schools the purchase and use of these magical devices to enhance the physical fitness and grace of their student bodies. Even today many an old high school will still have in storage the wands and dumbbells left over from this earlier day.

But almost to the year, 1891, the game of basketball was invented, a game of hypnotic charm. By the early 1900s basketball had routed gymnastics and forever after to the 1960s a high school gymnasium was designed to contain the game of basketball. While schoolboy football was being crowded by the professionals into "Friday nights under the lights" and baseball was dying at the gate, basketball was boffo at the box office, especially in the central states. Great arenas were built to contain the crowds that statewide tournaments could attract. Boys with serious pituitary derangements (extraordinary height being a selective factor for success in the game) were much sought after by colleges, including those who should know better.

Basketball became education's "sport biz." It was the first sport to be racially integrated, it made money at the gate, and it made a wasteland of physical education for all children, boys and girls, for three generations.

Not until the 1960s did physical fitness, health, and recreation emerge from the dominance of basketball. As recently as 1967 a school board member wrote plaintively to EFL asking for help in finding a protective covering for his high school gymnasium floor so that the people of the community, over the objections of the basketball coach, could dance there.

But in the late 1960s there emerged a new art form for physical education, health, and recreation—what might be called the poor man's astrodome, a great scoop of the sky, a great cavity of space, a simulated outdoor area, an acre of June, in which persons of all ages could play what they wanted to play, day or night, summer or winter, north or south. Weather was routed as a determinant of program. No longer could Barnaby Keeney, when he was president of Brown University, complain, "We don't play lacrosse at Brown; we only cancel it."

In these new mini-astrodomes, as at Graceland College, Lamoni, Iowa, all games can be played all seasons. These great inexpensive tents of space offer a protected environment the year round. In these great uninterrupted spaces the flooring will be layered according to the requirements of the program: a hard floor for basketball and similar games; a rolled-down field of artificial turf for activities normally conducted on grass; and a layer of plastic ice—not primitive frozen-water ice—for skating.

By 1980 these acres of June will have replaced the basketball box gymnasium and the facility will not only serve the young but the middle-aged who are jogging for their lives. It will serve everybody in the community. We have the technology to create these inexpensive enclosures; all we await is the desire.

And it is predictable that the desire will come—and it will come from, of all places, the students. By 1980 the opinion of high school students about interscholastic sports and physical activity will be heard. When these students learn how much it costs to train a few gladiators to entertain the populace, and learn what a redistribution of funds could do for all students, boys and girls, the reordering of priorities will ensue.

3. *The Science Laboratories.* By 1980, the high school laboratories as we have known them—chemistry, physics, and biology—will likewise have given way to the ravages of progress. The same influences that blended the library and its academic classrooms will blend the laboratories, each into the other, as the lines between the sciences blur.

By 1980, high school science laboratories will be neutral space with easy access to utilities located in both the floor and the ceiling. By 1980, science educators will have adopted the obvious economy already practiced in automobile service stations—the convenient availability of power, water, and gases through quick-connecting hoses pulled down from the ceiling, out from the wall, or up from the floor.

Many a high school laboratory will have instruments which today are found only in colleges, and the subspaces will be designed for teams of students just as industry research is now conducted by teams of scientists. Students in science will be taught to cooperate in group discovery rather than, as now, compete for individual prizes. The 1980 laboratories will provide storage for the apparatus of long-term investigations and not, as now, force the student to dismantle his equipment and obliterate the evidence of his quest when a bell rings in 50 minutes.

By 1980, the central thrust of science education will be ecological. Bio-systems and bio-ecology will be the overriding concerns as man seeks to undo the damage he did to his planet in the first two-thirds of the twentieth century.

The neat rows of rectangular islands in the typical laboratory will have given way to quickly rearrangeable space. The laboratories will be carpeted for the same reasons that kitchens and bathrooms are being carpeted today—to reduce fatigue and noise. And the laboratory can be expected to be open for business the same hours as the school library which in 1980 will be most of the time including evenings and Saturdays.

Expect, too, that earth science, oceanography, and marine biology will be lively subjects. Indeed, by 1980 the national interest in the ocean may be equal to our interest in outer space.

Even in the sciences the ultimate luxury will be universal space made special by specialized equipment. Schools can afford to write off the cost of equipment as it is obsoleted but they can't afford to write off space. Despite the constraints of plumbing and the prejudices of early settlers in the faculty, laboratories will increasingly be "open plan."

In sum, the high school of 1980 will be, in effect, a great tent-like structure offering freedom of movement to its occupants. No one knows what things will be talked about in the year 1984 or the year 2020, when the building built today is still standing, nor do we know what kinds of instruments for learning will be employed.

But we do know that students will be learning from teachers, from each other, and from things. The best school will be the one that not only supports learning but nourishes the spirit. Unlike the high schools of the mid-twentieth century which focused on efficiency and the fast processing of youth, the schools of the 1980s will seek both light and warmth. After all, as Unamuno said, "It is not the night that kills, but the frost."

Teaching Technology

John W. Loughary

In this paper, I will discuss some of the general kinds of change in educational capability that by 1980 should result from the effective utilization of appropriate technology in high schools, and will suggest implications of these changes, especially for future planning.

Specific technological developments are in part determined by the present state of the art, which can be assessed. They are also affected by a variety of other factors which are difficult to identify with any reliability, except to know that they are always potentially important. Economic conditions, congressional fads, rediscovering the poor, changes in the Department of Defense structure and concerns, modifications in corporate goals and teacher-student revolutions are illustrations of such variables. They can have surprising and unpredictable effects on advances in education.

World War II, in every sense, probably did as much to refine education as any other single phenomenon. The training demands of the massive military mobilization overwhelmed educational capabilities. The need for greater capabilities was extremely critical, and new ones were created almost overnight. But we cannot conclude that critical periods of national defense necessarily encourage the development of new educational capabilities. Conditions change. In the last few years, for instance, increasing educational capacity has been made available to the educational community itself. However, the continuing war has directly reduced this support.

There are other illustrations of the problems involved in forecasting specific developments and capabilities. In 1960, for example, programmed instruction appeared to be well on its way to becoming commonplace in classrooms throughout the country. Dozens of firms began marketing—or at least advertising—hardware and software; professional associations and publications devoted to programmed instruction were formed; and a few colleges began to offer course work in programming procedures. What appeared to be an obviously valid forecast did not materialize. Will the same be true, for example, of computer-assisted instruction? We hear much talk and promise about the impact of CAI in the near future. But many of my school district friends are asking; Where is the necessary software? Will it be developed, and when, and by whom?

Though planning for a 10 to 20 year time span can and should be flexible and amenable to changes because of revised technological forecasts, there is still a point at which educational leaders must make a commitment. We cannot wait until the technology has proven itself before deciding to go along with it—that is, to gear up our institutions to accept a capability. To do so would be to engage in a waiting game between those who are primarily concerned with developing technology, and those who are primarily interested in using it.

Furthermore, the nature of technology being what it is, and when the task is to develop strategy for the next two decades, I would argue that we should not rule out any kind of potential educational capability.*

With all of these challenges and cautions in mind, I want to suggest several kinds of educational capabilities growing out of the use of technology which we should explore carefully now. Such an exploration, I believe, will lead to more specific and valid forecasts for high school 1980.

What follows should be qualified by: "It could be possible." What takes place will depend in part upon what educators do about existing technology.

We are really only in the mechanical phase of the technological revolution in education. Nearly all of the man-machine systems now being operated in education, are clumsy. They are exciting—but so was the Model T as compared with the horse. Computer applications in education to date are quite cumbersome. They seldom work as well as predicted; they cause many inconveniences, and most require a fairly constant application of technological bailing wire. As a number of users have commented, for example, the only trouble with flexible scheduling is that it is highly inflexible. If its goal is

* An important problem in attempting forecasts about technological developments in education is that, as a result of our excitement about hoped-for improvements, we tend to be premature, in judging the readiness of a given technological development for use in schools. Many of us, in our enthusiasm, describe an idea to the practicing educator but fail to note what stage the idea has reached in the research and development process. We tend to get our tenses mixed. We often say *is* when we mean *will*, or *could*, or even *might*. The problem is that in the research and development process we learn more not only about the technology, but also about what we should be seeking to do in education. Many of us operate in blissful ignorance of recent findings and, more important, of revised decisions and plans.

to make possible individualized instruction, then flexible scheduling will have succeeded on the day that we no longer need to schedule students.

COMPUTER-BASED DATA SYSTEMS

Perhaps the most obvious increased capability which computers could bring to high schools is that of storing, retrieving, and manipulating large amounts of data about students. Large and flexible learning-data systems will have two main functions: (1) instructional management and (2) educational research. The first provides constant monitoring and analysis of student learning behavior absolutely essential for individualized instruction. The second offers one of the greatest opportunities for making substantial improvement in the teaching-learning process. It should be helpful to describe in at least some detail, the components of such a system. Several are under development, including one by American Institutes for Research and another by the Portland, Oregon, schools. The one with which I am most familiar is called System for Individualized Instruction Management (SIIM).

This system includes two basic computer files: a curriculum file and a student file. The system can have one or several input/output modes. Figure 1 shows the kinds of reports that can be generated, as well as the research and evaluation that can be undertaken by using the system. Probably types of output from an initial version include findings of immediate practical use, such as:

—student appraisal reports
—student status reports
—warning messages for students not meeting expectations
—suggestions for instructor-directed presentation groupings
—individualized instructional materials list
—instructional materials inventory lists
—indications of special interest groups

Research generated by the system would include:

—evaluation of specific materials for various kinds of pupils
—studies of objective sequence patterns
—studies of teacher and student use in reactions to various input/output formats and modes
—studies of information volume and space limitations and instruction
—studies of comparative instructional systems and procedures

There is a master curriculum file (map) for each course unit, as well as an individual curriculum map for each student. The master file contains performance objectives, and instructional-materials index, a test-item bank, sequence dependencies, and classifications of intellectual activity. All test items and instructional materials are indexed to the performance objectives. The curriculum file serves as a unique driver for the system that permits the development of generalized program design, applicable in different subject-matter areas and different environments.

The student file contains the individual curriculum map; characteristics such as age, aptitude, and interest; behavior records (materials and activities involved in the student's work; and his performance record (test scores).

Given the initial curriculum map and student file, daily or weekly recommended changes for the map are based on updated performance objectives. An analysis is made of the student's subject matter strengths and weaknesses, as well as of his intellectual activity. Recommendations might include: a change in the sequence of performance objectives, substitution for an objective where unexpected strength has been revealed, or the addition or repetition of an objec-

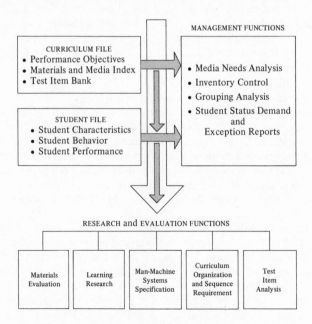

FIGURE 1. System for individualized instruction management.

tive to overcome an indicated weakness. (A print-out of this record would be provided at regular intervals as requested, or when changes are to be recommended.)

An analysis is made also of the instructional materials used, based on recorded data and student performance. It indicates materials best suited for a particular individual, as well as a broader evaluation of the effectiveness of the materials.

The test-item bank assembles tests and incorporates review items based on objectives already attained. Students concurrently working on the same objective could receive different test items, depending on analysis results. Extensive item-analysis procedures would include difficulty and discrimination indexes for test items.

An instructor might begin the day by studying a report summarizing the status of individual students. He would note who needed special attention, organize presentations, elect special instruction materials for the day, and determine the points of emphasis of the group's study. Instructor-aide assignments would be made and anticipated tests ordered and printed. He would make inputs on student behavior and performance during the day and he might receive warning messages regarding students having difficulty with their contracted objectives. Toward the close of the day, the instructor would put in requests for data and materials needed for the next day. The administrator, counselor, and other staff members would monitor the instructional program daily as a basis for guiding their own efforts. The system should be available to both students and staff on demand.

Consider the research function of such a system. Imagine that in 1980 50,000 students in several districts are all served by the system. Each student has a file containing data about personal and social characteristics, records of past achievement, and measures of interest and personality. As each student pursues an objective defined in operational terms, the following are put into the system: (1) descriptions of the material and procedures he uses; (2) his reactions to these; (3) teacher observations, and (4) the student's actual accomplishment.

The system could provide answers of several kinds. Relatively simple analyses of alternate materials designed to teach similar objectives could be made. For example, a sample of students could be drawn, each of whom had been pursuing similar objectives, but using different instructional materials—for example, three different texts. One could easily compare the learning achievement of each of the groups. A more sophisticated analysis would be a comparison of different sequence patterns. My guess is that instead of a single sequence, we would discover a number of ways of sequencing in-structional material. Most of us, I assume, have reacted—after reading a book, listening to a lecture, or viewing a film—with a comment such as "If I had known that earlier I would not have been confused all this time," and at the same time, being aware that the fellow in the next seat—no more or no less bright—*had* understood, that is, the sequence of presentation was right for him.

The capability of a research-based instructional system could, if we would use it by 1980, revolutionize education as it now exists. The capability obviously would not be limited to instruction per se, but could be applied to staffing and any other aspect of education.

SATELLITE-SUPPORTED INSTRUCTION

By 1980, one of the more exciting prospects will be *real time instruction* rather than historical instruction, through increased use of tele-vision, and especially through world wide satellite systems. Given increased technological facilities and staff, students even in the small-est and most remote schools should be able to observe and view events as they occur throughout the world. Whether it is a riot in Chicago, a debate in the British Parliament, or a ten-week series of half-hour programs on experimental farming in Arabia, students could observe what is taking place *at the time it takes place.*

This world wide communication facility has many obvious advan-tages for education. Not the least among them is counteracting the provincialism characteristic of much education, even in secondary schools. I am not suggesting that there is no value in acquainting students with a local and regional history.

At the same time, it is clear that high school 1980 must become more cognizant of a world society. Traditional schools have attempted something like this through the study of either ancient civilization or of a regional history. In my own region, for example, students spend an unreasonable amount of time examining the living habits of Northwest Indians, in part—according to curriculum guides—as a means of studying primitive and developing countries such as those in Africa. One reason that this is done of course, is that materials exist on the Northwest Indians, while they are much more difficult to find on the emerging African nations. The problem has been—and to some extent still is—one of educational capability. Movies are expensive and, in the area of social studies, they are frequently out of date before they are available for classroom use. Video tapes are relatively inexpensive, and the lag between recording and use is insignificant.

Grant then, if you will, the possibility of a rather tremendous world wide satellite-assisted audio-video network for education. It is clear, I believe, that some such system will develop. Even though the specific characteristics are unpredictable now, educators should begin thinking about how they can make the best use of a satellite system.

A number of serious problems and difficult tasks lie between an educational capability and its effective use. One problem is especially critical. It involves the level of inference of presentations and displays of the subject matter, whether it is by lecture, book, film, tour, or some other medium.

A certain amount of abstracting or selecting must take place in the preparation of content for presentation. The learner's time is too valuable to waste on irrelevant and needlessly repetitious materials.

Given the real time nature of an audiovisual world wide communications capability, we must deal with two kinds of questions: How can we be selective, given the short time frame? What shall we select, or more to the point, what shall we use as selective criteria? The first problem apparently can be solved satisfactorily. In general, experts suggest buffer systems in which "raw" information is temporarily stored, analyzed, edited, rearranged, merged, or whatever is appropriate, and then displayed to the learner. They are quick to point out that the more serious problem relates to what is selected, a problem basic to the whole technological revolution in education. The issue itself, particularly in a world-oriented educational enterprise, can be deceptively complex. It is even more complex when the educational vehicle has the real time characteristic noted above.

A good part of the deception results from the problem of omission because of unawareness. The current concern over whether or not history texts give adequate attention to Negro history and its contribution to the development of America is illustrative. It is apparent that the critics are correct. And while it could be that the omission was willful in the case of a few authors and publishers, the important reason for the omission is really insensitivity, or middle-class cultural blindness. The Negro was not maliciously left out of history books, (he was however, maliciously left out of history); he was simply seldom seen. How can we avoid the same kind of error in using an audio-visual technology capability?

The immediate interpretation of an event may be revised significantly with the perspective of time. When the publication lag no longer exists, how can we guard against teaching concepts which may soon need to be "untaught"?

PUBLISHING CAPABILITIES

By 1980, another capability resulting from computer technology and increased audio-visual reproduction devices can have great impact on the primary medium of instruction, namely books, and can destroy the basic one book, one course educational model. It will be possible to go from author manuscript to indexing to magnetic storage, to generating hard copies of such things as CBI (Computer Based Instruction) programs in response to teachers' specifications. Authors will not contract to write or revise texts, as is now the case, but rather to update data banks and materials. Ideally, a teacher—or "instructional team leader"—will indicate the learning objectives for one or more students, and the computer will search its files and produce a combination of materials best suited to the objectives. The chief problem, as always, will involve the issue of stating objectives. Whether we call them performance criteria or behavioral objectives, this kind of capability will make a significant contribution only after learning objectives are stated in precise terms. Our experience to date has taught us that this is an extremely difficult task. Until we master it, however, all we can do is to index the subsections of books, and treat these as entities. This, in itself, offers at least certain economic advantages and somewhat greater flexibility, but falls short of individualized or prescribed instruction which is truly responsive to the needs of pupils.

INSTRUCTION THAT IS INDEPENDENT OF TEACHERS

The technology to which I have alluded can be viewed from another perspective: that is, the changed role and function of the teacher and student in the educational process. Much has been written about the impact of technology on the role of teachers, but I would suggest that more attention should be given to the changed role and responsibilities of the student. We really cannot appreciate the importance of technology for the teacher's role without considering what will happen to students in 1980.

It appears obvious to many that the application of sophisticated technology in education will reduce the need for the teacher "interface" function between instructional materials (content or substance) and the learner. In other words, the capability for teacher-independent instruction will be increased.

By 1980, the high school teacher's function as a presenter of information could easily be eliminated entirely. He will continue to interpret, synthesize, and clarify information displayed in another mode. Whether teacher and student will spend less time together has caused concern among some educators, They ask if technology will dehumanize education. It could lead in this direction, but I doubt that it will. "Interaction" probably misstates what goes on in most lecture halls and classrooms today, where the student's role is largely passive. A reduction in this kind of student-teacher relationship, and a concomitant increase in true student-teacher interaction may in fact increase the humaneness of instruction in high school 1980.

A more important outcome of the teacher-independent instructional capability for students, is by definition, the increase in responsibility which students must assume for their own learning behavior —a radical change from the tight control teachers have maintained over students in the past. The freedom to explore and to set his own pace, plus a comprehensive in-depth instructional capability to support independent learning should lead to the development of a new breed of students. Their perceptions of "school" will be very different from that of present-day students.

Increased technological capabilities will profoundly affect the role of teachers, without a doubt. First of all, technology will provide both new educational tools, and thus change the teaching process. Secondly, technology will involve teachers in new functions. Most of what has been said so far has concerned the first kind of capability. A few comments about the second kind—namely changes in staff deployment—are appropriate at this point.

If we keep in mind that the labels are merely suggestive, it is reasonable to assume that by 1980 man-machine educational systems will require at least four kinds of nonteaching specialists: (1) content research specialists, (2) media specialists, (3) educational systems specialists, and (4) educational engineers. They will serve as a kind of support team to teachers. The team concept is critical and the maximum contribution by each area cannot be made independently of the others. Perhaps the most effective way to describe the function of each is to illustrate how they might operate in a high school that is fully exploiting new capabilities.

The teacher's first responsibility will be to determine the learning objectives for students and to communicate these to the specialists. Before members of the team can function, they must know what the teacher-leader wants to achieve. Precisely what behavior of his students does he think should be modified, promoted, or eliminated? Given a statement of objectives and information about the students to be taught (no easy task), the content researcher, media specialist, and systems specialist could assist the teacher to develop appropriate instructional systems.

Content Research Specialists. The content researcher will have the responsibility of identifying and synthesizing subject matter relevant to the particular objectives. In part a librarian, he will have at his disposal an information-retrieval system much more sohpisticated and sensitive than traditional manual classification systems. The task would be to identify the most appropriate materials for the instructional objectives stated—those which are most sensitive to the characteristics of the individual students.

Media Specialists. Given the learning goals, students' characteristics, and a pool of material from which to work, the media specialist will have to determine the most effective modes of presentation and then assemble and construct instructional materials. Besides available libraries of materials and collections of equipment, an equally important resource would be a media laboratory and production shop. Media specialists will include artists, audio-visual production specialists, material programmers, and so on.

Educational Systems Specialists. The educational systems specialist represents the greatest staff innovation required by man-machine systems in education, which embody such complexity, coordination, and knowledge of machines as the teacher cannot reasonably be expected to master. The systems specialist must put the various resources together and design a control procedure which will enable the teacher to exercise and maintain maximum surveillance and control over the teaching and learning processes.

The ultimate goal of man-machine systems in education is to achieve truly individualized instruction, and the closer one approaches this goal, the more complex the systems become. The potential for chaos—the failure to instruct anybody in much of anything—also increases. All of the "what happens if" and "what should be done when this takes place" questions must be anticipated and thought through, with solutions provided and built into the system. Thus, the task of the systems specialist is to assemble the components of instruction provided by the resource and material specialists according to the specifications determined by the teacher. In highly sophisticated systems, educational systems undoubtedly will require the skills of computer programmers.

Educational Engineers. In larger schools the efficient use, maintenance, and modification of complex man-machine educational systems will require a staff of engineers familiar with the school or school system and with education in general.

BIO-ELECTRONIC LEARNING

Only a few of the many kinds of possible new educational capabilities have been discussed here. However, I would not want to leave this brief exercise in forecasting, without at least mentioning a kind of future capability which represents a new dimension, rather than an extension, of education. The capabilities discussed to this point are all "outside" of the individual. They attempt to make it easier for the organism to change itself.

There will emerge by 1980, I believe, the capacity to make direct changes in human learning ability. Such things as laser beam technology, advances in endocrinology, biochemical control of genetics, and preconscious cognition techniques will provide an exciting and somewhat frightening prospect. They will be exciting because of the tremendous potential for enhancing learning—and frightening because they entail unprecedented moral, ethical, and philosophical problems. While these possibilities are more speculative than other kinds of emerging technology, educational planning that does not give them at least some serious consideration is short sighted.

The main obstacle to the development and use of sophisticated data banks and information systems, I suspect, is not any problems posed by the technology itself, but technology's putative threat to the educational establishment. American education operates on a set of myths dating from the time when few had access to stored knowledge (print on pages) and thereby had the power to influence tremendously who should learn what. The educational elite—that is, the establishment—guarded its capability closely, and carefully handed it down to each new generation. More recently the professors of administration largely decided what teachers could know and do, and the teachers (which is only fair, of course) decided what materials students should learn. (Somewhere in the shuffle professors of teacher education tended to get bumped aside.) But the bastion around the educational preserve is crumbling. The old restrictions on classroom content are made ineffective by information available through such sources as movies, television, and greater freedom in the printing and distribution of materials.

The point is simply that new and powerful educational capabilities exist outside the school, and out of control of the educational establishment. This emerging trend will continue, and educators will either "get with it" or find learners increasingly dissatisfied with school and teachers.

Preparing the Teacher and Administrator

Charles E. Brown

History suggests that the schools may not be very different at all in 1980. After all, the typical high school of today is not really very different, at least in style and form, from the school I attended some 28 years ago, and given the difficulties associated with major institutional change, 10 years does not seem very long. On the other hand, there are forces now at work in our society, particularly among the young people, that will very likely necessitate a more rapid response by the schools than we have been accustomed to in the past. In any event, let me talk about some of my hopes if not my confident predictions, for the schools a decade hence.

In expressing these hopes, I start with the conviction that a redefinition of the function of education is needed in this country, a definition that may enable us to meet more fully the human needs of our society. As I reflect on where we are now as a human group, I come to the conclusion that we have lost touch with ourselves, and with each other. In spite of our advanced methods of communication, we seldom really communicate with others, and find it difficult to establish the kind of empathetic relationship with others that might enable us to find out who they are and what they are all about. Similarly, we tend to evade even the seeking of a deeper understanding of ourselves, we tend to "protect" our inner lives from those kinds of experiences that probe beneath the superficiality of our daily existence, that may crack the veneer of reserve that seems to me to be characteristic of many Americans.

Hence, we have great difficulty in understanding our children, we are often unable to come to grips with the nature of prejudice, particularly white racism, the concept of loving others is too often regarded in only sentimental terms, and our acts of worship have become a kind of cultural habit rather than moving, fulfilling experiences. What I am saying is that the *quality* of our lives has diminished, and we find too many people living out their lives in a kind of mindless, sterile existence, with each day a foretaste of tomorrow, and each night bringing the same kind of tired resignation to the inevitability of it all. Too many of us feel that we are controlled by the seemingly inexorable forces of a bureaucratic and technocratic society that shape our lives in ways that we barely understand but against which we have little resistance. As a consequence, much of the sense of humanity that is so desperately needed in the determination of human affairs has gone from our individual lives and from the institutions of which we are a part. It was Lincoln who said that we cannot escape history. We can only fail to be aware of it. And one has to wonder if we are aware of the pageant of history to which we are contributing.

I believe that it is to this lack of awareness, to this indifference, to this mindlessness, to this absence of a real sense of humanity that the schools must address themselves. A new concept of public education is needed, a concept that will enable us to prepare a generation of men and women who are more able than we to cope with and to live fully with their world. I agree with those who say that we need to find ways to educate men not only to think, but to *feel*, and to *act*. Man's inhumanity to man is *real*, and more than anything else, the schools must educate for humanity—by helping people to understand who they are, how they and their institutions relate to other people, and how human behavior can be changed.

I am aware of the idealistic and perhaps naive nature of my statement but the trouble is that I am dealing with what we seem to regard as "soft" words or concepts—words like trust, respect, humanity, dignity, love. The "harder" terms that we have used in the past to talk about the school (such as discipline, intelligence, testing, homework, organization) are somehow easier to deal with, and even now I find it difficult to convince myself that we can ever think of the school in any other terms. But my conviction is that the words I have used to talk about the future are not "soft"—they are real, and the stuff of which a civilized society is made, and somehow we have to find ways to translate this conviction into new kinds of learning, teaching, and institutional styles. And if we are to do this, it will have to be done with the full involvement of those people who are legally and professionally responsible for shaping the school, the teachers and administrators. To be sure, it is increasingly evident that the community, and particularly the students, are going to be demanding changes in the high school, but in the final analysis, really significant change will come about only as teachers and administrators make it happen.

Because so much of the responsibility for change rests on teachers and administrators, the education of educators is crucially important, and we need to ask ourselves some hard questions regarding the

process. First, we have to think once more about the teacher and administrator as a *person,* and as I do this, I am drawn to the com-
panion volume of this text, *Campus 1980,* and the chapter in it en-
titled "The Future of Teaching" by William Arrowsmith. All that I
could say about the importance of educators as *men,* and more, is
said by Mr. Arrowsmith, and in my judgment, powerfully and elo-
quently. For example:

> We, too, lack educators—by which I mean Socratic *teachers,* visible em-
> bodiments of the *realized* humanity of our aspirations, intelligence, skill,
> scholarship; men ripened or ripening into realization. . . . It is *men* we need,
> not programs. . . . It is only in the teacher that the end is apparent; he can
> humanize because he possesses the human skills which give him the power
> to humanize others. . . . He is the student's only evidence outside the text
> that a great humanity exists: upon his *impersonation* both his text and his
> student's human fate depend. . . . *Men,* not programs; *galvanizers,* not
> conductors.

I concur. A friend of mine, who is himself a great teacher, puts it
simply when he talks about the need in teaching for what he calls
"whole men," and I suppose this is what Arrowsmith had in mind
when he, in more elegant words, talks about men who "represent
the integration of significant life and knowledge, of compassionate
study and informed conduct." And the point is important, for (once
more to quote from Arrowsmith), ". . . lacking such men, the student
distrusts the teacher and the culture he represents; the culture is
defeated in the teacher's failure."
It seems evident enough that we lack such men everywhere in our
society. Nonetheless, it is apparent to me that unless we can attract
more of this kind of person into teaching, the schools are not going
to change very much, and I believe that there are some steps we can
begin to take.
First, to put it bluntly—and to state the obvious—if prospective
teachers are not themselves well taught, by sensitive and humane
teachers, then we can have little hope that they will become the kind
of public-school teachers we need. And I believe that it will not be
enough to "just" improve college teaching: the whole question of
how a college student (and particularly an undergraduate) learns
best needs to be reexamined. In the Winter 1968 issue of *Daedalus,*
Martin Duberman describes an experiment in education in one of
his classes at Princeton. In this article he makes two statements
(among many others) which are pertinent to the point under discussion. He begins the article as follows: "I have been an educator
for ten years, but I have really been interested in education only

for the past year or so. Before that I was chiefly interested in my career." It is with this kind of honesty and candor that we must begin if we are to change the universities. And the direction of change is suggested by another line in his article: ". . . I do not know what 'education' is if not self-examination and change." If Martin Duberman's ideas, and the kind of experimentation in learning and teaching he has tried at Princeton can become commonplace among college teachers, then we may have a chance of finding more of the kind of men and women we need as teachers in the high school of 1980.

And the importance of this point cannot be overlooked, for people tend to teach the way they were taught. If college teaching is pedantic, dull, and stereotyped, what right do we have to expect anything different as the college student himself becomes a teacher? Indeed, there are those who believe that the current style of college and university teaching represents the greatest single weakness in the process of teacher education. And this is not a criticism of just the teacher's colleges, for the overwhelming majority of today's teachers are prepared in large, multi-purpose universities. So my earlier statement is worth repeating: if we want a new kind of high school teacher in 1980, then teaching at the college level is going to have to change first.

A second step we can take is to begin the process of preparation for teaching much earlier than has been the case, by involving children of all ages in teaching other children. By 1980 this should be done in a systematic way beginning in the elementary grades, and continuing through high school and at least the undergraduate years of college. Further, it should be a part of the education of all students, with special opportunities available for those who become particularly interested. Specifically, I would like to see some student-organized and student-taught "courses" or seminars in every high school, perhaps beginning with the summer school if people find it difficult to imagine this happening during the regular year.

Beyond this, we should organize "institutes for future teachers," both during the school year and the summer, drawing upon all available talent in a region or locality to staff such institutes. Because I would want these to be something more than a course in "how to teach," I hope they would at least originate as semi-independent institutes, rather than being the creation of a particular high school or college faculty. Thus, in the Greater Boston area, where I happen to live, such an institute might be put together through the efforts of several of the universities or colleges in the area and a number of school systems, but also involve a variety of community agencies and the local media. Such a coalition (as an example only) would not only bring together an outstanding variety of resources, human and otherwise, but would enable the group to develop a variety of learning opportunities for students. By 1980 I can see, for example, the systematic involvement via television of hundreds of students with such people as Jerome Bruner and Erik Erikson as they talk about learning styles, followed by locally-organized discussion groups staffed by sensitive public school teachers. I can see summer schools or, for the bolder types, "regular" schools being established around some of the experimental ideas of learning and teaching that we so desperately need to explore, and organized around the ideas of teachers *and* student-teachers. I can see in 1980, perhaps for the first time in our history, a thoughtful involvement of students in the study of education, which strangely enough, has never found a place in our public school curriculum. And as important as the potential benefit for future teachers would be, I can see a real possibility in such institutes for growth in those who are already teaching. I am aware of the sketchy nature of my description of this new kind of organization, but I remain convinced that it is a viable idea and one that is simply waiting for someone to start putting it all together. We must begin immediately because the teachers of the high school of 1980 are now students in our public schools, and we are doing precious little to encourage them in any systematic and sustained way to become teachers, let alone the *kind* of teachers the future needs. It seems to me that too much is at stake for us to neglect this opportunity.

By 1980 we must be more concerned and intelligent about the formal preparation of teachers. I guess this is a difficult subject and my confusion about it grows out of a number of things: my inability, after working with and interviewing thousands of teachers over the years to isolate one pattern of preparation that produced the better teachers I have known; my feeling, as stated by Peter Drucker in an article in the Fall 1968 issue of *Daedalus* that "so far we neither know what the skill of teaching is nor how to convey or acquire it;" and my uncertainty about the necessity of certain kinds of special preparation for particular teaching roles. So I can offer only the most general of observations. It seems to me that there should be five major parts to the process of preparing a teacher:

1. A careful screening of candidates is needed at the point when they indicate an interest in enrolling in such a program. Do we not know enough about the assessment of personality, attitudes, and other psychological and personal attributes to make at least a general screening of those who simply should not be teachers? If my friend James Koerner were looking over my shoulder at this point, he would

probably remind me again that the sheer size of the teaching force in this country makes such a process of screening an impractical wish. This may be the case, but I remain convinced that we should at least begin.

2. All teachers should be liberally educated, if we can ever decide what that means. For me, and for my purposes at the moment, it means a style of education, a process, rather than a particular pattern of courses. James Bryant Conant, in his book *The Education of American Teachers* talks about it as something that is "characterized by what it aspires to, rather than by what it embraces." I think the implications of what he says are important. Also, it suggests to me the word "open," which I think is what John Seeley had in mind when he wrote about education as a process of "building up" in "the sense in which a poem, a good love affair, or a good life builds up toward an ever-open, potentially ever self-transcendent, ever culminating non-conclusion."* I think if professional teacher preparation could be built on that kind of base, we might be able to move toward the kind of schools I discussed earlier.

3. Education *is* worth studying, we should take it more seriously than we do, and we should find the best people in our colleges and universities (from perhaps the disciplines of psychology, philosophy, history, sociology, and anthropology) to create new "cores of learning experiences" to provide an opportunity for a serious study of the learning process for every prospective teacher. I have deliberately avoided the use of the term "course" in this statement, since I am not sure what such a "learning experience" would look like. Clearly, however, teachers should benefit from a thorough knowledge of the history and philosophy of education, from a greater understanding of how an anthropologist or a sociologist might look at a school or at education generally, as well as from a study of the psychology of learning. At least we can try to understand what Israel Scheffler had in mind when he wrote:

If we . . . conceive of the education of teachers not simply as the training of individual classroom performers, but as the development of a class of intellectuals vital to a free society, we can see more clearly the role of educational scholarship and theoretical analysis in the process. For though the latter do not directly enhance craftsmanship, they raise continually the sorts of questions that concern the larger goals, the setting and meaning of educational practice. It is these questions that students need continually to have before them as they develop into mature teachers, if they are in-

* John Seeley, "Educational Policy Today," *Urban Review*, Vol. 3, No. 2, November, 1968.

deed to help shape the purposes and conditions of education. To link the preparation of teachers with such questions is the special opportunity of the university.

4. One should learn how to teach by teaching, and I would include an intensive and extensive internship as one of my major components. If we can find enough really qualified school systems, this function should be assigned to them, with carefully selected and trained "teacher trainees" taking on this task as their major responsibility. Such teachers may have "clinical" appointments with a college or university, or they might have some affiliation with the state department of education, but they must be selected much more carefully than is presently the case, and they should be paid well for their efforts. The development of such a cadre of people is a matter of high priority for the future, and I should think that by 1980 every state department in the country should have some plan developed by which this can be done.

I should add, however, that merely the creation of an extended internship will not help improve teaching. If possible, such an experience should be in a setting where the prospective teacher is taught in the style which most nearly approximates the style which we see the future demanding. This may be unrealistic, both because we may be uncertain about the style of the future and because we will not be able to find enough such places in which internes can work. But if we want to train teachers to value the things I talked about earlier—openness, trust, flexibility, student participation, being humane, etc.—then we will have to try to place them as internes in schools where these qualities are valued.

5. The entry into full time teaching should be more gradual than it is at present. There are a variety of ways in which this can be done (all of which will add to our school budgets, by the way, but it is an important point and worth whatever investment it requires). I suspect that many potentially fine teachers are either lost to the profession entirely or turn sour too soon simply because they are overwhelmed by the complexities of being thrown into a full teaching load (plus other responsibilities) before they are ready.

I do wish that I could say more about preservice programs for teachers, that I could offer some neat solution to the various problems that plague this field. But I am convinced that there is no such solution, and that improvement in teacher education will come about only as we tackle the broader factors mentioned above. For me, at least, the problem in teacher education is not one of developing a specific model that will produce the "best" teachers—I think there are a number of such models—but rather one of generating the kind of institutional change that will improve college teaching, involve the schools (and the broader community, too) more fully as responsible participants in the process, and help us become clearer than we are now about the basic purpose of education. The last point is particularly important; unless we know what we are seeking to accomplish in the name of education, then all the rest becomes a kind of mindless exercise in change for its own sake.

A fourth question we must face if we are to improve teaching is; Who is a teacher? By 1980 we must find room in the teaching field for a whole variety of people: community workers, parents, part-time teachers, college professors or others with specialized knowledge, poets, musicians and artists, retired people. And I do not mean that these would just be interesting people to have around; rather, I would like to see them incorporated fully into a teaching faculty, not on an ad hoc, occasional basis, but with a view towards utilizing as completely as possible their time and talent in a sustained, thoughtful way.

To do this may require the development of new kinds of institutions that help to prepare such people for their various roles, a process that may lead us to recognize that there may indeed be a variety of routes by which a person may become a teacher in the future. Also, it may require a reexamination of one of the major hurdles to change in the teaching profession: state certification and licensing requirements. Again, I wish it were possible for me to offer a formula for the solution of this problem, but once more I must confess to a feeling of frustration. My frustration centers around my conviction that certification laws as presently defined and implemented are all but meaningless, serve only a kind of nuisance value, and unfortunately keep some good people out of teaching. Let me rephrase that. What I mean to say is that the present philosophy of certification, based as it is on the accumulation of certain course credits, has no relationship to the quality of teaching, and it will not be until we begin to talk about *competence* and *performance* as a basis for licensing that any sort of desirable change will take place. Thus, if our whole approach to this problem is wrong, should we not admit it, and begin the process of making those changes that are necessary to make certification and licensing mean something? Or perhaps we should admit that the only place where standards can be applied is at the local level, when a teacher is either hired or rejected, and do away with certification laws entirely.

We must encourage some experimentation in a state where certification could be waived for, say, five years to see if such an apparently drastic step made any measurable difference in the quality of those coming into teaching for the first time. Or we might try an idea that was proposed in Massachusetts (and ultimately discarded by the way), which involved the establishment of an independent commission of scholars, lay people, teachers, and administrators whose responsibility it would be to establish initial criteria for entering teaching and periodically review those already holding certificates, both of which would be done around *performance* criteria, rather than the accumulation of course credits and semester hours. In short, if this whole problem is the disaster area that I think it is, then we need to experiment boldly if we are to find more intelligent solutions. Furthermore, if the schools are going to have to change in the ways that society (and particularly the students) almost certainly will demand, then school people will need all the flexibility and support that the state can provide as they go about the task of staffing their institutions, and they should not have to continue to live with the mindlessness of present certification regulations. Again, time is a factor, and it behooves all of us who can provide any assistance to support those state commissioners or any other state groups that are seeking to bring some new thinking to this entire matter.

While I am at it, I should like to comment briefly on two related problems: tenure laws and the single-salary schedule. As with certification, it seems to me that we should question the whole philosophy of tenure for public school teachers and administrators. One way to raise this question is to suggest that the burden of proof regarding the continuation of existing tenure laws rests with those in the profession; they should be willing to show evidence that the positive influence of tenure laws for the protection of able teachers from administrators, school boards or outside pressure groups of whatever kind exceeds the more negative possibility that these same laws are protecting a significant number of teachers and administrators who do not merit such protection, thus serving in a real way to perpetuate mediocrity in the profession at a time when we particularly need excellence. Similarly, the same sort of question should be raised about the single-salary schedule. To quote from a report by Henry Levin done for The Brookings Institution:

What is rational about a system of salary policies that leads to shortages of classroom teachers with certain backgrounds and surpluses of teachers with others; that is unable to differentiate among teachers on the basis of teaching effectiveness; and that provides the same incentive for a dull and unimaginative teacher as it does for a bright and creative person? This question remains unanswered by the profusion of literature which tacitly or actively supports the single-salary schedule as the *only* feasible salary policy.

It is to this argument that the various professional groups must respond if they are to justify their proclaimed interest in improving the profession.

Let me say a word more about these professional groups. While I have no doubt appeared critical of them, I recognize their dilemma. They do have a point when they insist that the teaching profession will not be improved until salaries are increased and working conditions improved, and I can understand their preoccupation with these problems. On the other hand, it seems necessary to me that they recognize the indefensible nature of the argument that the only way to improve salaries is to treat all teachers alike, or the only way to assure teacher's rights is to assure them for *all* teachers, whether they deserve to be protected or not, or that the way to combat the rigidity of administrators or school boards is to substitute their own brand of rigidity (i.e., in matters such as certification and working hours). I am, I think, teacher-oriented, and a strong believer in teacher power, but with this power must come a degree of accountability for their collective actions that has too often been missing.

By 1980 we must reevaluate the whole matter of the continuing education and the re-education of teachers. To state that we have not been as concerned about this problem as we should be is to state the obvious. Anyone who has taught knows that to work hard at it is to drain oneself both emotionally and intellectually, and when the only stimulation a teacher gets from his peers is during the coffee break, it is not surprising that intellectual and emotional bankruptcy sets in all too soon in too many teacher's lives. Beyond this broad need for self-renewal, there is the demand for renewal in one's discipline, plus the constant need for curriculum evaluation and development. And in the face of these realities of a teacher's life, all that we have been able to offer is an occasional summer workshop, or an afternoon or evening "course" at the local college, or a curriculum committee meeting "after school," or if one is lucky, a single sabbatical leave during an entire teaching career. Is it any wonder that teachers go stale—or quit? Indeed, the wonder of it is that so many good people have stayed with it, and even managed to grow as individuals and as teachers.

If we add to all of the above the need for a major *reeducation* of teachers, the problem becomes rather overwhelming. And in spite of my caution about the slowness of institutional change as expressed in the beginning of this chapter, I think there is some evidence that at least in the East and the Far West, we are on the verge of a student rebellion in the high school that will force teachers and administrators to reexamine completely their attitudes toward their roles, the student's roles, and, indeed, the whole style of the school itself. The closed, bureaucratic system that denies a student almost any opportunity to be an individual and to participate in shaping his own education is simply no longer realistic, and to change all of this is going to require a massive job of reeducating both teachers and administrators. (I should make it clear that I am not assigning blame for the current situation to all teachers and administrators. These are not evil people, conspiring against students. Rather, their inappropriate response to student rebellion usually results from the unthinking application of what they have been taught in the past to believe about school operation. At any rate, some of this reeducation will take place in an informal way as students begin to exercise their political power and force confrontations with the school, confrontations that might be difficult, but that also should be educating. But to assume that we can solve this problem by growing with each crisis that comes along is hardly a sufficient answer.

One of the problems we will have to face in this regard is that many adults, and perhaps particularly school people, regard conflict as a negative thing, and something to be avoided. It seems to me that to the extent that this attitude exists, it will have to be altered, for it is becoming increasingly clear that conflict is often a necessary ingredient in the process of change, and that we will have to learn not only to live with it, but to accept it in positive terms. Nonetheless, it is clear that what we have regarded as conventional wisdom will no longer do in many cases, and ways must be found to enable high school personnel to cope with an increasingly politicized student body. Clearly, the tired answers of the past will not do, and the high school of 1980 must try new approaches. Some come to mind:

1. The establishment of more experimental high schools, where students and teachers who are willing are asked to create their own institution. Obviously, much more needs to be said about such a process than that simple statement, but the need to learn *how* to create new institutions is so great that experimentation on a broad scale is very much in order.

2. The creation of "institutes," either on a local or a regional basis, that bring together administrators, teachers, students, parents, and appropriate professional people on a sustained and regular basis in order to at least bring out into the open the failures of the present institution. These people rarely talk (I mean really talk) with each other now, and such a process of self-examination would be a healthy

beginning toward change. I offer this suggestion as an alternative to sensitivity training sessions or seminars on institutional change at the local college or university because I think it is essential that *all* of the parties involved be a part of the process that leads toward change, and too often the training lab or the college course serves only a limited clientele. On the surface, this may not appear to be a bold step, but if it were done, it would represent a dramatic departure from the kind of relationship the people I am talking about have had with each other in the past.

3. Any attempt at widespread change requires leadership, and we should begin to experiment with new institutional forms that may help to prepare people for this function. Again, we cannot wait for graduate programs in administration to change, and indeed, we cannot wait for the whole process of graduate education to be completed. Instead, we need to invent new "centers," or "institutes," or call them what you will, that can respond more quickly and with greater flexibility to this need. Such centers would not need to be all hung up about degrees, or credits, or any of the other institutional traditions that a college or university finds difficult to avoid, and they could work more easily, not only with formal leaders (such as principals) but with teachers, students, community people and even school board members. Staffing such places would admittedly be a problem, but it seems to me that the situation is urgent enough to demand the assistance of a whole host of highly-trained university people who are now spending considerable time doing research or getting a book published.

4. Is it wholly naïve of me to imagine that we could convince the television industry that it might make available on a regular basis a block of prime time to be devoted to the reeducation of school administrators and teachers? I suppose it is, but I make the suggestion anyway. Imagine, if you will, an arrangement under which the commercial stations provided the time for a weekly or even semi-weekly presentation (lecture, panel discussion, film, etc.) to a nationwide audience, followed by an opportunity through the use of local ETV stations for interchange and discussion from the audience in a particular locality. Imagine, too, the resources, the "faculty" that *could* be pulled together for such a series—could, that is, if we were to take this problem seriously.

5. In connection with the "institutes" suggested earlier, we should experiment with new ways of helping people to look at themselves. For example, the use of video tapes that enable a person or a group of people to "look back" and reflect on their words, their actions and their behavior in a group situation may be a powerful tool in

generating the kind of attitudinal change on the part of teachers and administrators that I think is necessary if the schools are to change.

Above all, as we contemplate the education and reeducation of teachers, it is essential that we think of ways to generate changes in style, attitudes and educational values, and not just in techniques of instruction or in patterns of curriculum. I am convinced that it is here that most of our problems find their roots; that is to say, as important as the question of *what* teachers teach is, it may be that the questions of how they teach, how they ask students to learn, and how they are perceived, as men, by the students they teach are more important. The old saw about actions speaking louder than words has some truth for the schools: *what* they are, what they see as important, the values they hold in the eyes of the students may be the lessons students learn, and these characteristics of present schools will be changed only as the people in them change in real and fundamental ways.

Before anything can be said about the education of high school administrators for 1980 the prior question of the role, or roles, they are to be educated for must be raised. Clearly their role must be recast if the schools are going to change, but in what ways?

One approach to this question is to suggest that the characteristics of the school reflect in a major way the characteristics of the principal. Thus, if we want the schools to be more humane, then the principal must be humane; if the schools are to be "open" in their style, so must the principal; if values such as trust, respect, and individual freedom are to be honored by the school, so must they be honored by the administration.

Similarly, if we want the school, and the students, to be willing to take risks, to be bold in their attitudes toward change, then these traits will have to be part of the principal's bag. And if conflict is to come to be regarded as an inevitable part of change, it will be particularly important for the principal to understand and be willing to support this view.

Another approach to trying to redefine the administrative role is to ask what the kinds of changes I have implied for the high schools of 1980 will mean for what principals and other administrators actually *do*. It is clear, for example, that they will have to surrender or at least share some of their current responsibilities. They must come to understand, for instance, the wisdom of John Seeley's words regarding students: "We must learn the arts of parley and negotiation, rather than the tricks of administration and the methods of government." If that sentence is taken seriously, it means the death of student councils as we now know them, and the encouragement instead of a *real* role for students in setting school policy. The same point of view applies to teachers, and we will find emerging in the high schools a role for them in their own affairs and in school policy that at least approximates the role currently played by a college faculty. Other examples could be offered: a shared role in the appointment and evaluation of teachers and a willingness to *really* involve the community in school affairs being but two illustrations. There can be no doubt, then, that the administrator or 1980 must be an open, secure, and flexible person who does not feel threatened by the notion that he will no longer sit in splendid isolation as the ultimate decision-maker in matters that affect "his" school. Indeed, this is precisely the point—the school should no longer be *his*, but the student's, the teacher's, and the community's.

All of the above suggest a *changed* role for the principal, but not a *diminished* role. In fact, his role will be a critical one. For what he should become is a leader, a facilitator, and a staunch supporter of change. In any dynamic situation, leadership is crucial, and while it should be encouraged and allowed to emerge in a number of places in the school and the community, those holding formal positions of leadership will be particularly important. At a time when many people tend to look to a past that never really was for answers to present dilemmas, we need people who are willing to seek bold new answers. In an age of personal and institutional dysfunction and human conflict, we need those who can rise above the conflict and begin to point a way to some of the answers we so desperately need. In an increasingly technological and materialistic world, we need men and women who can see our problems—and those of the schools —in human terms. We are part of a society starving for such leadership, and nowhere is the need more apparent than in the schools. This is what the high school principalship in 1980 should be all about.

How to prepare people for these new roles? Again, there is no simple answer. For one thing, we cannot even agree on the characteristics of successful leaders, although we can make some educated guesses. For example, there is considerable evidence that intelligence is a major factor, so we should pay more attention to that than we have in the past. In addition, I am convinced that since the administrator of 1980 will not be able to function solely on the basis of being in authority, he will need to possess whatever personal characteristics we can identify as being related to a man who leads because he *is* a leader.

In any event, much of what I said earlier about the education of teachers applies to administrators as well. We need to be concerned about the administrator as a *person*, the *quality* of his education, the need for opportunities for his continued education once on the job, and his attitude toward education and its functions. This latter point is particularly important, in two ways: first, because the administrator is in a key position to help us redefine the aims of education, and second, because he must come to be more aware of what the process of education is all about. As I stated earlier, many people have come to regard the study of education with derision, and while that view may be justified in the light of what is happening in this field now, it need not be the case. The study of education, as such, is important, and should be a part of the intellectual baggage that every administrator brings to the job.

So what I want in the administrator of 1980 is a man (or woman, by the way) who is the type of person described earlier by William Arrowsmith, liberally-educated, open, and with a keen awareness of the possibilities of renewing education in this country. He may or may not have had teaching experience prior to becoming an administrator, but he should be capable of teaching while he is an administrator, and, indeed, should teach. (It should be noted in passing that the qualities I am describing have little to do with current certification requirements for administrators, and these will have to be either abolished or radically changed.) Further, I am convinced that a man can prepare himself for this role in a variety of ways, and therefore I am not prepared to offer a model for his preparation. It is his qualities as a person, rather than a particular pattern of previous experience that counts. It is the quality and style of his education rather than the accumulation of certain "preparatory" courses that matters and that will make a difference. As with Arrowsmith, "it is *men* we need, not program; *galvanizors*, not conductors." With both teachers and administrators the need is great, and we will underestimate it only at our peril as a civilized society.

The Administration of the Secondary School

Lloyd S. Michael

Forecasting, even in education, can be a precarious art in a rapidly changing world. A prediction of the high school a decade away may be more an exercise of fancy than of reason.

In several respects our perspective of the secondary school of the future will probably be correct. The surest thing we can say about the future is that we shall not have solved all of our educational problems. When our difficulties get too trying, then as now we shall exercise the art of "selective inattention." We have failed to find solutions to many educational problems in our day, and will probably fail in the eighties, for the same reason that we have failed to come up with final answers to other problems. We have not always succeeded because the problems are difficult and thinking is hard work. We have failed to resolve all our problems because in the immortal words of Allen's Law, "Everything is more complicated than it seems to most people." In the eighties as now, concerns about the role of educational leadership in the high school will continue to vex us.

There is the assurance that the future will reveal a continued increase in the quantity of education and in the size of schools that provide educational experiences for youth. Enrollments will be greater since entrants from lower schools will be more numerous for most of the period ahead and the holding power of the secondary school will increase. The ever-growing tide of persons interested in continuing education, shared with the community colleges, will add still another dimension to the quantity of education to be provided by our future high schools. The current trend toward consolidation, combined with increased enrollments, will ensure schools of greater size. The median secondary school today has an approximate enrollment of 400 students; the median school in 1980 may well double in size.

Another prediction can be made with reasonable assurance. By 1980 some of the high schools will be considerably beyond the standards expected of the schools of that period while others will undoubtedly be striving to achieve quality found in the average high school of the earlier decade. Despite efforts to attain greater standardization, wide variances in programs and services will persist.

Profound changes are taking place in the guardianship of public education. Today the high school administrator is confronted with many demands and pressures which are influencing markedly his role and status. The most critical problem areas include: (1) the rapid development of teacher power which demands greater participation in how schools are administered, (2) growing student unrest and a desire for a more influential part in school affairs, and (3) the movement of citizens to a power position by insisting upon a share in the process of decision-making. These forces, currently on the scene, will require realignments of authority and responsibility long before 1980, and hopefully will offer new direction and improved status to the role of the building principal.

Today the position of the princial is unclear and often confusing. Each problem points to the desirability of increased cooperative problem-solving and decision-making by administrators, teachers, specialists, students and citizens. Each group must be involved to a greater extent than is the case in most schools today. There may never be one best pattern of cooperation and involvement, because of wide differences among schools and communities and the nature of problems that confront them, but there will be increasing clarity with respect to the essential criteria and principles which should undergird such cooperation and involvement and the roles to be assumed by each participating group. The authority and responsibility of the building principal working with various segments of the school and its community need clarification.

THE SECONDARY SCHOOL IN 1980

The most important obligation of the secondary school of the future will be to develop and sustain high standards of excellence in our commitment to a program of universal secondary education. The comprehensive school will continue as the institution best qualified to meet the challenging demands of an ever-changing society and the educational needs of an increasing and widely diversified youth population.

An educational institution, and surely a secondary school, tends to look back over its shoulder rather than forward. Progress in education demands new ideas and novel approaches to many of our present practices. It is our thesis that dynamic educational leadership within the structure of the comprehensive high school can lead the way to the achievement of a quality program for all youth through the full, daring, and imaginative use of many resources including time, space, program, people, and money. The whole concept of the secondary school—its functions, its curriculum, its instructional methods, its staffing patterns, its facilities for teaching and learning, and its financing—must undergo basic and penetrating changes.

THE DISTINCTIVE ROLE OF THE FUTURE PRINCIPAL

The uniqueness of school administrations in comparison with the executive function in other organizations is their primary emphasis upon teaching and learning. All administrative decisions have as their highest value the learning of boys and girls. All administrative personnel are instructional officers, directly or indirectly. Some administrators merely have more instructional duties and responsibilities than others; principals are primarily instructional leaders.

The superintendent is the crucial person on a district basis. He must recognize that the strength of the school system is to be found in the quality of teaching and learning in each school in the system. The importance of his position is derived essentially from his authority to allocate resources and to coordinate educational programs which can in effect maintain the status quo or cause improvement in the school system. The increased specialization of staff personnel and the wide range of services provided in a school system and the growing rate of change emphasize the chief administrator's responsibility to select and develop an effective administrative team, including the building principals. In a large system the superintendent cannot work directly with large numbers of teachers, but he can influence them significantly through his ability to direct and coordinate the work of members of his administrative and supervisory staffs.

It is the building principal who has the strategic and vital role of leadership to ensure that the school provides appropriate and quality education for every learner who can profit from such education. The realization of this objective in our day has been less than adequate largely because the principal has been unable or unwilling to make the transition from administrative management, concern about "running the school" and undue attention to housekeeping chores, to institutional leadership, which presumes a high level of educational vision and statesmanship. There are only a relatively few principals who are committed to such a role and are performing at a level to give them status as an effective instructional leader.

The principal in the future must stimulate, coordinate, and direct a vastly improved learning environment. As an educational leader and statesman, he will be an able facilitator of change and innovation, playing a responsible role in policy development and implementation, clarifying and interpreting the aims and functions of the school, fostering the full professional growth and participation of all staff members, selecting with staff cooperation new programs and services to guarantee equal educational opportunities for all students in the school, and enlisting community understanding of and support for those resources that will provide instructional and learning effectiveness. Only to the degree that the principal assumes this distinctive position of institutional leadership will the high school in 1980 fulfill its mission.

The principal in the future secondary school will perform many functions that will give him high prestige and influence as an educational leader in his community. The more important of these administrative functions are identified and discussed.

THE ORGANIZATION FUNCTION

To achieve maximally the aims of the high school of the future, greater attention will be given the problem of how schools should be administered. Structure is a means, not an end, in the realization of the goals of the school. A school is well organized when it is organized for its improvement. The best organizational arrangement is that which facilitates the attainment of the highest possible level of teaching and learning. Organization is the facilitating agency through which the larger and more demanding purposes of the secondary school in 1980 will be achieved.

Current organizational practices set rigid, outmoded educational standards. These barriers to quality education relate to untenable policies and practices about the length of the school day and the school year, pupil programs, class size, grade-level and pupil-progress requirements, teacher assignments and load, and building facilities.

These uniform organizational patterns preserve the status quo and stultify change and innovation by their denial of the need for a functional purpose and flexibility in all school arrangements.

As a facilitator of improved teaching and learning, the principal in 1980 will have an important organization function. He will organize the school day, the school year, the staff, the curriculum, instruction, and the facilities so that optimal learning will be realized.

Changes and innovations in organization, now present in a relatively few schools, will have been adopted by most schools in the decade ahead. Many novel ideas and improved practices will have been introduced and diffused among many high schools. The principal's role as an organizer will be recognized particularly through his successful efforts to achieve significant improvements in the internal structure, staff utilization and differentiation, and institutional arrangements for teaching and learning. The internal structure of the school will deal creatively with the differing needs of the small school and the very large, complex institution. Appropriate organizational models will enhance the advantages associated with either large or small schools and will lessen the disadvantages attributed to them. The principal will prove to be the key person in the way the school is organized so that teachers can make maximum use of their individual abilities and gain optimum success and satisfaction in their teaching. Organizational changes will be effected that provide teachers with time during the school day to prepare better, to keep up-to-date in their subject field, to confer with colleagues, to work with individual students, and to improve appraisal practices and reports. Schools will be organized so that variations in time and student groupings will contribute to the varying needs and interests of students. A functional and dynamic concept of organization and its application will pay rich dividends in the utilization of staff talents, individual study, individualization of instruction, and the use of physical facilities. The school administrator will use his organizational skills to achieve the aims of the school.

In most school districts today the high school principal is one of a number of administrators responsible to the superintendent. Administrative regulations and formulae too frequently control organizational practices in individual schools and restrict the principal's autonomy to initiate changed procedures in organization. The changing role of the principal will, it is predicted, be accompanied by changes in the roles of other administrators and all will work together, as a system-wide team, to facilitate the implementation of the changes desired and to encourage innovations in organizational practices in individual schools.

THE MANAGEMENT FUNCTION

The principal in the future will continue to be responsible for the total educational enterprise in the school he serves. Management is an essential function that must be executed effectively to ensure the most efficient operation of the school. The principal will determine operational duties that must be done, and then decide those tasks that he must perform and those that can be assigned to other members of the school's administrative team. He retains the responsibility for the successful execution of all managerial phases of the administration.

Today's principal averages a 50-hour week on school work and other directly related activities. He spends most of his time on the management function, either because he views his role as the proprietor of the operation, or the administrative structure is so inadequate or inefficient that he has difficulty in delegating managerial responsibilities to others. It will be the principal's obligation in the future to select and supervise a staff capable of the successful performance of most managerial tasks. The principal in most high schools will employ a staff of specially trained assistants to assume many duties related to the daily operation of the school, including discipline, attendance, scheduling, guidance and testing, finance and business management, and public relations. These assistants, the number depending upon the size of the school and the organization of the district, would carry out most of these managerial phases of administration thus releasing the principal and his instructional assistants for educational leadership roles.

THE INSTRUCTION FUNCTION

It is imperative that the high school in the eighties be organized, administered, and programmed so that the educational experiences of all youth contribute maximally to their development and self-realization. The curriculum of the school must provide authentic and relevant content that will guarantee a meaningful and satisfying education to every youth. Every subject field must do soul-searching to meet this test. The wise determination of relevance and authenticity in curriculum content can be gained through cooperative analyses by teachers, students, and the principal.

Educational opportunities in the community will be an increasing resource to enhance and enrich the education of youth. A few schools are now planning, and others intend to institute, school-community organizations to provide cooperative work-study programs, community-service programs, and other means by which youth can be actively involved in work experiences, in community services, and in joint civic participation with adults. These are significant developments in youth education.

More than instructional content will undergo profound changes in the future school. New patterns of instruction will result from the active involvement of teachers under the inspiring leadership of the principal. Current innovations in class size, length of class meetings, number and spacing of classes, types of instructional grouping, team teaching, nongradedness, programmed learning, and modular scheduling will become common practice after careful testing and evaluation. New approaches to independent study and individualized instruction will have even greater impact upon educational excellence.

New patterns of staffing are emerging and others more striking will be developed, despite Brickell's prediction that very probably if one opens the door of a typical 1980 classroom and walks inside, the teacher will be standing up front talking. The most significant trend presently is the increase in the ratio of professional persons to students. It is estimated that 45 professionals per 1000 students represent the average in schools today. By 1980 a majority of schools will seek to achieve a dubious standard of at least 65 professionals; 50 will be classroom teachers and 15 will be specialists.

Currently there are no acceptable criteria for defining the "best" staffing pattern for a school or a school system. Under the leadership of an able principal, a good school will develop educational quality goals. Research findings will reveal the effects of various staffing models upon the accomplishment of these goals. Innovative schools, through careful experimentation and valid appraisal, will determine how many professional staff members in relation to a given number of students are needed and how they should be deployed. Such a school will also decide the desirable ratio between classroom teachers and specialists with evaluative and supportive functions, and the number of professional persons that can be reduced through the wise utilization of auxiliary personnel and instructional technology.

The principal will have the primary responsibility, delegated by the superintendent to effect continuous improvement in curriculum content and in the instructional roles of teachers to the end that the professionalization of teaching and the attainment of each student's potentialities will be significantly increased. It is essential that schools continually seek the highest dividends in their investment in school personnel and instructional tools if they are to reach our aims in secondary education.

THE COMMUNITY INVOLVEMENT FUNCTION

By 1980 we will have answered the problem of how to best finance public education. Essentially a major portion of financial support for public elementary and secondary education will come from state and federal sources. Probably not more than 10 to 15 percent will be derived from local property taxes assessed in many fewer school districts.

This development will not lessen the need for a dynamic program of school-community relations. Lay participation and control will continue to be the cornerstone and foundation of public education. Public opinion, as in the past, will be the force that operates to determine ultimately the progress of a school system. The need for an effective instrument for the exposition, clarification, and promulgation of the public will, with respect to the schools, is the reason for a program of community-school relations, and the justification for its refinement and improvement in the future. There are two means through which the objectives of community-school relations will be realized in the future. The first consists of institutional interpretation which seeks to acquaint the people with their schools by providing opportunities for them to know, to understand, and to influence the development and direction of their schools. The second means is that of community interpretation through which the conditions and needs of the community are made known to the school personnel. Together the two methods can result in a high degree of intercommunication and interaction between the public and the schools that will give purpose and value to the school as a democratic institution. It will provide a means whereby the public can identify and support the desirable aims and program of the schools, and the schools can contribute effectively to community betterment. It will assert that the school is a vital community institution in which citizens are interested and active participants.

In the future, school authorities will be expected to give citizens the opportunity to know, understand, and influence the development of their schools. Community involvement will be essential to the resolution of problems and issues related to (1) the role of the school,

(2) change and innovation in school programs and practices, and (3) decision-making about school matters.

The high school in 1980 will be in a much more independent, autonomous position in most school districts than now. Currently there is a high correlation between the number of secondary schools in a given district and the degree of centralization and uniformity of program and administrative practice imposed upon the various school units. This characteristic of most school systems will gradually lessen as citizens demand a greater voice in the affairs of their schools, and as principals show their willingness and ability to function as institutional leaders in the development of schools that are uniquely adapted to the needs of a particular student population and sensitive to the community environment. In such a setting the principal will exercise his leadership in involving parents, staff members, and students in the quest for better answers about the aims and purposes of their school. He will interpret the need for change and innovation and provide the means for staff and community involvement in the change process. Decision-making about school policies and procedures will also include citizen participation. Procedures will be established, through maximum involvement of individual, committee, and large-group activity, to guarantee effective relationships and mutual understandings among parents, administrators, teachers and other staff personnel, and students to the end that the quality of the school may be fostered and extended.

THE PRINCIPAL AS A CHANGE AGENT

The secondary school must be sensitive to the needs and opportunities of a society characterized by ever-accelerating change. The nature and direction of these changes in 1980 are less predictable than that they will have great impact upon education and its inevitable restructuring and development to provide the kind and quality of education demanded in the future. Educational leadership of the highest order will be required to adapt and change our schools in the light of new situations and needs.

The principal will have an unique and challenging role to effect changes and introduce innovations which hold promise for the continued improvement and expansion of youth education. He will think wisely and act vigorously for the comprehensive betterment of the school. There are important strategies that the principal must implement if educational change is to take place and be accepted by the profession and the public. These procedures require the school to (1) assess its efforts, (2) determine what changes should be made, (3) decide how they can be accomplished, (4) introduce the revised practice or innovation, (5) appraise the results, and (6) disseminate the values of the change. Subordinate duties must not conspire to prevent the principal from fulfilling his role of institutional leadership. The local school is where the action is and will be in 1980.

The principal today must prepare the way for tomorrow's high school by becoming more aware of the dynamics in the present educational scene, and more committed to his leadership role in building a school that will ensure an appropriate and superior education for every youth in the community. A strengthened educational system is the first and most important responsibility that each generation must pass on to the next. The school principal is the indispensable agent in the realization of this purpose.

Evaluation

William W. Turnbull

Developments in evaluation during 1970 and 1980 will both reflect and shape developments in the rest of education. It will reflect them, inevitably, since evaluation is an integral part of a total educational structure. It will shape them because many of the most exciting prospects for new ways in education depend critically on new and improved methods of evaluation.

It will help if we tackle separately the two sharply different components of what is usually thought of as "evaluation": (1) the measurement of individual student attainments and (2) the assessment of the effectiveness of entire educational systems. Developments in both areas are likely to grow out of the current wave of experiments and innovations in instruction and lead to quite new systems of guidance, selection and placement over the next decade.

TESTS AND THE SINGLE CHILD

There is every reason to think that within the next decade the individual learner—the fellow it's all about—will finally come into his own. Individualized instruction, so long a pious hope, is now becoming a reality in innovative high school systems across the country. It's what's happening.

In an individualized system, of course, each high school student works on a given unit of instruction for as long or as brief a time as *he* requires to master it. He becomes the determiner of when he is ready to be tested. He then proceeds to a subsequent unit that is appropriate to his own past preparation and his present educational interests.

Such a system places an enormous demand on its evaluation procedures. First, there is a need for a reliable measure that will tell teacher and student alike when the initial unit has been mastered. Second, there is a need for a system whereby this evidence of mastery is added to the student's previous record of accomplishment. Third, the system must point to the next unit of instruction that the student is prepared to undertake and that is most consistent with his educational interests. The evaluation system, then, must function both as a gauge of distance traveled and as a guidepost at each fork of the road. We simply do not have the instrumentation that will be needed to allow the system to work efficiently, but there is little doubt that it can and will be developed, and on a large scale.

There will probably be a need for a very large number of unit tests—general-purpose measures of mastery of material taught in the schools. The teacher can then lay out a learning plan for each student and use the test results to determine the instructional sequence each student should follow, as well as to pace his progress.

More typically, however, a teacher may elect an instructional program designed as a total entity, including film strips, textbooks, physical objects to be studied, programmed workbooks, and incorporating sets of questions designed to help each student check the extent and precision of his learning along the way. The curriculum reform movement that began in the fifties and gained momentum in the sixties seems likely to be extended in the seventies and eighties and to place increasing emphasis on multi-media approaches and on integrating media and content within comprehensive teaching-learning systems.* Tests will be essential components of these systems. The curriculum-embedded test seems likely to be designed not only to measure but also to bear some of the teaching load itself, as indeed it does almost wholly in the case of programmed instruction. Attempting to distinguish between the medium of the question and the message of instruction will be pointless—an observation that owes less to McLuhan than to Socrates.

The traditional concept of evaluation has been tied to judgments of results—of end products. Increasingly, it is being recognized that evaluation has a critical role to play as part of the developmental process. As instructional units are developed, they can be pretested with groups of students so that their effectiveness can be judged, then modified experimentally, tried out again, and progressively refined until they are highly effective for the instructional task at hand. In this process, it will be especially important to ask for what kinds of students a particular procedure is effective; it is at this point, perhaps, that we can gain the greatest efficiency by

* The center of these activities may well lie within the new "learning corporations" that are springing up as big business discovers the education market.

capitalizing on interactions between teaching materials and learning styles, to design instructional systems that will be particularly effective with particular kinds of learners.

To date, most of the large curriculum development efforts have been directed toward academic disciplines. It is also fair to say that the problems of measuring student attainments for purposes of placement or guidance in academic areas have received disproportionate attention in relation to the problems in vocational, technical, commercial or other "career" programs. The latter problems may assume even greater importance as the trend toward universal school attendance moves upward in age levels, and it is predictable that strong efforts will be made to develop sound evaluation procedures in the job-oriented programs during the 1970s. Success here is likely to depend directly on the speed with which we can break the habit of thinking of evaluation in terms of paper-and-pencil exercises, and develop a whole new array of work-sample procedures requiring performance in realistic, on-the-job settings, whether real or simulated.

Other underdeveloped areas of evaluation at present relate to the personal and social development of learners: the noncognitive domain. Here the lack of progress stems not from a lack of effort but from the intransigence of the measurement problems. Again, the key to improvement may lie in developing testing situations of life-like complexity. In fact, it may well be that the most progress will result not from paper-and-pencil tests at all but from finding ways of recording and categorizing peoples' nontest behavior. An analogy might be drawn to judging writing ability by what students produce in their courses other than English composition in addition to their work on set pieces in English classes.

Psychologists have, of course, been intent on extending their understanding of personality structures and dynamics, and further progress in measurement will no doubt come from the studies undertaken for that purpose. A sharper focus of interest, however, is the personal characteristics of students that may affect their learning: the interest patterns, cognitive styles, problem-solving skills, preferences for instructional media, or readiness to identify with particular kinds of teachers. Even small gains in our ability to describe individual differences in these areas and to capitalize on them might pay big dividends in learning. And the more pointed emphasis on learning-related characteristics may contribute to progress by providing an available and valid criterion: the amount and kind of learning that takes place.

As computer technology is developed further for educational uses, at least some instruction is likely to be computer-based. The potential gain in individualization is tremendous. The selection of successive units of materials will be mediated by the computer on the basis of the student's responses to questions embedded in the teaching units. Thus the computer will supply a kind of micro-guidance, or perhaps mini-placement, within the minute-to-minute interactions of the student with the instructional program. It will also accumulate the responses over longer sequences of material and display the record for the information of the student, the teacher, and the guidance counselor at educational decision points. In this way, at least some of the functions now requiring special external examinations may be performed on the basis of a record generated automatically as part of the instructional process itself.

When tests are given outside of the instruction itself, they may also use the computer's power to tailor successive experiences to fit the cumulative evidence of the student's ability to perform. The selection of each question will be based on the student's pattern of success and failure on prior questions. The number of questions to be asked will not be predetermined: the student will be asked to keep answering until his response level has reached a desired stability and a profile of his capabilities can be produced with some confidence. This approach is analogous to sampling techniques in other fields, where one keeps adding to the sample until fluctuations in results reach an acceptably small level. Each student will spend virtually all of his testing time on questions that are appropriate for him, rather than wasting time on large numbers of questions that are either much too easy or far beyond him. This will increase the efficiency of the procedure substantially and at the same time will remove a common source of student frustration.

Implicit in the foregoing observations is the view that evaluation should be an aspect of instruction rather than something apart from it. It should, moreover, be a device for continuous feedback of information to the student to guide him along alternate pathways, rather than a reward-punishment device whereby the teacher conveys approval or disapproval of a student's effort.

As education becomes truly individual, the importance of "norms" will fade away. The concept of mastery as a basis for subsequent learning will, for most purposes, replace the concept of finding one's place on the normal curve. It will become apparent that the teacher and the student are on the same side in the educational game, both working to see that the student reaches the level of attainment needed for success at the next stage for him.

As student progress comes to be marked by hard evidence of educational attainment, the need to depend on time as a marker will diminish. A school year will become an administrative convenience rather than an implied educational stage. Reports of progress to students, teachers, and parents will be more descriptive of the nature of the particular student's accomplishments, and in many high schools will probably be produced by the computer in the form of verbal summaries to supplement more traditional numerical or letter grades.

An interesting question is, What happens to college entrance examinations under these conditions? With a rich source of data available from classroom testing built into specific courses of study and used in successive course placement decisions up through grade 12, by 1980 it will perhaps seem less sensible than it now does to contemplate a duplication of existing information through an external examination program at one arbitrary point in the student's educational progress. The processes of college guidance and college selection, now separated by a large chasm, are likely to grow together as they draw upon a common base of student data, at least within systems (such as state systems) that are homogeneous in some fashion and can cooperate in the research needed to make external examinations redundant in light of the extensive student information already organized and at hand.

The importance of having an evaluation program of high quality in such an educational system is apparent if the results are to carry the principal load of certifying student progress. Having good evaluation steps built into curriculum materials from the beginning will be the principal method of ensuring good measurement. To ensure quality in the tests that are prepared by the school itself for its own special purposes, it seems highly likely that much more attention will have to be given to the field of evaluation in teacher preparation and through in-service training. Test-building may become largely a function of departmental teams rather than of individual teachers, and the teams may draw on evaluation agencies for consultation and for basic materials they can adapt to their own situation.

TESTS AND THE GROUP

By 1980 much of the work in evaluation will properly focus on the progress of the individual high school student and on techniques for monitoring and guiding his development. Virtually all programs of measurement and evaluation are now built around those concerns and are based on measures designed to assess individual student attainment. In many cases, however, the results are used principally in attempts to evaluate the effectiveness of educational systems rather than of individual students.

The urge to look at measures of student performance in order to evaluate a system is both understandable and laudable. It grows out of the widespread recognition that an enumeration of resources or a description of teaching processes will not suffice. The number of days of schooling in a year, the expenditure per pupil, the size of the library collection, the presence or absence of a language lab, of team teaching or of programmed learning, refer to means rather than ends. The question is how well the *system* works. The taxpayers' revolt of the late sixties may stem in part from the public's unwillingness to accept the idea that simply pouring more and more money into the community's school system will automatically make it better.

Although looking at the end results of education is a step ahead of just tallying resources invested in it, it is far from a sufficient basis for evaluation. To begin with, the initial competence of the students must be taken into account. The fact that two high schools show identical patterns of achievement test scores for their seniors at time of graduation is by itself a useless bit of information as far as any judgment of the respective efficiencies of the schools is concerned. It is quite conceivable that one school has done a magnificent job of pulling up a group of students who started at a handicap, while the other was blessed with a group of youngsters who at the time of their entrance *already had* most of the proficiencies they later exhibited at graduation, little thanks to the school. The touchstone for judging the effectiveness of instruction is not what students can do at a point in time, but how much growth the instruction has produced.

Using results from present testing programs—composed of the long tests needed to evaluate individuals accurately—to evaluate whole school systems presents some thorny problems. Invariably, such a testing program measures only a very small proportion of the student characteristics that are of interest to the school system. There just is not time in the school schedule to administer many of the full-length tests required to assess individual growth. *Ergo*, the measures are usually confined to academic aptitude and subject-matter achievement tests. They do not extend to vocational or artistic abilities, let alone to attitudes, values, or learning styles. They stick to conventional paper-and-pencil approaches. Unobtrusive measures such as library withdrawals by type of book, or attendance at school and community functions, are seldom incorporated systematically in an assessment of what the school is accomplishing.

School administrators are frequently advised that the effectiveness of the school's program must be assessed in the light of the home environments of their students and the characteristics of the community, but they are never told how this is to be done, and they seldom have measures of those characteristics available in any case.

Notwithstanding these problems and more, the pressure for comprehensive evaluation is growing. This pressure has been increased by the new federally supported educational programs that require evaluation of innovations introduced with federal funding. In fact, we may have here the basis for a law: The pressure for formal evaluation reports varies directly with the distance between the source of the money and the place where it is spent. But the concept of cost effectiveness, newly popular as applied to education, presumes the existence of techniques to measure *system* effectiveness.

In this climate, it is predictable that organized programs for the evaluation of educational systems will be developed and applied widely by 1980. They will be built around techniques by which school administrators and others can assess the progress of *groups* of students toward educational objectives judged to be important by the school system in which the students are enrolled. And they will provide also for description of pertinent characteristics of the community within which the school system is functioning, as well as the teaching procedures actually used, down to the classroom level. They will provide techniques for integrating all this information so that student progress can be seen in relation to the whole context in which it has taken place.

These elements of educational context include such enduring influences as the proportion of the adult population that endorses college as an educational goal for their children, and such transitory events as a month-long display of modern art or a period of racial rioting. What relation did the school program bear to these occurrences—and *vice versa*?

What is visualized for the high school of 1980, then, is a continuous program to monitor changes in the effectiveness of instruction as shown by a broad system of sensitive indicators that measure group rather than individual characteristics. These will be based not only on test performance but on many varieties of observable high school student behavior, both in and out of the school setting. They will include the expressed attitudes of students, parents, and teachers. The evaluation mode suggested may be thought of as a running quality control or continuing audit of accomplishment.

In such an effectiveness information program, for most school systems, academic achievement measures are likely to command only part of the attention of the school administration or of the community. It is important for the people concerned with any system to stipulate in a comprehensive way what they want it to accomplish; otherwise, progress will be charted on only a few dimensions of concern. "Comprehensive" means inclusive, not vague. The specification of goals has to be precise enough to permit later measurement of results and comparison of accomplishments with goals.

GOAL STATEMENTS

It is no mean accomplishment to be both comprehensive and precise in framing the educational goals of a school system. An illustration may help to indicate what is meant.

Some four years ago, a committee of educational leaders in Pennsylvania set out to appraise the "adequacy and efficiency" of education in the state. After lively debate, the group decided upon a broad interpretation of what was meant by the adequacy and efficiency of educational programs. The goals they proposed covering the personal, academic, social, and civic development of students, were formulated into ten general statements, here paraphrased for brevity:*

Quality education will help every child to
  I. understand himself and appreciate his own worth as a member of society
  II. understand and appreciate persons of social, cultural, and ethnic groups different from his own
  III. acquire to the fullest extent possible for him mastery of basic skills in the use of words and numbers
  IV. acquyre a positive attitude toward school and the learning process
  V. acquire the habits and attitudes associated with responsible citizenship
  VI. acquire good health habits and an understanding of the conditions necessary for maintenance of physical and emotional well-being
  VII. be creative in one or more fields of endeavor
  VIII. understand the opportunities open to him for preparing himself for a productive life—and take advantage of them

* For the complete statement, see *A Plan for Evaluating the Quality of Educational Programs in Pennsylvania: Highlights* (Educational Testing Service, Princeton, New Jersey, 1965).

IX. understand and appreciate as much as he can of human achievement in the sciences, the humanities, and the arts

X. prepare for a world of change in which education will continuu through life

Following each general statement was a paragraph or two of elaboration, which made the brief goal statement precise enough to suggest lines of evidence that could be sought in order to assess the degree to which the goal was being reached. The point made by the Pennsylvania example is simply that it is both undesirable and unnecessary to exclude or ignore an important goal because it lies outside the realm in which we usually look for systematic or "standardized" measurements. One of the most important jobs for the evaluation research specialist in the next decade will be to improve upon the crude measures now available for some student characteristics—like self-understanding—which are of paramount human and educational concern. The fact that present measurement techniques are crude is no reason to disregard the objective, but rather a reason to extend research and development.

It is undoubtedly true that not all goals are shared by all school systems, and that differences in the priorities assigned to various objectives are even more widespread. Each system should select and define its own goals. But it will be important to gather an array of information that goes far enough beyond the specifics of the school's objectives to shed light on things the educational system may be accomplishing that it does *not* want to accomplish. For example, by doubling the amount of required reading, a high school may be producing higher scores in English literature but dulling the reading interest of a large segment of the class. In education, as in pharmacology, side effects are important, and they may show up in only a fraction of the population.

THE INTERACTION OF TEACHING AND LEARNING

A vital point in the example just cited is the fact that a heavy program of required reading might be just the thing for some students and a disaster for others. Most educational practice and almost all educational research have proceeded as if what was good for one would be good for all—an assumption contradicted by common sense and casual observation. We have accepted the assumption, or at least we have acted as if we accepted it, because the alternatives have been so hard to handle either in educational administration or in research design. The teacher or principal has had to seek the best compromise procedure for a whole class. The research has typically been designed to answer such questions as "Is algebra taught better by method A or method B?" and the studies have not included the large numbers of students needed if one is to find that method A produces better results with boys who have previously done well in arithmetic while method B seems to be more effective with all other groups. It is, in short, the quality of *interaction* of a learning style and a teaching method that determines the effectiveness of instruction, not the method by itself. Similarly, it is the interaction of a particular student and a particular teacher that establishes the right or wrong climate for learning. Recognition that different people have different learning styles and respond differently to the same teaching procedure or to the same teacher is one of the brightest hopes for the improvement of learning—provided we have ways of getting the information systematically and acting on it intelligently.

In an effectiveness information program, all students in an entire school system will be the group studied, and so there will be no problem about assembling the numbers of learners needed to explore interactions. The problem is, rather, how to assemble the large quantity of information needed to discover which characteristics of the students predispose them to respond better to one teaching strategy than to another. After all, present testing programs touch only a fraction of the abilities and interests that might be pertinent.

The key to this problem lies in recognizing that it is the group—indeed, the system—that is being described in such an information program, rather than the individual student. It is entirely feasible, then, to collect data about the total group on a wide variety of characteristics by gathering only partial information from each individual; with an adequate sampling design, the reliability of the description of the total group and of most subgroups will be enough to permit conclusions about program effectiveness both over-all and as it interacts with specific kinds of learner characteristics.

The gain in the comprehensiveness of measurement—the number of student characteristics described—is bought at the expense of reliability of information about the individual child. The latter is, needless to say, vital for many purposes. Indeed, individual measurement would still be necessary for student abilities central to decisions in individual guidance and instruction, and the results of the measures used would be cumulated for the entire school system and entered into the effectiveness information program. Through group measurement, however, the information about individuals could be extended very widely to other characteristics of possible importance.

By 1980, it may well be that the United States will have developed a variety of "social indicators"—indices of status and progress in each of many facets of national health, housing, participation in civic and cultural activities, and the like—and that indices of educational accomplishment will be among them. The National Assessment Program, initiated in 1969, seems likely to constitute a significant first step toward providing some educational components of such a system of social indicators.

The possibilities for 1980 appear to bear out E. B. White's prediction of a bright future for complexity. The future of evaluation may be equally bright if we recognize the complexity inherent in the teaching-learning interaction, build our programs of research and evaluation to reveal how the interaction operates, and learn to turn it to the learner's advantage.

Educational Change

Anthony G. Oettinger

The tradition of all the dead generations weighs like a nightmare on the brain of the living.—Karl Marx, The Eighteenth Brumaire of Louis Napoleon.

It is curious how the educational community changes its words but not its deeds.—Paul Brandwein, in a report to the Committee on Labor and Public Welfare of the United States Senate.

We find it easy to respond to inquiries on what the secondary schools will be like ten years or so from now. Our unhappy conclusion, pressed upon us by examining the facts rather than giving free rein to wishful thinking, is that ten years or so from now the schools will be pretty much as they are today. The American school system seems almost ideally designed to resist change. It combines the rigidity of a military organization with the fragmentation of small business. But it lacks both the centralized authority that can make the military move or the initiative and flexibility of response of the innovative entrepreneur.

To be sure, appearances may differ, but that is an old story: Old wine in old bottles with new labels has been encountered in education before. A report to the Committee on Labor and Public Welfare of the United States Senate on the use of funds under the Elementary and Secondary Education Act noted:

'Learning by doing' is replaced by 'learning through discovery,' the 'discovery method,' or the 'problem solving method' by 'inquiry.' Yet observations will show that in the majority of high schools, teachers of science lecture 80 percent of the class time and that laboratory time is given over to 'doing experiments' with equipment laid out in advance, hence, the results are postulated in advance. Yet teachers and administrators will assure the observer that the new curriculums (PSSC, CHEMS, BSCS, and the like) are being used and 'inquiry' is the mode of instruction.

We will concentrate in this essay on the future of educational technology and individualized instruction, although most of the constraints on developments in these fields can be expected to have similar effects on other attempts at innovation in secondary education.

THE TECHNOLOGICAL FIX

Experience in defense, such as the Manhattan Project, the development of national air defense, the design of the Polaris submarine, and the space efforts has suggested to many that the application of advanced technology and a systems approach may lead to equally dramatic developments in social areas. All of these examples, however, are in areas that are so far beyond the experience of the ordinary taxpayer that even without the secrecy that commonly prevails in such projects it was possible to push them through with the support of the President and a relatively small number of scientists, engineers, military men, administrators, and congressmen.

The setting of education is radically different. There is no one in education with anything like the power of the secretary of defense or the Joint Chiefs of Staff, to say nothing of the presidency. Rather, there are 27,000 local autonomous lay school boards. Furthermore, schools are a familiar experience for nearly everyone and consequently nearly everyone has an opinion on how they should be run. Putting technological innovations into meaningful use in such an environment requires the active and enthusiastic cooperation of an educational establishment of legendary inertia. Innovation from the top is virtually impossible because of the lack of line organization and central authority. Innovation from the bottom is virtually impossible because the lower ranks of education lack the training, the resources, and the individual independence necessary to begin. The educational establishment has been tempted with innumerable new dishes which it sniffs at, kicks over, or proudly displays, but only very rarely eats.

Even the children, the supposed beneficiaries of any change, often show a great capacity for resistance. As the language coordinator of one suburban school system once put it in conversation: "The language laboratory is a magnificent environment for daydreaming. Kids who are used to having blaring transistor radios around them every waking moment have trained themselves to ignore anything coming into their ears, and therefore hear very little of what comes out of the earphones they wear in the lab."

Finally, there is the little matter of knowledge. The Manhattan Project relied on major developments in physics during the previous 30 years and the space effort relies on physical theory from as far back as Newton. Can anyone seriously argue that educators of today know as much about teaching and learning as Newton did about gravitation and motion three centuries ago?

Since the foregoing analysis of the problems of finding technological fixes in secondary education is not very deep and in fact is obvious in some respects, it is worth seeking the reasons for the appeal of the idea. Perhaps the most important reason is the universally accepted proposition that the schools *must* change. Add to this the glamour and modernity of technology and the systems approach, the widespread publicity for successes like the space program and the lack of knowledge of the fundamental reasons for failures like the M-14 rifle and the F-111, and we are close to an answer.

Consider these altogether typical examples of what educators and laymen are hearing about educational technology. The first is from a *Scientific American* article by Patrick Suppes, who has conducted extensive experiments with computer-assisted instruction: "One can predict that in a few more years millions of school children will have access to what Philip of Macedon's son Alexander enjoyed as a royal prerogative: the personal services of a tutor as well-informed and responsive as Aristotle." The second is from a Republic Steel advertisement. It drops no names but it makes a promise that even Aristotle couldn't fulfill: "Someday a single computer will give individual instruction to scores of students—in a dozen subjects at the same time." Now "a few more years" and "someday" are phrases sufficiently vague as to elicit agreement from almost anyone. We can only say that in more than two years of research for *Run, Computer, Run* we found that most experiments in utilization of educational technology gave results more akin to those Our Miss Brooks might have achieved than to those of Aristotle and that the best experiments depended, as did Philip of Macedon, on the presence of a charismatic and imaginative teacher. Such an item is rarely listed in glossy brochures of the manufacturers of educational hardware or mentioned in the enthusiastic reports on technological experiments of academic educators.

The conclusion seems inescapable: neither the state of basic knowledge about educational processes nor the people and organizations now responsible for education offer fertile ground for technological fixes to blossom quickly enough to affect the secondary schools seriously in the next decade.

SOME ECONOMIC CONSIDERATIONS

Suppose that to confound the fallible analysis of the preceding section a genuine breakthrough occurs, that a technical idea so grand, so powerful, and so well realized emerges that no rational man can quarrel with its claims of ability to cure the ills of education. If we further suppose that developing, introducing, and operating such an innovation will either cost nothing or be paid for, because of its recognized importance, by whatever fraction of the gross national product it requires, then nothing further need be said in this section.

If, however, one assumes more realistically that the innovation, no matter how brilliant, must take root within the economic boundaries now projected for the coming decade, then there are gounds for serious concern. In his *Goals, Priorities, and Dollars: The Next Decade,* Leonard Lecht has sketched those economic boundaries. While Lecht found the nation's economic resources sufficient to maintain the status quo in the face of population growth between 1965, when he wrote, and 1975, when he added the estimated costs of some very modest *improvements,* he saw serious problems. Postulating the elimination of most dropouts, adding more teachers and paying them all better, and constructing or remodeling the educational plant where needed, he estimated the cost at $54 billion in 1965 dollars for operating the nations public and private elementary schools. Yet the U.S. Office of Education estimates that only $39.5 billion in 1965 dollars will be available. Since Lecht's projections amount to a per pupil expenditure of about $1000—many systems, including New York City's, already spend as much—it is difficult to see how any room can be made for more radical departures in education without major, unforeseen changes in school economics.

One must conclude that widespread introduction of innovation, far from merely having to fight for a slice of an existing pie, must make a case for adding to the already large deficit. Certain school systems will be able to afford at least pilot projects in innovation, but any change nationally will be exceedingly difficult. Projected enrollment in public elementary and secondary schools in 1975 is 46.5 million. It is obvious that every additional dollar spent per child per year represents an addition of $46.5 million to the national educational budget. To put it another way, an increase of one billion dollars per year in the national educational budget of 1975 would add only $21.50 per child, hardly enough to put a movie projector in each classroom, much less a computer terminal.

It is failure to recognize this multiplier effect that makes pilot applications of educatioal innovations so deceptive. Pilot projects almost never involve more than a single school, often only a single class. They are run by highly qualified and highly motivated specialists. Because they involve only a small number of children, it is easy to boost the amount of money spent per child. In 1959, New York City sought "to raise the educational, vocational, and cultural aspirations of elementary and junior high school students born and brought up in the slums" through its Higher Horizons program. Early applications of the program were successful, but the city failed in its attempt to expand the project to include 100,000 children. The reasons are simple. In the experiments, an additional $250 per child per year was spent, but the city was simply unable to spend the $25 million to add as much for 100,000 children. Taking New York City's attempt to provide such enrichment for one-sixth of its pupils and applying that low proportion to the nation, we find that an additional $2 billion dollars would be needed to pay for the program in 1975. Since the figures clearly preclude a national application of the program, we need not even ask where all the qualified and motivated teachers for these nearly 8 million pupils would come from.

In any case, we must remember that we are dealing here with only one of the numerous possible organizational or technological changes now competing for attention and resources. When any single one of these, translated onto the national scale, yields cost estimates in the billions, there clearly arises a problem of planning for resource allocation and decision-making, to say the least. To all appearances, very little attention has been paid to this problem.

SOME ADMINISTRATIVE CONSIDERATIONS

To these purely economic difficulties, one must add the administrative difficulties—encountered in every area—of translating an enterprise from the laboratory to full-scale application in realistic circumstances. We have touched on these above in noting the enthusiasm, expertise, and committment common to participants in experiments, but we would add that not only is it next to impossible to call forth such resources for routine operations, it is also next to impossible to find in education the intellectual and administrative ability to see such large projects through.

Gordon Raisbeck and his associates at the management-consulting firm of Arthur D. Little, Inc., have analyzed the problems of scale-up of experiments, using again defense and aerospace projects. We have already cautioned against drawing educational analogies from successes in these areas, but since no comparable studies of educational development are available, we will simply have to use what we have and proceed with caution.

The Little group's first conclusion was that the transition from research to development to use is not straightforward. This may seem obvious, but we found in our observations of language laboratories that while the investment was usually justified on the grounds that language instruction would be improved and individualization of instruction facilitated, in practice the labs are viewed by both teachers and students as another study hall, that even the limited potential for individualization (limited compared, say, to a library) was rarely exploited, and that attempts to integrate classroom instruction with lab work were very rarely successful. While the labs had facilities for running four to eleven lessons at one time, for instance, program materials were few and ordinarily not available to the teacher, with the result that all 30 students in a lab received a single lesson, just as in an ordinary class. One language lab we visited included in its instruction sheet for students the frank warning, "No one is an individual in the laboratory."

As for the initial requirements for setting out on a development project with a chance for success, Raisbeck and his associates named three, all of which must be present: "An explicitly understood need, goal or mission. A source of ideas, typically a pool of information, experience and insight in the minds of people who could apply it. Resources, usually facilities, materials, money, and trained and experienced men, who could be committed to do a job." In education we cannot state needs or goals explicitly and clearly until we have more knowledge of the learning process and more sophisticated theories of the goals of education. Ideas abound, certainly, but without the meeting of the first requirement, they tend to be unrelated and difficult to accomodate to one another. Finally, no schoolman, no intelligent and informed citizen, would claim that present resources come close to meeting the third requirement listed.

And once these requirements were met, the Raisbeck group found that a long wait between initial discovery and application was to be expected. For half their cases, the technological base had existed for five years before the project even began. Not only will it be difficult for those who hope for technological salvation of education to meet the initial requirements, but it is exceedingly difficult to regard present technological accomplishments as any sort of base for future improvements. The conclusion must be that all these ingredients—goals, ideas, resources, knowledge—while not absent altogether from the educational scene, are found as nuggets and not as rich veins.

The Raisbeck group also found that communication in research and development tends to be informal and person to person. We have mentioned the fragmentation of education already, but we must also note the reluctance of academic educators to spend time teaching in the public schools. And although various summer institutes and collaborative curriculum development projects from the universities have drawn on classroom teachers, school administrators are reluctant to release their teachers for such participation because many find that their new experience and training will mean higher paying and more interesting jobs elsewhere while those who return find their missionary zeal unappreciated and become frustrated and quit or revert to their former passive state.

A corrolary conclusion by the Little researchers was that "In studying the various R&D events it was found over and over that the pushing through of an original idea from the research stage to the actual application involved the same people and the same management as were involved in the original idea or discovery." Few educational experiments qualify, for the ideas come from the universities and industry, the experiments are carried out by industry and single schools, while the application must be to entire districts or systems.

The Little study further points out that a strong guiding spirit is essential to success. There is plenty of enthusiasm and dedication in education, but it is often uncomprehending to the point of fanaticism and total blindness. The extent of "true believership" is hard to assess, but the comments quoted earlier on old wine in new bottles suggest either a high capacity for self-delusion or else a great innocence. Part of this failure stems from the lack of clearly defined goals and part from the misplaced faith of educators in technology. At any rate, the evidence points overwhelmingly toward a profusion of enthusiasm in the sense of flagwaving and exorcism rather than toward enthusiasm tempered by deep understanding but challenged by a terribly complex problem. We are speaking here, it is important to note, not only of the proverbial bureaucrat incapable of handling ideas, but also of the university professor and the industrial executive. All have been guilty of just-around-the-corner thinking about educational technology.

One criterion from the Little study can provoke only sardonic laughter when applied to the school context: Successful projects ordinarily operated under loose and untidy funding controls. Few teachers have access to even petty cash. One experimental school in Boston's Roxbury district has evoked the gratitude of its teachers by giving each one a few dollars to buy such things as a stick of butter from the corner store to pop corn with in a kindergarten class. Raisbeck also insisted on a generally adaptive environment, with decisions being made all over the organizational pyramid, with communications made directly rather than through channels, and no prescribed authority meeting out punishments and bestowing rewards. It is as though they had studied the schools and then advised doing the opposite in every case. In many systems, the superintendent is so hampered by the school board in matters such as the price of floor wax or the color of band uniforms that he cannot even discuss more important matters with them for lack of time. And the controls on teachers are, of course, more restrictive. When one reflects that teachers are subjected to the authority of principals who must answer to superintendents who are in turn responsible to lay boards themselves hemmed in by state legislation, federal regulations, political and parental pressures, and so on and on, it is clear that there is a long way to go.

Given our extensive and detailed pessimism, the reader may reasonably ask if any efficient and effective educational technology can ever be developed. The central problem, we believe, is the lack of goals. If everyone agrees that a certain percentage of children making a certain score on such-and-such an achievement test is an appropriate embodiment of educational goals, then present technology can be of help. But what are the appropriate achievement criteria? All one need do is ask to find whether a child has learned that $2 + 2 = 4$, but how will one know whether a child has learned to be a good citizen, to be creative, to work well with others, typical "goals" stated by educators? The line must be drawn somewhere, and while this point has received little consideration in education proper, we would suggest that the line is much clearer in the military and industry. Both these institutions know quite well what they want to teach and who they want to teach it to. It seems to us that it is thus in industry and the armed forces where educational technology must be developed before it is foisted off on children in any but experimental situations.

THE LAST BARRIER

Let us once again be hypothetical, even more so than earlier. Let us suppose that the technology is available and that the problems of economics, administration, development, and theory have been surmounted. Let us suppose that the best possible machines are in the hands of teachers in the tens of thousands. What will they do?

Philip W. Jackson has provided an excellent description of the confrontation of the teacher and the machine:

> If there is one thing the teacher, particularly the female teacher, is not, it is an engineer. Indeed, it is difficult to think of two world views further apart than those symbolized by the Golden Rule on the one hand and the slide rule on the other. The one calls to mind adjectives such as romantic, warm, tender-minded, naïve; the other calls to mind adjectives such as realistic, cold, tough-minded, efficient. One is essentially feminine; the other masculine. These two lists of adjectives undoubtedly exaggerate the real differences to be found between these two groups, but they do give us pause when we consider the likelihood of increasing the dialogue between the tender-minded teachers and the tough-minded technicians. To say that they do not speak the same language is a gross understatement.

Our observations support Jackson's imaginative survey. In one new high school, overhead projectors were introduced because the blackboards had not been delivered on time. The projectors remained after the blackboards were installed but older teachers had complained all along that they felt they needed a pilot's license to use them. These teachers abandoned the projectors as soon as possible. The younger teachers were said to be more enthusiastic, but we saw no evidence that any extensive use of the projectors was made by anyone.

Perhaps Jackson exaggerates. Perhaps we observed only atypical situations. Nonetheless, regardless of what their attitudes might be, most high school teachers do not have the training to make use of present or future educational technology. Nor, at present, are they rewarded for a receptive attitude towards innovation. Instead, they are rewarded for accurate records, neat and quiet classrooms, certification and educational credits, and, particularly, longevity.

If indeed it makes sense to introduce advanced technology into the high school classroom—which we will assume for our present hypothetical argument—then massive education and reeducation of teachers and administrators will be absolutely necessary. How this will be done is not clear, but for the sake of the argument, let it be said to be done.

The kind of training in writing computer programs, running new curricula, and implementing new learning theories that will be necessary will not only suit the trainees for technological schools, it will suit them for working in technological industries, which already pay much more than any existing or projected school system. How much devotion can we call on our teachers to have?

Enough to forego a starting salary in industry that exceeds their own top salary by thousands of dollars?

The alternative of introducing technicians from industry into the schools is equally unattractive. Not only is there no money to pay them, but the existence of parallel staffs at disparate salaries and with disparate educations and personalities raises problems of administration of gigantic proportions.

It is hardly necessary to state our conclusion again. We stated it at the beginning of this essay: ten years or so from now the schools will be pretty much as they are today. Most of the school buildings that will be in use in 1980 are in use today. Most of the teachers who will be teaching in 1980 are teaching today. The absurdity of our hypothetical examples is apparent, yet even with such absurd premises it appears that change is virtually impossible. It may be, now that the college troubles of the 1960s are beginning to show up in the high schools that the student body will be very different. If so, then administration and teaching may change in response, but as for any revolution founded on technology, we see none. Given the intellectual and social complexity of education and the weakness of its weapons of attack, we will simply have to grit our teeth, try as hard as we can to implement change, but muddle through as best we can no matter what happens.

PAUL F. BRANDWEIN is president of the Center for the Study of Instruction, a division of Harcourt, Brace & World, Inc. He is also an Adjunct Professor in Education and Conservation at the University of Pittsburgh. He has served on the steering committees of the Physical Sciences Study Committee, the Biological Sciences Curriculum Study Committee, and the Advisory Board of Harvard Project Physics. He is an author of 33 books in the natural and social sciences.

CHARLES E. BROWN is a program officer in the Public Education Division of the Ford Foundation. Formerly he was superintendent of schools in Newton, Massachusetts, and a lecturer at the Harvard Graduate School of Education.

SAMUEL M. BROWNELL is Distinguished Professor of Education at the University of Connecticut and Consultant on Urban Education at Yale University. He was formerly U.S. Commissioner of Education, superintendent of schools in Detroit and Grosse Pointe, Michigan, professor of educational administration at Yale University, and president of New Haven State Teachers College.

KENNETH B. CLARK is president of the Metropolitan Applied Research Center, a member of the New York State Board of Regents, and professor of psychology at City College, City University of New York. His many publications include *Prejudice and Your Child* and *Dark Ghetto.*

JAMES CONANT'S studies of American schooling have resulted in many publications including *The American High School Today, Slums and Suburbs,* and *The Education of American Teachers.* He has served as president of Harvard University, United States High Commissioner for Germany, United States Ambassador to the Federal German Republic, and director of several Carnegie Corporation supported studies of American education.

ROBERT B. DAVIS is professor of mathematics and education at Syracuse University and visiting professor of mathematics at Cornell University. He is the creator and director of the Madison Project, a program sponsored by the National Science Foundation which uses a concrete approach to teach mathematics in grades K-9. Among Dr. Davis's publications are *Discovery in Mathematics* and *Explorations in Mathematics.*

DOUGLAS D. DILLENBECK is director of guidance services of the College Entrance Examination Board. Formerly a school counselor and guidance director, he has been president of the American School Counselor Association and has served on the editorial board of the *Personnel and Guidance Journal.*

ALVIN C. EURICH is president of the Academy for Educational Development, a nonprofit organization specializing in the field of educational planning, and chairman of the Educational Research and Development Division of FAS International, Inc. Formerly he was president of the Aspen Institute for Humanistic Studies, vice-president and director of the Fund for the Advancement of Education, executive director of the Ford Foundation's Education Program, first president of the State University of New York, and vice-president and acting president of Stanford University.

MARVIN J. FELDMAN is a program officer of the Ford Foundation in the Division of Education and Research—Public Education. He is a member of the National Advisory Council on Vocational Education of the Department of Health, Education and Welfare and has served on the U.S. Office of Education's Committee on Planning Major Curriculum Development. He has served as a Foundation consultant in Colombia, Nigeria, Japan, and Israel, surveying technical and vocational, as well as general, education programs. His publications include "The Richmond Plan," "Making Education Relevant," "Public Education and Manpower Development," and others on comprehensive education.

EDGAR FRIEDENBERG is professor of social foundations and sociology at the State University of New York at Buffalo. He is the author of *The Vanishing Adolescent, Coming of Age in America,* and *The Dignity of Youth and Other Atavisms.*

A. BRUCE GAARDER is chief of the Basic Studies Branch of the U.S. Office of Education, where he has also served for five years as chief of the Foreign Language Research Section, and later as head of the sections concerned with establishing training programs for teachers of modern foreign languages and for teachers of disadvantaged youth. He has taught Spanish at all academic levels. He is the author of numerous published essays on foreign language teaching and on bilingual education.

HAROLD B. GORES is president of Educational Facilities Laboratories, a nonprofit corporation founded and supported by the Ford Foundation to help schools and colleges with their physical problems. Prior to EFL's establishment in 1958, Mr. Gores was superintendent of schools in the city of Newton, Massachusetts. He has served on several presidential advisory committees, including the President's Task Force on Education in 1964, and is an honorary member of the American Institute of Architects.

HAROLD HOWE, II, is Program Advisor on Education to the Ford Foundation in India. He was United States Commissioner of Education for three years during the Johnson Administration. Before that, he directed the Learning Institute of North Carolina, an agency to encourage educational experimentation in that state. Mr. Howe has been a high school principal in Newton, Massachusetts, Cincinnati, Ohio, and Andover, Massachusetts, as well as superintendent of schools in Scarsdale, New York. He has served on the Board of Trustees of Vassar College and the College Entrance Examination Board and is currently a trustee of Yale University.

FRANK G. JENNINGS is Director of College Relations at Teachers College, Columbia University, and editor-at-large of the *Saturday Review*. He was formerly education consultant for The New World Foundation in New York City. Mr. Jennings is the author of *This Is Reading*, published in 1965, and frequently contributes to journals and books concerned with education, including, most recently, *The Preparation of Educators to Meet Emerging Needs*, published by Designing Education for the Future.

CHARLES R. KELLER, for many years professor of history and chairman of the history department at Williams College, was the first director of the College Board's Advanced Placement Program and later the director of the John Hay Fellows Program. He is now an educational consultant.

JOHN W. LOUGHARY is professor of education and chairman of the Counseling Psychology Department at the College of Education, University of Oregon. He has been involved in the development of man-machine systems in education for the past ten years. Among Professor Loughary's publications are *Man-Machine Systems in Education* and *Educational Information System Requirements: The Next Two Decades*.

SEMA MARKS is a resident consultant to the RAND corporation and is finishing her doctoral dissertation on educational technology for the Harvard Graduate School of Education.

LLOYD S. MICHAEL, professor of education at Northwestern University, was formerly superintendent of Evanston, Illinois Township High School. He is a member of the National Advisory Board of National Instructional Television Center and of the National Committee on Secondary Education. He served as chairman of the Administrative Internship Project in Secondary School Improvement and as chairman of the Commission on the Experimental Study of the Utilization of the Staff in the Secondary School.

ANTHONY G. OETTINGER is professor of linguistics and mathematics at Harvard University. He is a former president of the Association for Computing Machinery, has served as chairman of the Harvard Computing Center, and is chairman of the newly created Computer Science and Engineering Board of the National Academy of Sciences and director of Project TACT (Technological Aids to Creative Thought) at Harvard. He is the author of *Automatic Language Translation: Lexical and Technical Aspects* and of *Run, Computer, Run: The Mythology of Educational Innovation.*

NEIL POSTMAN is professor of English education at New York University and director of its graduate program in language and communications. He is the author of *Language and Reality, Television and the Teaching of English,* and coauthor of *Teaching as a Subversive Activity.*

OLE SAND is director of the National Education Association's Center for the Study of Instruction. Prior to assuming those duties in 1960, he was professor of education and chairman of the Department of Elementary Education at Wayne State University. He has served as a visiting professor at Harvard University, the University of California—Berkeley, Stanford University, the University of Wisconsin, and the University of Washington. He serves on a number of national boards and commissions and is probably best known for his leadership of the NEA Schools for the 60's program.

SIDNEY G. TICKTON is executive vice-president of the Academy for Educational Development. He has acted as staff director for long-range planning studies of educational systems in a number of states and served formerly as executive director of the National

Commission on Instructional Technology and as program associate in the Ford Foundation education program.

J. LLOYD TRUMP is associate secretary of the National Association of Secondary School Principals. Currently he is directing an international five-year NASSP Model Schools Project with partial support from a Danforth Foundation grant. Formerly he was professor of education, University of Illinois and served as teacher, principal, and superintendent in Illinois and Indiana elementary and secondary schools. His best known publications are *Images of the Future— A New Approach to the Secondary School* and *Focus on Change—Guide to Better Schools*, both concerned with reports of and projections from staff utilization studies which he directed with partial support from Ford Foundation grants.

WILLIAM W. TURNBULL, president-elect of Educational Testing Service, has been associated with that organization since its formation in 1948. He has served as vice-president for Test Development, Research, and Statistical Analysis; then as vice-president for Testing Operations; and executive vice-president.

CHARLES WEINGARTNER is coordinator of secondary education, Queens College of the City University of New York. He is coauthor with Neil Postman of *Linguistics: A Revolution in Teaching* and *Teaching as a Subversive Activity*.